Market Dynamics and Productivity in Developing Countries

Khalid Sekkat
Editor

Market Dynamics and Productivity in Developing Countries

Economic Reforms in the Middle East and North Africa

Springer

International Development Research Centre
Ottawa · Cairo · Dakar · Montevideo · Nairobi · New Delhi · Singapore

Editor
Khalid Sekkat
University of Brussels
1050 Brussels
Belgium
ksekkat@ulb.ac.be

A copublication with the
International Development Research Centre
PO Box 8500
Ottawa, ON, Canada K1G 3H9
info@idrc.ca / www.idrc.ca

e-ISBN (IDRC e-book) 978-1-55250-459-8

ISBN 978-1-4419-1036-3 e-ISBN 978-1-4419-1037-0
DOI 10.1007/978-1-4419-1037-0
Springer New York Dordrecht Heidelberg London

Library of Congress Control Number: 2009939074

Printed on acid-free paper

Springer is part of Springer Science+Business Media (www.springer.com)

Contents

About the Editor and Contributors

Editor

Khalid Sekkat holds a Ph.D. in Economics from the University of Brussels (ULB). He is Full Professor of Economics at the ULB and a member of the Royal Academy of Sciences and Technologies (Kingdom of Morocco). His fields of interest are industrial organization, international economics, and development economics. He has published numerous articles in international refereed journals (including *Journal of Industrial Economics, Journal of International Economics and European Economic Review*), and several books, including *Trade and Jobs in Europe* (co-editor, Oxford, 1999), *Vertical Relationships and the Firm in the Global Economy* (Elgar, 2006), *Competition and Efficiency in the Arab World* (editor, Palgrave-McMillan, 2008), and *Industrial Policy in Europe, Japan, and the USA* (co-author, Palgrave-McMillan, 2009). He was economic adviser at the European Commission and has acted as a consultant to the European Parliament, the European Commission, the World Bank and the OECD.

Contributors

Lahcen Achy is Professor of Economics at the *National Institute of Statistics and Applied Economics* (INSEA), Morocco. He has a Ph.D. in International Economics and Finance from the *Université Libre de Bruxelles* (ULB), Belgium. His fields of specialization are international economics and trade policy, competition policy, and manufacturing sector issues. Lahcen Achy has several publications in internationally referred journals such as *Review of Development Economics* and *Applied Economics*. He has also contributed to a number of books on finance, competition, globalization, and income distribution in developing countries. Lahcen Achy has been adviser and consultant for a number of international organizations such as

UNIDO, WIPO, WHO, ILO, the World Bank and the European Commission. He is also a Research Associate of the DULBEA (Department of Applied Economics at ULB), Research Fellow of the Economic Research Forum (ERF), member of the Global Development Network (GDN), and the academic liaison of Research Alliance for Development (RAD).

Nesreen Barakat is the Managing Director of "To Excel Consulting & Associates" – a consulting firm based in Amman (Jordan) specialized in strategic planning, institutional strengthening, policy advocacy, and economic research. Nesreen Barakat holds an MBA degree from Durham University Business School in the UK and a BSc in Computer Science from the University of Jordan. Previously she managed the Policy Support and Institutional Strengthening Component of the Euro-Jordanian Industrial Modernisation Programme. She also worked as the Director of the Competitiveness Unit (TCU) at the Ministry of Planning and International Cooperation and was assigned as an official counterpart to the World Economic Forum (WEF) to follow up on Jordan's competitiveness ranking in the Global Competitiveness Report (GCR). Additionally, Nesreen Barakat was a member of the Technical Policy Analyst Team to support the official negotiators during Jordan's accession to the Jordan-EU Association Agreement.

Riadh Ben Jelili is Ph.D. in Economics and Econometrics. Since September 2005, he is Economic Expert and Coordinator of the Consultancy Committee at Arab Planning Institute. From 1994 to 2005, he was Associate Professor at University of Rennes 1 and University of South Britain. His fields of specialization are performance, competitiveness and investment decision in manufacturing sector, rural–urban migration, international migration, and simulated methods in econometrics. He published in books and international journals (e.g. Palgrave-Macmillan, *Journal of Development and Economic Policies*).

Mohamed Goaied is Professor of Econometrics and Statistics at the Institute of High Business Studies in Carthage and Polytechnic School of Tunisia. He is Ph.D. in Mathematical Economics and Econometrics from University of Bougogne in Dijon, France (1988). He published many papers in academic journals including: *Journal of Productivity Analysis, Econometric Reviews, International Review of Finance and Economie et Prevision*. His fields of specialization are productivity analysis, firm efficiency, demand systems, and poverty analysis. He served as a Managing Director of The Institute of High Business Studies in Carthage (2002–2005) and is Director of the Laboratory of Applied Economics and Empirical Finance at the University of 7 November in Carthage, since 2005. He also served as a consultant for national and international institutions. He is a fellow of the ERF.

Teoman Pamukçu is currently Associate Professor at the Department of Science and Technology Policy Studies at the Middle East Technical University, Turkey. He previously worked as teaching and research assistant at the ULB, and was an expert at the Belgian Federal Planning Bureau and Research Fellow at the University of Luxembourg. He holds a BA degree in economics, a MA degree in econometrics and a Ph.D. in economics from the ULB. He worked on issues relating to the emergence and development of information society, on labor market polices and on the determinants of innovation activities of firms in developing countries. His current research interests are foreign direct investment, clusters of enterprises and their impact on innovation and economic development. He has published articles in journals and chapters in books. Teoman Pamukçu is a Research Associate of the ERF, a Research Associate of the DULBEA and member of the International Joseph A. Schumpeter Association.

Ibrahim Saif is an Economist at the Economic Studies Unit at the Center for Strategic Studies at the University of Jordan. He obtained his Ph.D. from the School of Oriental and African Studies; University of London. Ibrahim Saif has taught both at the University of London (UK) and Yale University (USA) where he offered courses on the Economies of the Middle East. He also worked as a consultant to international organization such as the World Bank, the IMF and the ILO. He is a Fellow of the ERF and a member of the GDN. His core research areas include international trade and structural adjustment programs in the developing countries and his regional interest in addition to Jordan includes Middle East region. Currently he is working on regional project on competition and the political economy of Euro-Med Association Agreement. He is a member of the Competition Committee in Jordan.

Erol Taymaz is a Professor of Economics at Middle East Technical University (Ankara, Turkey). He was educated in mechanical engineering at METU. He received his M.S. degree in Economics at METU (1985), and Ph.D. degree in Economics at Case Western Reserve University, USA (1989). He worked as a Research Engineer at Aselsan Electronics Industries (Ankara, 1982–1985), Research Assistant at CWRU (Cleveland, 1985–1989), and Research Fellow at Industrial Research Institute (IUI, Stockholm, 1989–1992). He is at the Department of Economics of the Middle East Technical University since 1992. His current research interests include economics of technology and innovation, industrial and technology policy, industrial dynamics, small business economics, and microsimulation modeling.

Chapter 1
Reforms, Market Dynamics and Productivity in Developing Countries

Khalid Sekkat

1.1 Introduction

Between the end of World War II and the mid-eighties, development strategy in a number of developing countries was based on the protectionist "Import substitution" (IS) concept. Many of these countries' governments were of the opinion that maintaining free trade would prevent their economies from industrializing and would therefore render them vulnerable to long-term adverse movements in terms of trade, and impact their growth and welfare. However, during the 1980s, both economists and policy-makers became skeptical about the beneficial impact of the IS strategy. The difference in performance between the outward-oriented Asian and the inward-oriented Latin American economies clearly called for a reconsideration of the strategy. Empirical evidence (Sachs and Warner 1995) also suggests that open economies tend to adjust more rapidly from primary-intensive to manufacture-intensive exports, and to achieve sustained growth. Since the mid-eighties, many LDCs have engaged in a process of economic reform, involving a more outward orientation of their economies, the lowering of trade barriers, privatization of many industries and reform of the foreign-exchange market.

The rationale behind reforms is that increased competition is an important driver of economic performance. Economists agree, in general, that fair competition is beneficial to growth because it induces efficiency gains. Among the latter, productive efficiency is of particular importance. It brings the output-input combination to the optimal production frontier and induces firms to produce at lowest costs. This is achieved by fighting overstaffing, sluggish response to new opportunities and poor management. It forces inefficient firms either to exit the market or to take necessary actions to reduce costs and rationalize production and management processes. The outcome is an increase in productivity, both at micro and macro levels.

K. Sekkat (✉)
University of Brussels, Belgium
e-mail: ksekkat@ulb.ac.be

K. Sekkat (ed.), *Market Dynamics and Productivity in Developing Countries: Economic Reforms in the Middle East and North Africa*, DOI 10.1007/978-1-4419-1037-0_1,

Recent analyses (see Hoekman and Winters (2005) for an overview) of the impact of liberalization on efficiency in developing countries (LDCs) lend support to the role of such "natural selection" process among firms. For instance, Wacziarg and Wallack (2004) analyzed a set of 25 liberalization episodes in developing countries and found a strong effect of intra-industry reallocation on economic performance.

While there has been a profusion of theoretical work on entry and exit of firms, there is comparatively little empirical work in the area even for developed countries (Disney et al. 2003a, b). Firm entry and exit is a part of the market selection process by which resources are reallocated within or across industries. The process of entry and exit influences economic performance through firms' internal restructuring, reallocation of resources among firms, and changes in market shares of incumbents. It also induces the introduction of new technologies, thereby improving economic performance.

This chapter presents a brief review of the knowledge about firms' entry and exit and economic performance. The objective is to set the stage and motivate the researches presented in the subsequent chapters. Section 2 presents the conceptual framework underlying the determinants and impacts of firms' entry and exit. Section 3 summarizes the main finding in developing and transition economies. Section 4 concludes.

1.2 Firms' Entry and Exit: Determinants and Impacts

A series of firm, industry, and country specific factors determines the extent of entry and exit. The process of entry and exit has impacts on economic performance. However, such relationships are not unidirectional, and literature documents various cases where performance affects either firm, industry, or country determinants as well as the process of entry and exit itself (Tirole 1988). For clarity, we do not discuss the latter links in this chapter (Fig 1.1).

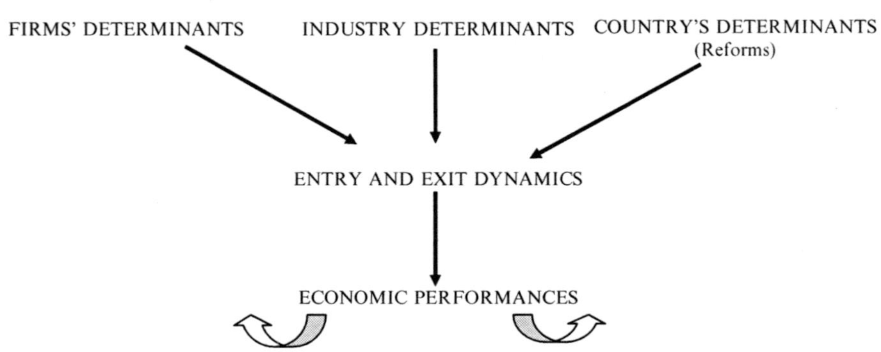

Fig. 1.1 Firms' entry and exit: determinants and impacts

1.2.1 Determinants

1.2.1.1 Firm Determinants

There is a relationship between firm entry and size. Entrants tend to have a size which is lower than the average firm size found in the industry (Boeri and Cramer 1992). Some authors (Audretsch and Mahmood 1995) have uncovered evidence that firms that enter the market with a small size do so because they consider that their chance of success is small. However, if after entry, results seem promising, small sized firms have the option of investing heavily.

A relationship was also found between firm exit and size. Firms exiting the industry have a smaller size than the average size of the industry. Moreover, many small firms exit the industry before reaching their efficient scale of production, which may reflect the intensity of the market selection process.

Another finding is that young firms tend to exit the market after a relatively short period of activity. This may be linked to the fact that newly created firms generally enter the market with a small amount of own funds. As they are not competitive enough during the first years of their existence, they make losses which decrease the level of their own funds. After 2 or 3 years, the latter become insufficient to allow the firm to pursue its activity, and its goes bankrupt. The result may even happen to newly created firms gaining market shares if they have no access to external funding and if the level of their own funds does not allow them to finance their expansion. So, one important element among the determinants of exit is the initial amount of own funds and more generally the financial structure of the company.[1]

In terms of firm survival, research shows that the survival of entrants is low, with a large number of entrants failing within the first year (Churchill 1955; Baldwin 1995). The firms that survive need 5–10 years to properly compete with incumbents and their failure rates decrease over time. Firms that survive in the market have a larger size than those that exit and also have a more rapid growth rate which declines with age however.

1.2.1.2 Industry Determinants

Industry's characteristics include profit margins, concentration ratio, growth rate, capital intensity and specific workers skills. Profit margin determines the attractiveness for new firms to enter into the industry, but it could also be associated with imperfect competition. In the former case, the expected effect on entry is positive, while in the latter, the reverse is expected. The concentration is an indicator of the easiness to enter a market. It is easier to enter perfectly competitive industries in which many small firms produce standard products. The growth rate of the industry is a proxy of its life cycle. New firms prefer to enter rapidly growing industries. Capital intensity captures "natural" barriers to entry. It may discourage entry because if the industry uses capital-intensive technology, the cost of the initial investment could be substantial. Finally, the requirement of specific workers' skills could also deter entry if not enough is available in the country.

Regarding exit, similar variables are in play, but with an effect opposite to the one on entry. For instance, capital intensity (because of potential sunk costs) delays exit and high industry growth rate allows firms' survival despite their low performance. Finally, high concentration ratio reduces competition among firms and may reduce exit.

According to Caves (1998), entry and exit rates tend to be positively correlated in industries with steady states of maturity, but varying structural entry barriers. The correlation between the two is negative during the early and late phases of a product's life cycle. During the expansion phase, industries have both high entry rates and high exit rates. The overall impact on employment tends to be small, given the lower than average size of both entering and exiting firms.

1.2.1.3 Country Determinants

Entry and exit are affected not only by firm and industry characteristics, but also by country characteristics such as macroeconomic shocks. More importantly, researches suggest that a firm's investment decisions are highly sensitive to the country's institutions and policies. Such policies, by affecting the business climate, can either promote or deter firms' willingness to enter or stay in the market. To our knowledge, there are little studies focusing on the impact of policies and institutions on firms' entry and exit. Indirect insights can be gathered from the studies concerning firms' investment. Some of them focused on trade and foreign exchange policies and found that the size and openness of a country are important determinants of investments (Lucas 1993; Cushman 1985). Others looked at policies such as grants, subsidies, tax abatement, loan's guarantees, and interest subsidies. They found that the impacts differ between developing and developed countries (Grubert and Mutti 1991; Loree and Guisinger 1995).

Another strand of empirical literature, inspired by Douglas North's works, is increasingly dealing with the role of institutions. These refer to a large set of factors including political instability, corruption, investment regulation, democratic accountability, and bureaucratic quality. For instance, Schneider and Frey (1985) found that both economic and political factors are crucial to fostering investment. Mauro (1995) found that corruption depresses domestic investment; a result confirmed by Wei (2000) regarding foreign investment. Brunetti and Weder (1998) used various indicators of the quality of institution (e.g., voice and accountability, government effectiveness, regulatory burden, and rule of law) and found that their deterioration decreases investment. Finally, Henisz (2000) examined the effect of commitment to rules on growth and investment. He focused on the effect of frequent or arbitrary changes in taxation, regulation and other relevant economic policies. He found that commitment to rules has a statistically and economically significant impact on investment. Although indirect, these findings suggest that taking account of institutions and policies is important for the study of firms' entry and exit.

1.2.2 Entry, Exit and Economic Performance

A large part of the studies on the impact of firms' entry and exit on economic performance concentrates on productivity growth. The impact of firm entry and exit on aggregate productivity growth is decomposed into three sources. First, the "within effect," or restructuring effect, refers to factors internal to the firm such as organizational change, the introduction of new technologies, R&D activities or a change in the mix of labor and capital. Second, there is a process of creative destruction by which low productivity firms exit the market and are replaced by new entrants. Among them, the most efficient will survive, while the least efficient will exit the market in subsequent periods. Third, there is a change in market shares among incumbents which will also have an impact on aggregate productivity growth. There are also a number of important interactions between the various sources of aggregate productivity growth.

Entry and exit of firms is generally found to have an important contribution to aggregate productivity growth. Scarpetta et al. (2002) analyzed several OECD countries and found that entry and exit contributed between 20% and 40% of aggregate productivity growth. There were significant differences in the contributions of entry to aggregate productivity growth across sectors however. In high technology sectors, the entry of new firms has a larger than average contribution to total growth, whereas in mature industries, the exit of firms has larger contributions to growth. The results also differ according to whether aggregate productivity is measured by Total Factor Productivity (TFP) or labor productivity. Disney et al. (2003b) found that, in the UK, the contribution of entry and exit to TFP growth was sensitive to the business cycle and was larger in periods of economic expansion. Martin and Jaumandreu (1999) uncovered evidence that entry and exit play an important role in aggregate productivity growth in Spain. The impact was stronger in the period before Spanish integration in the EU.

The contributions of the three sources of growth to aggregate productivity growth varies from one study to another, depending on the method of decomposition used, the measurement of aggregate productivity, the time horizon over which changes occur, the business cycle, as well as on the country and the industry under investigation. The contribution of the "within effect" was found to be an important source for aggregate growth by Foster et al. (1998). Scarpetta et al. (2002) uncovered evidence that the within effect had larger contributions to growth in mature industries. It also has a higher contribution to growth in periods of economic expansions. The contribution of the "within effect" to aggregate productivity growth remains important, but is smaller when productivity is measured by TFP than when it is measured by labor productivity. The results on the contribution of market share reallocation to aggregate productivity growth are mixed. Aw et al. (1997), Hahn (2000) and Griliches and Regev (1995) found that the contribution is small, whereas Baily et al. (1992) and Foster et al. (1998) found that the contribution is important among US industries. According to Scarpetta et al. (2000), the contribution of market share reallocation is positive, but typically small and varies widely from one country to another. It also increases in periods of economic slowdown.[2]

1.3 Entry, Exit and Economic Performance in LDCs

1.3.1 Entry, Exit and Reforms

To date, a major reference about manufacturing firms in developing countries is the survey by Tybout (2000). He documented entry rates, exit rates, net job creation and net job destruction patterns among the population of plants with at least ten workers. The survey shows that there is more plant and job turnover in a number of developing countries than in the United States and Canada. In Chile, entering plants with at least ten workers captured 15% of the market and in Colombia they captured 20% of the market. In terms of job creation and job destruction, Chile and Colombia average 25 and 27% annual turnover rates, respectively. In Morocco, even more flux in plants and jobs were found. The annual manufacturing job turnover rate was 31%. Finally, in Korea and Taiwan, new entrants captured an average of 33 and 44% of the market, respectively

The reasons for such high turnover are different among countries. In Latin America, high turnover seems to reflect the dramatic business cycles. In Korea and Taiwan, it partly reflects rapid expansion of the manufacturing sector. Policies also seem to matter. Market shares and turnover rates are higher in Korea and Taiwan than they are in Latin America. This can be linked to labor markets regulation. For instance, Taiwan's labor markets are less regulated than in Latin America, and sunk entry costs are relatively modest, because the business environment makes subcontracting easy.

However, it seems that the turbulence takes place among plants with 10–50 workers. Moreover, the moderately small producers never seriously challenge the larger incumbents. Hence, high turnover rates in LDCs may simply reflect the relative importance of small and medium enterprises and not necessarily imply that large firms' market shares are more at risk. Studies for Chile and Colombia suggest that all of the market share loss comes at the expense of small producers. Here again, one finds a contrast between Latin America and Asia. Studies for Korea and Taiwan show that large plants suffer important market share losses.

It seems that there are marked contrasts among countries about the profile and the reasons of entry and exit. The contrast is related to countries' institutions, policies and economic environment. This implies that detailed country studies should be more helpful to provide policy recommendations than aggregate cross-countries analysis. Some recent country studies are presented in what follows.

Fajnzylber et al. (2001) focused on the role of trade reform in Chile and Colombia. It used establishment level data to document patterns of job creation, destruction and turnover. It also assesses the share of employment changes due to within-firm versus entry and exit effects. The paper established that the contribution of entering and exiting firms to employment change is almost as important as that of continuing firms. However, the paper failed to show whether job creation, destruction and turnover are due to trade reform or to business cycle. Campos and Iootty (2005) used Brazilian data for the manufacturing sector (at the 3-digit level) for the period 1996–2002 and found that the share of exports in the sector's output is one main determinant of entry and exit rates. It also identified a relationship between the impact of export orientation and the business cycle. In years of real per capita GDP decline, entry rates increase with the export propensity, in years of GDP expansion, net entry increases with domestic growth. Masso et al. (2004) focused on Estonia and showed that firm turnover has been rather high during the period 1995–2001, thanks to low institutional entry barriers and the emergence of numerous SMEs. Moreover, new firms achieved higher productivity compared to incumbent and, therefore, exhibited high survival rates. Yang (2004) examined the impact of the transition to the "socialist market economy" in China on firms' entry, exit and survival in the electrical and engineering industry. The analysis suggested that the competitive selection process is taking place, with entrants contributing substantially to both output growth and productivity growth. Old firms are, however, still important in the economy. Kaya and Ucdogruk (2002) analyzed the case of the Turkish manufacturing industry (at the 4-digit level) over the period 1981–1997. The findings are that entry rates are highly affected by profit margin, capital intensity, concentration ratio and growth rate. The main determinants of exit are growth rate, capital intensity and concentration ratio. The entry rate is highly correlated with the exit rate.

Finally, Klapper et al. (2004) used a comprehensive database of firms in Western and Eastern Europe to study how regulations governing entry drive the creation of new firms. They found that entry regulations hamper entry, especially in industries that naturally should have high entry. Also, value added per employee in naturally "high entry" industries grows more slowly in countries with onerous regulations on entry. Interestingly, regulatory entry barriers have no adverse effect on entry in corrupt countries, but only in less corrupt ones. Taken together, the evidence suggests that bureaucratic entry regulations are neither benign nor welfare improving. However, not all regulations inhibit entry. In particular, regulations that enhance the enforcement of intellectual property rights or those that lead to a better developed financial sector lead to greater entry in industries which do more R&D or need more external finance.

1.3.2 Entry, Exit and Economic Performance

Regarding economic performance, Roberts and Tybout (1996) provides evidence supporting a positive relationship between high turnover and gains in productivity in LDCs. Other studies confirm the relationship in different countries. For Korea, Hahn (2000) found very large effect of entry/exit on aggregate productivity growth.

Aw et al. (1997) focused on Taiwan and found that entry and exit processes are important sources of aggregate growth. Pavcnik (2002) finds that exiting plants are substantially less productive than surviving plants in Chile. Griliches and Regev (1995) showed that most of the growth in labor productivity in Israel is due the "within effects." This fits with Tybout (2003) findings that competition (through openness to trade) induces markets for the most efficient plants to expand, but at the same time large import-competing firms tend to contract. Palangkaraya and Yong (2006) found that Indonesian incumbent plants, are on average, more productive than entrants and exitors in every year between 1990 and 1995. New plants are relatively less productive than the exiting plants in the early years, but they are more productive in the later years. They also exhibit the highest productivity change during the early years. Decomposition in the change of productivity suggests that such high productivity growth is due to a movement toward the frontier. In Brazil, Campos and Iootty (2005) found that exit (and to a lesser extent, entry and net entry) is a very robust determinant of total factor productivity across industrial sectors.

The transition from a centrally planned economy to a more market oriented one offered an important opportunity to further document whether the competitive selection process induces any improvement in productivity. Masso et al. (2004) focused on entry and exit in Estonia and decomposed productivity change into components consisting of resource reallocation across existing firms, firm entry and exit, and productivity growth within continuing firms. The decomposition shows that the high productivity growth has been mostly from within-firm productivity growth (e.g., the adoption of new production technologies and organizational changes), but the reallocation of production factors (especially the exit of low productivity units) has played an important role as well. Brown and Earle (2004) studied productivity enhancing reallocation for Russia and Ukraine. Before reforms in Soviet Russia, the reallocation rates were low and bore little relation to relative labor and multifactor productivity across firms. After reforms, increasing resource flows have contributed to aggregate productivity growth through both increased flows from less productive to more productive continuing firms, and the exits of less productive enterprises. Orazem and Vodopivec (2003) showed that in the Slovenian manufacturing, competitive pressures sorted out the most efficient firms, and the entry of efficient new private firms was the major source of TFP growth. De Loecker and Konings (2003) showed that more than 40% of average productivity growth in Slovenian manufacturing was due to firm entry and exit. Warzynski (2002), focusing on Poland, found that more job reallocation was connected with more productive industries. Finally, Yang (2004) focused on the Chinese electrical and engineering industry. Productivity decomposition suggests that exits contribute to productivity improvement especially within the small firms. In these firms, as well as in the collectively owned ones, the competitive selection process operates like in a private market economy. However, for state owned enterprises the rate of exit is much slower, and compared with new entry, the contribution of exit to productivity growth is trivial.

1.4 Conclusion

The process of firm entry and exit is a part of a "natural selection" by which resources are reallocated within or across industries. It influences economic performance through firms' internal restructuring, reallocation of resources among them and changes in their market share. The theoretical literature on entry and exit of firms and their impacts on economic performance is rich but its empirical counterpart is very limited especially on developing countries. The latter have adopted important reforms over the past three decades with the objective of improving their economic performance. The process of firm entry and exit can play an important role in this context.

This chapter briefly reviewed the economic rationale behind the process of firm entry and exit and its impact on economic performance. It first explained how a series of firm, industry and country specific factors affect the process. It subsequently documented the relationship between economic performance and firm entry and exit in developing countries.

The analysis showed that there are marked contrasts across countries about the determinants and impacts of entry and exit. Such contrasts are related to countries' institutions, policies and economic environment. It follows that detailed country studies should be more helpful to provide policy recommendations than aggregate cross-countries analysis. This is the purpose of the following chapters.

1.5 Notes

1. The literature also found that manager turnover in small businesses had a tendency to predict sales or closures of the firm shortly afterwards.
2. There is also an indirect effect via innovation. Firm entry and exit can also affect productivity growth by stimulating innovation (see Aghion et al. 2003).

References

Aghion P, Blundell R, Griffith R, Howitt P, Prantl S (2003) Firm entry and growth: theory and micro evidence. Harvard University, miméo

Audretsch DB, Mahmood T (1995) New firm survival: new results using a hazard function. Rev Econ Stat 77(1):97–103

Aw BY, Chen X, Roberts MJ (1997) Firm-level evidence on productivity differentials, turnover, and exports in Taiwanese manufacturing. NBER working paper 6235, October

Baily MN, Hulten C, Campbell D (1992) Productivity dynamics in manufacturing plants. Brookings Papers on Economic Activity (Microeconomics), pp 187–267

Baldwin J (1995) The dynamics of industrial competition. Cambridge University Press, Cambridge MA

Boeri T, Cramer U (1992) Employment growth, incumbents and entrants: evidence from Germany. Int J Ind Organ 10:545–565

Brown JD, Earle JS (2004) Economic reforms and productivity-enhancing reallocation in the Post-Soviet transition. IZA discussion paper no 1044
Brunetti A, Weder B (1998) Investment and institutional uncertainty: a comparative study of different uncertainty measures. Weltwirtsch Arch 134(3):513–533
Campos NF, Iootty M (2005) Firm entry and exit in Brazil: cross-sectoral evidence from manufacturing industry. Proceedings of the 33th Brazilian economics meeting
Caves RE (1998) Industrial organization and new findings on the turnover and mobility of firms. J Econ Lit 36(8):1947–1982
Churchill B (1955) Age and life expectancy of business firms. Surv Curr Bus 35(12):15–19
Cushman DO (1985) Real exchange rate risk, expectations, and the level of direct investment. Rev Econ Statist 67(2):297–308
De Loecker J, Konings J (2003) Creative destruction and productivity growth in an emerging economy: evidence from Slovenian manufacturing. IZA discussion paper no 971
Disney R, Haskel J, Heden Y (2003a) Exit entry and establishment survival in UK manufacturing. J Ind Econ 51:93–115
Disney R, Haskel J, Heden Y (2003b) Restructuring and productivity growth in UK manufacturing. Econ J 113(489):666–694
Fajnzylber P, Maloney WF, Ribeiro E (2001) Firm entry and exit, labor demand, and trade reform evidence from Chile and Colombia. World Bank Policy Research Working Paper 2659
Foster L, Haltiwanger J, Krizan C (1998) Aggregate productivity growth: lessons from microeconomic evidence. NBER working paper 6803
Griliches Z, Regev H (1995) Firm productivity in Israeli industry 1979–1988. J Econometrics 65:175–203
Grubert H, Mutti J (1991) Taxes, tariffs and transfer pricing in multinational corporate decision making. Rev Econ Statist 5:285–293
Hahn C-H (2000) Entry, exit, and aggregate productivity growth: micro evidence on Korean manufacturing. Korea Development Institute, Seoul
Henisz WJ (2000) The institutional environment for economic growth. Econ Politics 12(1):1–31
Hoekman B, Winters A (2005) Trade and employment: stylized facts and research findings. ECES working paper no. 102 May 2005
Kaya C, Ucdogruk Y (2002) The dynamic of entry and exit in Turkish manufacturing industry. Middle East Technical University, Ankara, ERC working papers in Economics 02/02
Klapper L, Laeven L, Rajan R (2004) Business environment and firm entry: evidence from international data. NBER working paper no. 10380
Loree DW, Guisinger SE (1995) Policy and non-policy determinants of U.S. equity foreign direct investment. J Int Bus Stud 26(2):281–299
Lucas REB (1993) On the determinants of direct foreign investment: evidence from East and Southeast Asia. World Dev 21(3):391–406
Martin A, Jaumandreu J (1999) Entry, exit, and productivity growth in Spanish manufacturing during the eighties. Documentos de trabajo, Fundacion SEPI, Programa de investgaciones economicas, Madrid
Masso J, Eamets R, Philips K (2004) Creative destruction and transition: the effects of firm entry and exit on productivity growth in Estonia. IZA discussion paper 1243
Mauro P (1995) Corruption and growth. Q J Econ 110(3):681–712
Orazem PF, Vodopivec M (2003) Do market pressures induce economic efficiency: the case of Slovenian manufacturing, 1994–2001. IZA discussion paper no 901
Palangkaraya A, Yong J (2006) Entry, exit and productivity of Indonesian electronics manufacturing plants. Melbourne Institute working paper no. 8/06
Pavcnik N (2002) Trade liberalization, exit and productivity improvements: evidence from Chilean plants. Rev Econ Stud 69(1):245–276
Roberts M, Tybout J (eds) (1996) Industrial evolution in developing countries: micro patterns of turnover, productivity and market structure. Oxford University Press, New York
Sachs J, Warner A (1995) 'Economic Reform and the Process of Global Integration', Brookings Papers on Economic Activity 1:1–117

Scarpetta S, Hemmings P, Tressel T, Woo J (2002) The role of policy and institutions for productivity and firm dynamics: evidence from micro and industry data. Economic working paper (2002)15, OECD: Paris

Scarpetta S, Phillip H, Thierry T, Jaejoon W (2002) The role of policy and institutions for productivity and firm dynamics: evidence from micro and industry data, Working paper No. 329, Economics department, OECD

Schneider F, Frey BS (1985) Economic and political determinants of foreign direct investment. World Dev 13(2):161–175

Tirole J (1988) The theory of industrial organization. M.I.T. Press, Cambridge, MA

Tybout J (2000) Manufacturing firms in developing countries: How well do they do and why? J Econ Lit XXXVIII:11–44

Tybout J (2003) Plant- and firm-level evidence on the 'new' trade theories. In: Kwan Choi E, Harrigan J (eds) Handbook of international trade. Basil-Blackwell, Oxford

Wacziarg R, Wallack JS (2004) Trade liberalization and intersectoral labor movements. J Int Econ 64:411–439

Warzynski F (2002) Do Schumpeterian waves of creative destruction lead to higher productivity? Panel data evidence from Poland. LICOS discussion paper 120/2002

Wei S-J (2000) How taxing is corruption on international investors? Rev Econ Stat 82(1):1–11

Yang OG (2004) Entry, exit and the dynamics of productivity growth in Chinese manufacturing industry. ESRC Centre for Business Research, University of Cambridge, Working paper no. 284

Chapter 2
Exit–Entry Dynamics: Case of the Manufacturing Sector in Jordan

Nesreen Barakat and Ibrahim Saif

2.1 Introduction

The manufacturing sector in Jordan is the most important sector in terms of its contribution to the GDP at constant basic prices. Relative to other sectors, the manufacturing sector has been increasing from 18.4 to 21.3% during the period of 2003–2006. This sector has been playing a very important role in boosting growth in Jordan over the last few years and therefore, it is pertinent to take a closer look and analyze the dynamics of entrants, survivors and exitors in the manufacturing sector.

Traditional analysis in this sector focuses on the main indicators. Very few studies went further to investigate the internal dynamics of the sector, especially the dynamics between new entrants, exitors and the survivors as this study intends to do.

This study will examine the structure of the manufacturing sector and its main parameters. The study will cover the following aspects of the manufacturing sector:

- Main salient features,
- Institutional arrangements,
- Characteristics of the entrants, exitors and survivors,
- Productivity and efficiency through adopting accounting and econometrics techniques to measure the main indicators and the determinants for entrants and exitors at a sectoral level,
- Conclusion and recommendations.

N. Barakat
To Excel Consulting & Associates, Amman, Jordan
e-mail: nesreen.barakat@to-excel.com

Ibrahim Saif (✉)
Centre for Strategic Studies, Jordan
e-mail: ibrasaif@gmail.com

K. Sekkat (ed.), *Market Dynamics and Productivity in Developing Countries: Economic Reforms in the Middle East and North Africa*, DOI 10.1007/978-1-4419-1037-0_2,

To achieve the above, the study is divided into the following sections:

- *An overview of the manufacturing sector* which will present a historical view of the manufacturing sector in Jordan. This would provide an insight into the extent of the impact of the entry and exit dynamics.
- *The regulatory environment* which governs the manufacturing sector in Jordan and an overview of the relevant legislations and regulations. The overview of the regulatory environment would provide insight into the legal aspects that affect the dynamics of entry and exit of manufacturing companies.
- *An entry and exit dynamics analysis* covering data collected during the period of 1999–2004 and an in-depth study of those firms within the manufacturing sector.
- *A summary* to provide conclusions stemming from the analysis of the entry and exit dynamics.

2.2 Overview of the Jordanian Economy

Jordan is a small country, with limited natural resources, situated in the heart of the Middle East. Debt, poverty, and unemployment are fundamental challenges for Jordan. Average economic growth during the period of 2000–2006 was 5.9% with the lowest rate of 4.2% registered in the year 2000 and the highest rate of 8.4% in 2004 (Department of Statistics 2004).

Jordan has been facing an accelerated pace of change brought about by globalization and trade liberalization with simultaneous opportunities and risks. Jordan had entered into an Association Agreement with the European Union (1997), signed a free trade agreement with the United States (2001) and successfully joined the World Trade Organization (2002).

Jordan's economic performance has been impressive. During the period 1999–2001, Jordan's annual real GDP growth averaged 4.2% compared to an average of 6.4% from 2005 to 2007 (Central Bank of Jordan 1999–2007). One of the reasons behind this growth has been the establishment of Qualifying Industrial Zones (QIZs) that allows for privileged access to the USA market. This has resulted in the expansion of exports in the garment and textile industry which amounted to 30.8% of total exports during 2006 (Department of Statistics 2007).

This strong economic performance was also driven by domestic consumer demand and supported by a booming construction and real estate sector. Additionally, high levels of remittances from the Gulf, and growth in the services sector boosted private consumption. Other economic indicators have followed similar patterns to the growth rate. The private sector has also assumed a larger role in the economy, especially with respect to investment, with public sector demand decreasing from about 30% of GDP in the late 1980s, to about 23.2% in 2003. Private nonresidential investment has increased from 4 to 7% of GDP in 1990 to 10% by 2003. At present, however, exports amount only to half the level of imports, and competitiveness is hampered by the limited capacity to export high-quality products.

The Jordanian economy continues to exhibit high levels of dependence on the oil economies of the Gulf. One of the major recent developments in the Jordanian economy is the impressive boom in foreign direct investment which has taken place since 2003. In 2002, FDI in Jordan was JD 52.8 million and in 2003, it increased almost sixfold to JD 309.3 million. FDI increased to JD 461.6 million in 2004, and then doubled in 2005 to JD 1.086 billion. In 2006, FDI doubled again, to JD 2.2 billion and accounted for over 20% of Jordan's GDP. The proportion of FDI to local investment has also increased over the past few years. During the period 1995–2002, FDI in Jordan accounted for less than 1% of the total investment, with the exception of anomalous years, such as 2000, in which proceeds from privatization were recorded as foreign investment. FDI accounted for 3.9% of total investment in Jordan in 2002, 17% in 2003 and 18% in 2004, the most recent year for which gross fixed capital formation figures are available (Saif and DeBartolo 2007).

Remittances from Gulf countries continue to play an important role in the Jordanian economy. Remittances accounted for 17.6% of GDP in 2006, with Jordan ranking sixth in the world in terms of remittances as a proportion of GDP (World Bank 2007). The vast majority of these remittances are transferred from Gulf Cooperation Countries (GCC).

However, it is important to note that despite these reforms and some of the positive results that were realized, the underlying structure of the economy has not changed significantly. An analysis of recent growth trends suggests that Jordan's service sector continues to play a significant role in the economy, accounting for over 70% of the GDP at basic prices.

Also, after more than 15 years of the economic adjustment process, the main conclusion regarding sectoral growth and output composition of the economy is that it has not changed substantially. The services sector is the fastest growing sector, owing mostly to the growth in banking and financial services.

The industrial sector in Jordan is divided into the manufacturing sector and the mining and quarrying sector. The mining and manufacturing sectors averaged nearly 24–26% during the period throughout 1989–2005. The manufacturing sector has been growing steadily, with its share in the GDP growing from 11% in 1989 to 17.9% in 2005. Recently, the contribution of mining and quarrying to GDP has increased because of high international prices for potash and phosphates, the main Jordanian products in this sector. While there has been growth in the manufacturing sector, boosted over the past few years by the establishment of QIZs, this does not constitute a major economic shift towards industrialization. The main indicators of the industrial sector for the period 2003–2006 are displayed in Table 2.1.

2.3 Manufacturing Sector

This section of the study presents data about the manufacturing sector and specifically those subsectors selected for the study. The data would give an indication on the magnitude of entrants, exitors and survivors.

The importance of the manufacturing sector to GDP at constant basic prices, relative to other sectors over the period 2003–2006 has been increasing, as displayed below, from 18.4% in 2003 to 21.3% in 2006[1]. The manufacturing sector is the most important sector in terms of its contribution to GDP (Fig. 2.1).

Table 2.1 Main indicators of the industrial sector 2003–2006

Main indicators of the industrial sector 2003–2006	2003	2004	2005	2006
Value added at current prices (JD million)	1274.7	1544.0	1790.7	2045.3
Growth rate at constant prices (%)	2.1	14.2	9.7	8.6
Deflator of the industrial sector (1994 = 100)	109.2	115.8	122.4	128.7
Industrial exports (JD million)	1518.4	2105.7	2295.2	2606.7
Domestic exports excluding agricultural exports				
Mining and Quarrying and manufacturing industrial production quantity index	116.2	130.1	143.5	151.0
Number of registered industrial companies	704	981	1,125	1,425
Capital of registered industrial companies (JD million)	20.9	111	87.9	176.4
Outstanding credit facilities extended by licensed banks (JD million)	879.4	973	1038.1	1135.9
Outstanding credit facilities extended by the IDB (JD million)	76.7	62.2	80.6	108.2

Source: CBJ Annual Report 2006

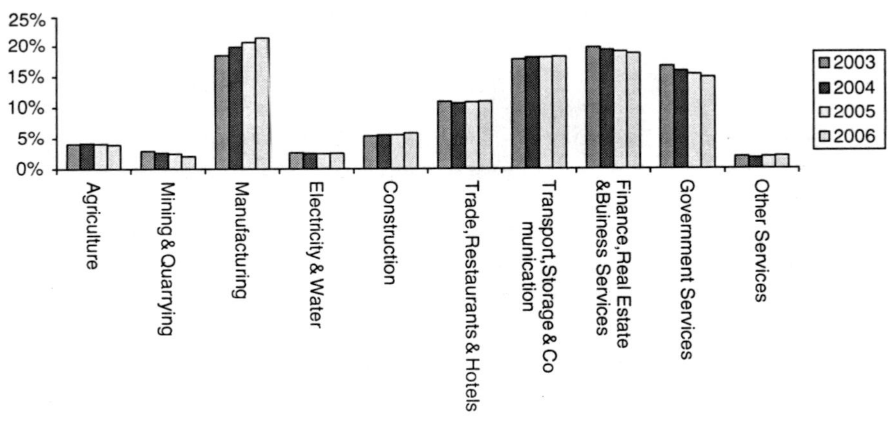

Fig. 2.1 Relative importance of economic sectors to GDP at constant basic prices, 2003–2006

2.3.1 *Labor Force in SMEs in the Manufacturing Sector*[2]

Figures.2.2 and 2.3 shows the number of establishments in the manufacturing sector that had 1–19 employees, during the period 2000–2004 as well as the total number of employees those establishments employed. The number of establishments that had between 1 and 19 employees grew from 17,154 in 2000 to 19,778 in 2004. Consequently, the number of employees in these establishments grew from 61,732 to 68,823 during the period of 2000–2004.

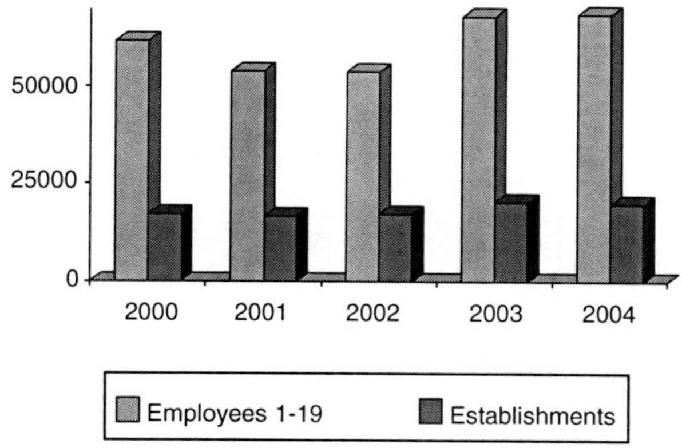

Fig. 2.2 Establishments (1-19 employees)

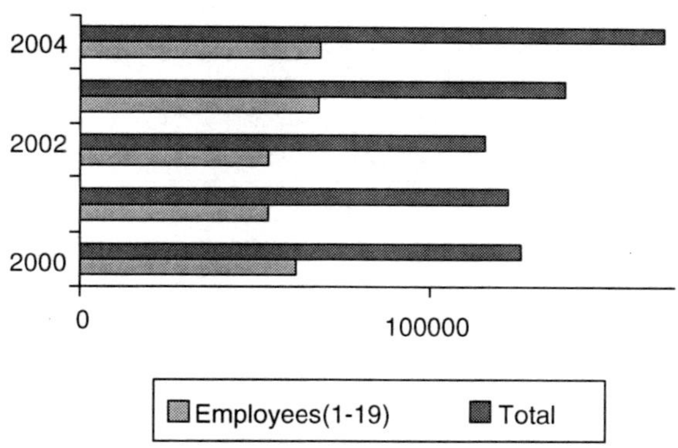

Fig. 2.3 Establishments (1-19 employees)

2.3.1.1 Employment in the Manufacturing Sector

Figures 2.4 and 2.5 display the total number of employees and establishments for establishments with 20 employees or more. As the figure below indicates, the number of establishments with 20 employees or more is drastically lower than the total number of establishments that employ 1–19 workers. Accordingly, the number of establishments that had more than 20 employees amounted to only 929 in 2004. Furthermore, the number of employees in these establishments grew from 64,498 to 98,148 during the period of 2000–2004.

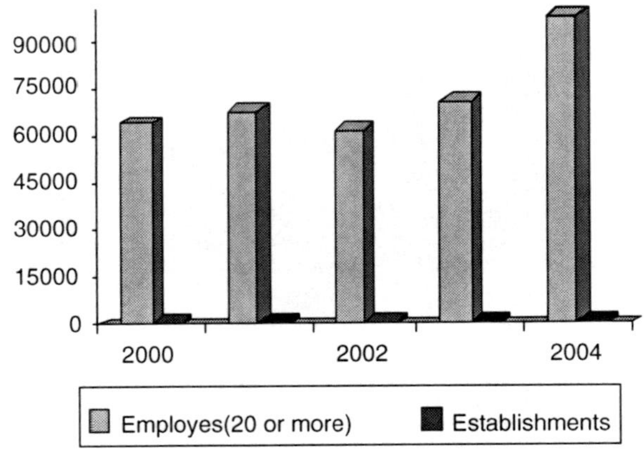

Fig. 2.4 Establishments (20 or more employees)

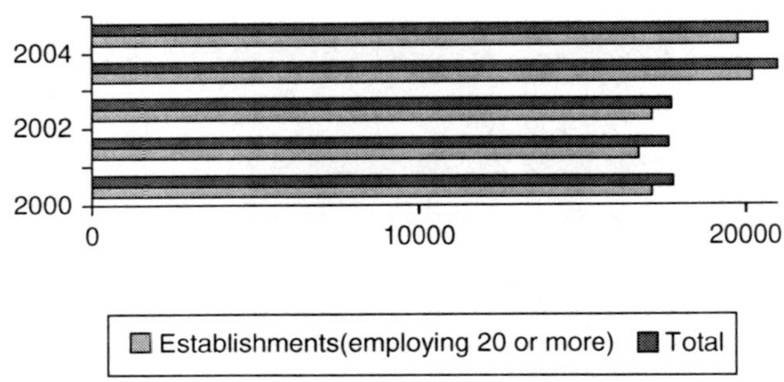

Fig. 2.5 Establishments (20 or more employees)

2.3.1.2 Employment by Establishment Size

Accordingly it is deducted that by 2004:

- Almost half of all employees in the manufacturing sector, 41.2%, were found in establishments that had (1–19) employees.
- Establishments that employed between 1 and 19 employees, as a percentage of the total number of establishments amounted to 95.5% of all manufacturing establishments. This figure fluctuated from 96.3% in 2000 to 96.7% in 2002 and to 95.5% in 2004.
- Around 4% of establishments in the manufacturing sector in Jordan employ more than 20 employees.

2.4 Entry Exit Dynamics

2.4.1 *Methodology*

This section will examine the determinants of firms' entry and exit and their impacts. To guide the choice of the explanatory variables and the specific hypotheses to test, before going further, a clarification of the classification of firms should be presented. For a given year, if a firm was present in $t-1$ but absent in $t+1$, it will be classified as an exitor. If a firm was absent in $t-1$ but present in $t+1$, it will be classified as an entrant. A firm that was absent in $t-1$ and $t+1$ (i.e., it is only present on t) is both entrant and an exitor. It will be put in a "one-year-live" category. Finally, a firm that belongs to none of the three categories will be classified as a survivor. For comparability across sectors, entry and exit rates are defined with respect to the current year's stock of establishments:

$$\text{Entry rate in } t = \frac{\text{Number of new firms from } t \text{ to } t+1}{\text{Number of firms in } t\text{; including entrants but excluding exitors}} \tag{2.1}$$

$$\text{Exit rate in } t = \frac{\text{Number of firms that exit between } t \text{ and } t+1}{\text{Number of firms in } t\text{; including entrants but excluding exitors}} \tag{2.2}$$

Overall, experience shows that there are marked contrasts among countries regarding the determinants and the impacts of entry in developing countries and the relationship to trade liberalization. The literature shows that these contrasts are related to the countries' institutions, policies and the economic environment.

2.5 Determinants of Entry and Exit in Jordan

Over the period throughout 1999–2004, the survival rate among firms that employ 20 employees or more was estimated at nearly 90%. The exit rate reached its highest rate in the year 2000 at 10% and its lowest rate in 2003 at 5%. On the other hand, the highest entry rate was registered in 1999 at 4% and the lowest rate of 1% in 2004. Overall, for this group of firms, the entry rate was lower than the exit rate. Not much can be inferred from the pattern of entry and exit over the period 1999–2004, since exit and entry were not associated with major economic events in the country over the period under investigation.

The dynamics of exit and entry seems to result mainly from intra-sectoral reallocation rather than inter-sectoral reallocation. Those firms that exited the

Table 2.2 No. of Firms, Totals, Survivors, Entrants and Exitors

Year	Survivors	Entrance	Exitors	Total	Survivors/ Total (%)	Entrants/ Total (%)	Exitors/ Total (%)
More than 20 employees							
1999	460	19	0	479	96	4	0
2000	446	17	50	513	87	3	10
2001	458	10	31	499	92	2	6
2002	443	4	40	487	91	1	8
2003	464	8	23	495	94	2	5
2004	444	3	38	485	92	1	8
Less than 20 employees							
1999	695		41	736	94	0	6
2000	654	67	72	793	82	8	9
2001	649	74	79	802	81	9	10
2002	644	70	82	796	81	9	10
2003	632	84	92	808	78	10	11
2004	624	48	114	786	79	6	15
Total							
1999	1,155	19	41	1,215	95	2	3
2000	1,100	84	122	1,306	84	6	9
2001	1,107	84	110	1,301	85	6	8
2002	1,087	74	122	1,283	85	6	10
2003	1,096	92	115	1,303	84	7	9
2004	1,068	51	152	1,271	84	4	12

Source: Industrial Census and Survey, Department of Statistics (DOS), (Jordan)

market went out of business more often than they shifted to other sectors where they could survive (Table 2.2).

The survival rate within firms that employ 10–20 employees was also high and averaged 82.5% over the period 1999–2004. The entry rate within this group was higher than in the larger group of firms with 20 employees or more. This might be the case because capital requirements and other institutional barriers are lower for firms to start this type of business. The exit rate was also high in this group and it seems to follow an upward trend averaging 10% and reaching as high as 15% in 2004. Small firms demonstrated more flexibility in entering and exiting the market, in contrast to the larger firms. This might be the case because costs associated with entering and exiting the market is lower for small firms. This also might reflect a lower degree of specialization and professionalism as far as small firms are concerned. Normally, small projects start without proper feasibility studies or a clear business model and hence their failure rate tends to be higher (Table 2.2).

For the entire manufacturing sector, the survival rate averaged 86%, while the entry rate averaged 5%, and the exit rate registered around 8.5% (Table 2.2).

Table 2.3a presents the number of firms exiting the manufacturing sector, by the number of their survival years. As can be seen below, 63% of all the companies that exited the manufacturing sector between the years 2000 and 2004 had been established for 10 years or more, depicting a trend towards the erosion of long-time established businesses. Very few firms exited the market after 1 or 2 years, and most of them seemed to have spent several years before exiting the market.

For firms with 20 employees or more, Table 2.3b shows that the average median size of employees for surviving firms was nearly double the size for entering and exiting firms for most of the years under investigation. Taking the mean exitors suggests that their employee size is much lower than for survivors or entrants. The mean size for entrants is similar and sometimes higher than for survivors. This means that in order to be able to compete and later to survive in the market, average employee size must be close to the mean of the survivors.

For smaller firms with 10–19 employees, as Table 2.3c depicts, the average employee size of the three groups of firms is similar, and it revolves around 12 employees. In all the cases, it was always less than 14 employees. This suggests that within small firms, size measured by the number of employees, does not influence the firms' competitiveness and hence, its survival ability. Management and the field of work is more likely to influence performance, than the mere size of the firms. This also suggests that there are other factors such as capital intensity and access to market and funding that may decide the exit and entry rate within this group, as we illustrated in section one of this study when securing finance emerged as one of the major challenges facing the SMEs in Jordan. One may also consider technical and marketing techniques that these firms need, in order to remain in the market. At present, there is little institutional support in Jordan with the aim of overcoming problems facing these small firms.

Clearly firms that enter the market tend to expand in terms of the number of employees as more time elapses. Average size for firms that entered the market in 1999 has increased from 93 to 131 after 5 years in the market. The same applies to the median size, which increased from 40 to 70 employees. Firms that managed to survive began to expand their sizes, reflecting their increase in market share and their confidence. It also exhibits the fact that economies of scale are important for such firms. Increase in the number of employees was gradual and consistent over the 5 year period we are covering.

On the other hand, an identification of a consistent trend within firms that are exiting the market was not allocated as shown in Table 2.4. It seems that firms, in order to survive, were trying to hold on to their share in the market. There was no trend which showed that firms were dismissing their employees and consolidating their expenses as normally would be expected from troubled firms. However, for some years as in 2002, the number of employees was halved just 1 year before exiting the market, while in other years almost the same number of employees was maintained. This may indicate that there is rigidity in firing labor in Jordan. This is confirmed by the "World Bank 2008 Doing Business Report," according to which Jordan suffers from a high difficulty of firing index (60) covering workers' legal protections against dismissal, including the grounds permitted for dismissal and procedures for dismissal which indicates rigid regulation in this area. Moreover, firing costs measured as the cost of advance notice requirements, severance payments and penalties due when terminating a redundant worker amount to an equivalent of a 4-week salary (Table 2.5).

Table 2.3 (a) Exitors by number of survival years. (b) Mean and median firm (20 employees and more). (c) Mean and median size firm (10–20 employees)

Year of exit	1	2	3	4	5	6	7	8	9	10+	Grand total	Percentage of total
(a)												
2000	1	1	4	1	5	4	6	2	3	24	51	28
2001		2		3	1	1	3		1	21	32	18
2002		2	3	3	2	6		1		26	43	24
2003				2		2		1	2	17	24	13
2004						1		4	1	26	32	18
Grand total	1	5	7	9	8	14	9	8	7	114	182	100
Percentage of total	1	3	4	5	4	8	5	4	4	63	100	

	Median			Average (mean)				
	Survivors	Entrants	Exitors	Survivors	Entrants	Exitors	Total median	Total average (mean)
(b)								
1999	61		32	128		50	48	104
2000	60	31	35	126	98	57	51	109
2001	60	37	32	127	123	51	50	112
2002	60	44	33	124	138	43	53	116
2003	65	42	31	129	140	38	58	124
2004	60	43		133	149		60	135

	Median			Average (mean)		
	Survivors	Entrants	Exitors	Survivors	Entrants	Exitors
(c)						
1999	13	12	10	13	12	10
2000	13	11	9	13	11	10
2001	13	11	10	13	12	11
2002	13	12	10	13	12	11
2003	12	11	10	12	11	11
2004	13	12	10	13	12	11

Source: Industrial Census and Survey, Department of Statistics (Jordan)

Table 2.4 Mean and Median Entrants Size (20 employees and more)

		After 1	After 2	After 3	After 4	After 5
1999	Average	93	102	112	122	131
	Median	40	45	54	65	70
2000	Average	164	179	190	205	
	Median	22	27	28	30	
2001	Average	145	172	190		
	Median	39	43	60		
2002	Average	54	48			
	Median	26	25			
2003	Average	129				
	Median	36				
2004	Average					
	Median					

Source: Industrial Census and Survey, Department of Statistics (Jordan)

Table 2.5 Mean and Median Exitors Size (20 employees or more)

		Before exit 1	Before exit 2	Before exit 3	Before exit 4	Before exit 5
1999	Average					
	Median					
2000	Average	36				
	Median	25				
2001	Average	44	42			
	Median	31	33			
2002	Average	53	77	67		
	Median	25	50	46		
2003	Average	46	46	51	61	
	Median	26	31	33	48	
2004	Average	39	42	51	61	66
	Median	31	33	35	35	39

Source: Industrial Census and Survey, Department of Statistics (Jordan)

At a subsector level, exit, entry and survivor rates vary to some extent. In general, as noted earlier, the survivor rate is high. It went down to 50% in other manufacturing items (390) and manufacturing of rubber products. The survival ratio was also low in subsectors such as manufacturing of leather products ISIC (323) (0.67) and manufacturing of wood and wood products (ISIC 331) (0.70). Notably, the survival rate of the manufacture of wearing apparel, except footwear ISIC (322) went as low as 0.65. These subsectors have witnessed a major shift over the last few years and there were many new entrants that boosted productivity within the subsector. Hence, this is a case where productivity was increasing, while many firms exited the market. This supports the argument that competitive pressure may boost efficiency. The entry rate in this subsector was estimated at 8% which is the second highest ratio within the entire manufacturing sector. The same trend was almost repeated in the manufacturing of wood and wood products with the highest entry rate at 20%.

In the case of the remaining subsectors with high exit rates, the story was different. It seems that low productivity in few instances such as manufacturing of leather products has pushed some industries out of the market. In this particular case, there were certain arrangements between these firms and the government in place regarding securing public procurements for certain companies. Once these arrangements had been terminated, incumbent firms could no longer survive and there was no incentive for new firms to enter the market (Table 2.6).

As witnessed earlier there is no clear pattern that emerges between entry and exit of firms. In order to determine if there is any significant relation between these two variables, an estimation of the correlation between entry and exit was conducted. Findings suggest that there is no significant correlation between exit and entry as Table 2.7 exhibits. The correlation between entry and exit was found to be negative, suggesting that as more firms exit the market, entrepreneurs would find it less attractive to enter into the same sector. This is a process of learning developed over time. However, since the correlation was not significant, this interpretation should be viewed with some caution.

The same exercise was repeated at a subsector level, as exhibited in Table 2.8. Again, no clear trend emerged concerning the correlation between exiting and entering firms at the subsector level. The sign of the coefficient was sometimes positive and sometimes negative, but not statistically significant. It seems that the decision to exit or enter any market depends on several factors, with the exit rate playing a marginal role in such a decision. This finding is consistent with the earlier conclusion regarding entry and exit by year, when no significant correlation was found between entry and exit for the entire period under investigation.

The impact of some correlation between entry and exit rates may vary across time. It could be negative during the early and late phases of a product's life cycle but it is positive during the expansion phase of industries. For this reason, interaction terms of explanatory variables should be considered later in this study, since not much can be inferred from this analysis.

2.5.1 Productivity Analysis

The importance of analyzing exit–entry dynamics is particularly important to aspects related to productivity and the manner by which this dynamics helps in boosting productivity and hence competitiveness in certain markets. In the following section, we will investigate issues related to productivity and how it evolves over time.

Table 2.9 presents the average productivity measured as the value added per employee for entering, exiting and surviving companies in the manufacturing sector. As can be seen from the figures, over the period from 1999 to 2004, average productivity fluctuated for entrants with an upward tendency. It has significantly decreased for surviving enterprises. For the entire period from 1999 to 2004, average productivity of exitors amounted to JD 7,621 per employee, which is lower than JD 11,290 per employee for survivors, and JD 8,711 per employee for entrants.

Table 2.6 Survivors, Entry and Exit by Industry

		Total firms	Survivors number	Survivor Percentage of total	Entry number	Entry Percentage of total	Exit number	Exit Percentage of total
Industry311	Whole period	595	555	0.93	16	0.03	24	0.04
Industry312	Whole period	19	18	0.95	1	0.05		0.00
Industry313	Whole period	72	71	0.99		0.00	1	0.01
Industry314	Whole period	20	17	0.85	1	0.05	2	0.10
Industry321	Whole period	118	105	0.89	3	0.03	10	0.08
Industry322	Whole period	112	73	0.65	9	0.08	30	0.27
Industry323	Whole period	6	4	0.67	0	0.00	2	0.33
Industry324	Whole period	20	17	0.85	1	0.05	2	0.10
Industry331	Whole period	10	7	0.70	2	0.20	1	0.10
Industry332	Whole period	120	116	0.97	3	0.03	12	0.10
Industry341	Whole period	121	111	0.92	4	0.03	6	0.05
Industry342	Whole period	164	155	0.95	2	0.01	7	0.04
Industry351	Whole period	473	446	0.94	3	0.01	24	0.05
Industry352	Whole period	333	320	0.96	5	0.02	8	0.02
Industry353	Whole period	6	6	1.00	0	0.00	0	0.00
Industry355	Whole period	2	1	0.50	1	0.50	0	0.00
Industry361	Whole period	6	5	0.83	0	0.00	1	0.17
Industry362	Whole period	30	29	0.97	0	0.00	1	0.03
Industry369	Whole period	180	167	0.93	3	0.02	10	0.06
Industry371	Whole period	73	69	0.95	1	0.01	3	0.04
Industry372	Whole period	30	26	0.87	0	0.00	4	0.13
Industry381	Whole period	172	155	0.90	2	0.01	15	0.09
Industry382	Whole period	96	88	0.92	0	0.00	8	0.08
Industry383	Whole period	88	86	0.98	2	0.02	0	0.00
Industry384	Whole period	50	48	0.96	1	0.02	1	0.02
Industry385	Whole period	36	32	0.89	0	0.00	4	0.11
Industry390	Whole period	14	7	0.50	1	0.07	6	0.43

Source: Industrial Census and Survey, Department of Statistics (Jordan)

Table 2.7 Correlations between entry and exit rates by year

		Entry	Exit
Entry	Pearson correlation	1.000	−0.639
	Sig. (2-tailed)		0.172
	N	6	6
Exit	Pearson correlation	−0.639	1.000
	Sig. (2-tailed)	0.172	
	N	6	6

Source: Authors' calculations based on Industrial Census and Survey, Department of Statistics (Jordan)

Table 2.8 Correlations between entry and exit rates by industry

	Pearson correlation	Sig. (2-tailed)
Industry311	0.811	0.050
Industry314	0.430	0.395
Industry321	0.074	0.890
Industry322	0.722	0.105
Industry324	0.430	0.395
Industry332	−0.081	0.879
Industry341	0.514	0.296
Industry342	−0.345	0.502
Industry351	−0.122	0.818
Industry352	0.133	0.802
Industry369	−0.343	0.506
Industry371	−0.057	0.914
Industry381	−0.358	0.486
Industry390	0.802	0.103

Source: Authors' calculations, Industrial Census and Survey, Department of Statistics (Jordan)

Table 2.9 Average of productivity

Average of productivity			
Year of entry	Entrants	Exitors	Survivors
1999		12.890	15.422
2000	8.305	8.080	9.822
2001	8.051	6.884	9.799
2002	5.487	4.183	10.143
2003	14.143	6.070	10.622
2004	7.571		11.933
Grand total	8.711	7.621	11.290

Source: Authors' calculations, Industrial Census and Survey, Department of Statistics (Jordan)

These differences between entrants and survivors on one side and survivors and exitors on the other side indicate an increasing average productivity over the life cycle of a firm in the manufacturing sector, resulting from the advantages of an increasing company size and the competition of other enterprises in the manufacturing sector.

Table 2.10 Average labor productivity

Average of productivity			
Isic2 4d	Entrants	Exitors	Survivors
311	5.907	7.950	9.493
312	2.571		11.539
313		5.585	11.396
314	5.733	12.727	12.031
321	4.609	9.377	9.624
322	2.478	5.702	7.106
323		16.381	8.956
324	2.069	8.945	5.061
331	22.457	11.313	9.464
332	9.664	4.578	7.154
341	8.495	21.484	11.638
342	21.073	7.222	9.908
351	12.481	9.606	12.011
352	7.364	5.831	14.931
355	3.024		
361		4.933	11.177
362		21.616	9.563
369	11.495	7.583	10.656
371		27.579	18.580
372		9.562	10.793
381	18.346	7.320	11.583
382		4.251	13.766
383	8.587		16.828
384	8.625		8.928
385		7.804	8.379
390	3.353	5.755	9.228

Source: Authors' calculations, Industrial Census and Survey, Department of Statistics (Jordan)

However, findings so far suggest that liberalization by forcing the exit of the least efficient producers, contributes to productivity growth since as can be seen from the table average productivity among exitors is lower than that among, survivors and entrants.

Depending on the subsector within the manufacturing sector, Table 2.10 shows that development in the average productivity widely varied over the life cycle of the firms in the respective subsectors. Overall, the sectors of manufacture of Paper and Paper Products (341), Printing and Publishing (342), as well as Iron and Steel (371) exhibited the highest average productivity per employee.

Table 2.11a depicts the productivity changes of companies entering the manufacturing sector from 1999 to 2003 up to the year 2004 according to subsector. As for firms entering in 1999, companies active in the subsectors of manufacture of wearing apparel, excluding Footwear (322), Printing and Publishing (342) and Iron and Steel (371) displayed substantial increases in productivity. These

Table 2.11 (a) Productivity change of entrants (average). (b) Average labour productivity

Year of entry	Isic2 4d	After 1	After 2	After 3	After 4
(a)					
1999	311	0.030	−0.641	0.487	0.312
	312	0.325	1.037	1.814	2.010
	321	−0.007	0.193	0.228	0.638
	322	0.003	−0.078	−0.057	−0.063
	332	6.834	3.258	1.288	0.959
	341	0.748	1.883	3.037	4.554
	351	−10.322	−10.322	−10.322	−11.400
	352	−0.016	−0.016	−0.016	−0.016
	371	0.366	4.001	11.956	13.637
2000	311	−0.170	2.070	1.719	1.816
	322	0.292	0.691	0.669	1.086
	324	0.042	0.042	0.104	1.507
	341	0.389	−1.163	2.131	3.225
	351	1.314	0.766	1.754	2.884
	352	0.275	0.216	0.421	0.554
	369	1.806	3.014	4.508	2.638
	381	3.304	4.087	4.929	4.695
2001	311	0.428	0.067	0.573	
	322	−0.455	0.364	−0.444	
	331	2.159	2.159	2.159	
	355	3.024	3.024	3.376	
	369	7.456	6.650	6.650	
	383	13.460	13.460	13.460	
	384	8.625	9.335	9.447	
2002	311	4.368	4.313		
	314	−1.518	2.338		
	331	25.943	29.827		
	383	−0.603	−0.781		
2003	311	20.898			
	322	1.743			
	332	−2.086			
	351	18.702			
	352	16.650			
	369	−2.015			
	390	−0.004			

Average of productivity	Entry						
year of entry	After 1	After 2	After 3	After 4	After 5	After 6	Grand Total
(b)							
1999	5	9	13	11	11	19	11
2000	8	8	8	9	10		9
2001	3	5	6	6			5
2002	9	14	16				14
2003	12						12
Grand Total	5	9	10	9	10	10	9

Source: Authors' calculations, Industrial Census and Survey, Department of Statistics (Jordan)

developments are an expression of the advantages gained through an increasing company size in these subsectors, e.g., economies of scale. In addition, technological progress and competitive pressure are factors leading to a boost in subsector productivity. As for the manufacture of paper and paper products, it can be noted that firms in this subsector displayed the highest productivity of all subsectors listed, but faced a stagnant productivity level over the following years. This picture slightly changed for the subsector of paper and paper products in 2000, as firms were able to register small productivity gains over the subsequent years. Furthermore, the subsector of food products (311) showed markedly higher levels of productivity for companies that entered the subsector in 2001 than for companies which entered the subsector in other years. Moreover, in 2001, entering firms in the subsector of the manufacture of wood and wood products, excluding furniture (331), exhibited a very low productivity of JD 1,000 per employee, which remained stagnant during the following years.

It should also be noted that special treatment was given to the manufacture of wearing apparel under the QIZs arrangements so that they were exempted from income taxes, and the government facilitated their work by ensuring good infrastructure and access to the US market (saif 2005).

Overall, there was some productivity gain for entrants, which varied across subsectors, as the table exhibits for the period under investigation, productivity improved over time for new entrants.

Regarding companies that entered the manufacturing sector in the years from 1999 to 2002, it can be seen from Table 2.11a and 2.11b that the average productivity per employee of those companies, showed an overall increase over the following years. This rise can be traced back to the productivity gains received from the advantages of an increasing firm size as well as an upward sloping learning curve. It seems also that competition from other companies forced the manufacturing companies to be more productive and efficient. As more time elapsed and firms managed to pass the critical first few years, their productivity exhibited an upward trend.

In order to complete the analysis, examination of productivity development of exitors was conducted. As can be seen from the below, there was a significant decline in terms of productivity of exitors just 1 year before they exited the market.

The overall trend in productivity was negative for most of the years preceding the firms' exit from the market. Productivity deterioration was clear just 1 year before exiting the market which suggests that firms spend some years striving to survive. They only exit when they can no longer stay in the market.

On a subsector level, the subsector of food products (311) exhibited the biggest average declines in productivity for firms leaving the subsector throughout 1999–2002. Firms exiting this subsector in 2002 recorded an average productivity loss of JD 67,616 over the past 4 years which accounted for the greatest average decrease of all sectors during the years 1999–2003. None of the subsectors registered an increase in average productivity for more than 1 year during the covered time period. This means that exiting companies did not manage to continuously reach productivity increases on average over their last years of business in any of the covered subsectors, which indicates weak, and even decreasing, competitiveness of exiting companies in those subsectors.

Overall, the highest loss in productivity for the, entire sector occurs in the year that precedes the year of exiting the market. It is also clear that lower productivity is associated with other variables such as profitability, which will be analysed later together with the determinants of exiting in the econometric section.

As expected, firms exiting the manufacturing sector during 2000 the period of 2004 showed a decreasing average productivity per employee in the last year before their exit. Table 2.12a and 2.12b depicts a considerable decrease in average productivity for exiting companies when compared to the productivity level 5 years before their

Table 2.12 (a) Productivity change of exitors (average). (b) Productivity Change of Exitor

Productivity change of exitors (average)

year of exit	Isic2 4d	Before 1	Before 2	Before 3	Before 4	Before 5	Grand (average)
(a)							
1999	311	−16.041					−16.041
	321	−12.596					−12.596
	322	−8.161					−8.161
	324	−8.724					−8.724
	331	−11.313					−11.313
	332	−7.924					−7.924
	341	−22.429					−22.429
	342	−10.340					−10.340
	351	−17.265					−17.265
	361	−4.933					−4.933
	369	−13.429					−13.429
	371	−40.405					−40.405
	372	−15.712					−15.712
	381	−10.072					−10.072
	382	−9.470					−9.470
	385	−7.518					−7.518
	390	−6.230					−6.230
Total		−13.092					−13.092
2000	311	−6.210	−1.141				−3.675
	313	0.000	5.585				2.792
	314	−14.426	−1.699				−8.062
	322	−5.525	0.124				−2.700
	323	−3.572	−3.572				−3.572
	324	0.000	9.166				4.583
	341	−7.647	8.348				0.351
	342						
	351	−21.820	−3.710				−12.765
	352	−7.962	−4.349				−6.156
	362	−24.504	−2.889				−13.697
	369	−10.096	−0.951				−5.524

(continued)

Table 2.12 (continued)

Productivity change of exitors (average)

year of exit	Isic2 4d	Before 1	Before 2	Before 3	Before 4	Before 5	Grand (average)
	381	−8.054	−3.989				−6.021
	382	−11.717	−9.440				−10.579
	385	−19.299	−6.696				−12.997
	390	−6.328	−3.539				−4.934
Total		−9.811	−1.250				−5.530
2001	311	−26.520	−20.544	−20.124			−22.396
	321	−13.779	−9.951	−3.711			−9.147
	322	−6.510	−5.192	−0.945			−4.216
	323	−16.157	−16.157	0.224			−10.696
	332	−23.936	−20.200	−20.285			−21.474
	341	−22.140	−2.946	3.887			−7.066
	342	−10.955	−4.788	−5.162			−6.968
	351	−2.879	−0.514	1.644			−0.583
	352	0.000	12.647	8.607			7.085
	369	−17.801	−10.859	−12.032			−13.564
	372	−8.110	−2.290	−2.290			−4.230
	381	−6.571	8.966	4.126			2.174
	382	−6.037	−1.965	−2.639			−3.547
Total		−12.415	−5.676	−3.746			−7.279
2002	311	−72.144	−61.207	−64.970	−72.144		−67.616
	314	−2.021	−0.045	1.349	−2.021		−0.684
	321	−5.480	−1.049	0.272	0.728		−1.382
	322	−8.263	−4.393	−4.393	−4.810		−5.465
	332	0.000	14.588	3.447	4.419		5.613
	351	−14.337	−9.542	−11.011	−11.134		−11.506
	352	−5.524	−0.741	−1.262	−5.524		−3.263
	369	−13.120	−8.800	−8.789	−8.542		−9.813
	372	−20.990	−9.055	−12.024	−13.837		−13.977
	381	−4.221	−0.739	−0.987	−0.689		−1.659
	382	−3.341	−2.717	−3.130	−2.849		−3.009
	385	0.000	0.000	4.118	3.290		1.852
	390	−6.929	−5.255	−4.449	−3.453		−5.022
Total		−12.029	−6.843	−7.833	−8.967		−8.918
2003	321	−9.803	−1.598	−3.589	−2.899	−1.168	−3.811
	322	−6.999	−1.764	−0.941	−0.490	−0.306	−2.100
	332	−11.125	−6.911	−7.009	−6.160	−7.113	−7.664
	351	−6.780	−0.789	−0.852	−0.799	−1.850	−2.214
	352	−15.668	−9.795	−10.004	−10.310	−10.393	−11.234
	369	−3.589	0.030	0.327	1.141	1.404	−0.137
	371	−15.972	−3.571	−0.866	−2.155	−1.219	−4.756
	381	−17.557	−7.765	−8.462	−8.843	−9.323	−10.390
	382	−10.381	−2.228	−3.773	−3.771	−4.764	−4.984
	390	−5.648	−1.632	−1.935	−1.826	−1.837	−2.576
Total		−10.35	−3.602	−3.710	−3.611	−3.657	−4.987

(continued)

Table 2.12 (continued)

Productivity change of exitor						
	Befoe 1	Before 2	Before 3	Before 4	Before 5	Total
(b)						
2000	13					13
2001	8	10				9
2002	7	6	16			10
2003	4	4	5	14		7
2004	6	6	6	6	9	7
Total	7.6	6.5	9.0	10.0	9.0	9.0

Source: Authors' calculations, Industrial Census and Survey, Department of Statistics (Jordan)

market exit. Overall, firms that exited in 2001 possessed an average productivity of JD 7,600 per employee compared with nearly JD 9,000, 5 years before they exited the market. Moreover, productivity seems to be declining over time.

2.5.2 Analysis of Productivity Change

The analysis of the productivity change for each group (entrants, exitors, and survivors) has so far been conducted separately. The picture will become clearer if there is a combination of the three groups with a decomposition of productivity changes in order to determine which group contributes more to productivity change.

Labor productivity will be decomposed into the contribution of "internal restructuring" (i.e., productivity growth within the surviving establishments, or the "within" effect), changes in the market shares of the survivors (i.e., productivity grows further if the shares of higher productivity establishments increase, or the "between" effect) and the contribution of entry and exit.

2.5.3 Productivity Change for Entrants, Survivors and Exitors

As Table 2.13a and 2.13b shows, productivity varied across subsectors, with some subsectors achieving strong growth while others suffered from productivity losses. However, the general findings suggest that over the period 2000–2004 positive productivity growth was registered.

Sectors such as wearing apparel, non metallic industry as well as iron and steel scored high levels of productivity growth. Improvements in these sectors can be attributed to favorable economic conditions. For example, the textile industry performance has been boosted by the QIZs and exports to the US market. In the iron and steel industry, the strong growth can be attributed to the expansion in the construction sector.

Table 2.13 (a) Productivity change for entrants, survivors and exitors. (b) Productivity change for entrants, survivors and exitors

	2000				2001				2002			
	Entrants (%)	Exitors (%)	Survivors (%)	Total (%)	Entrants (%)	Exitors (%)	Survivors (%)	Total (%)	Entrants (%)	Exitors (%)	Survivors (%)	Total (%)
(a)												
311	−2.31	−6.26	108.57	100	−6.81	−172.39	279.20	100	0.00	7.64	92.36	100
312	0.00	0.00	100.00	100	0.00	0.00	100.00	100	0.00	0.00	100.00	100
313	0.00	−1.10	101.10	100	0.00	0.00	100.00	100	0.00	0.00	100.00	100
314	0.00	73.09	26.91	100	0.58	0.00	99.42	100	−41.03	−2.48	143.51	100
321	0.00	0.00	100.00	100	0.00	105.24	−5.24	100	0.00	42.02	57.98	100
322	−8.84	−6.73	115.58	100	0.00	30.06	69.94	100	0.00	−66.26	166.26	100
323	0.00	0.00	100.00	100	0.00	694.06	−594.06	100	0.00	0.00	100.00	100
324	−4.99	−64.45	169.44	100	0.00	0.00	100.00	100	0.00	0.00	100.00	100
332	0.00	0.00	100.00	100	0.00	−293.85	393.85	100	0.00	8.68	91.32	100
341	−6.93	−12.82	119.75	100	0.00	38.17	61.83	100	0.00	0.00	100.00	100
342	0.00	−19.21	119.21	100	0.00	17.08	82.92	100	0.00	0.00	100.00	100
351	−11.29	−33.72	145.01	100	0.00	−59.32	159.32	100	0.00	22.59	77.41	100
352	1.66	0.81	97.53	100	0.00	−7.03	107.03	100	0.00	7.30	92.70	100
361	0.00	0.00	100.00	100	0.00	0.00	100.00	100	0.00	0.00	100.00	100
362	0.00	−14.31	114.31	100	0.00	0.00	100.00	100	0.00	0.00	100.00	100
369	0.82	1.27	97.91	100	0.00	1.25	98.75	100	0.00	45.66	54.34	100
371	0.00	0.00	100.00	100	0.00	0.00	100.00	100	0.00	0.00	100.00	100
372	0.00	0.00	100.00	100	0.00	11.26	88.74	100	0.00	48.67	51.33	100
381	−7.70	−1.10	108.80	100	0.00	28.32	71.68	100	0.00	33.78	66.22	100
382	0.00	−0.20	100.20	100	0.00	128.76	−28.76	100	0.00	0.18	99.82	100
383	0.00	0.00	100.00	100	0.00	0.00	100.00	100	21.98	0.00	78.02	100
384	0.00	0.00	100.00	100	0.00	0.00	100.00	100	0.00	0.00	100.00	100
385	0.00	−179.46	279.46	100	0.00	0.00	100.00	100	0.00	10.42	89.58	100
390	0.00	−88.53	188.53	100	0.00	0.00	100.00	100	0.00	88.78	11.22	100

(continued)

Table 2.13 (continued)

	2003				2004		
	Entrants (%)	Exitors (%)	Survivors (%)	Total (%)	Entrants (%)	Survivors (%)	Total (%)
(b)							
311	0.00%	−17.47%	117.47%	100%	0.00%	100.00%	100%
312	0.00%	0.00%	100.00%	100%	0.00%	100.00%	100%
313	0.00%	0.00%	100.00%	100%	0.00%	100.00%	100%
314	0.00%	0.00%	100.00%	100%	0.00%	100.00%	100%
321	0.00%	22.08%	77.92%	100%	103.33%	−3.33%	100%
322	30.77%	92.04%	−22.81%	100%	0.67%	99.33%	100%
323	0.00%	0.00%	100.00%	100%	0.00%	100.00%	100%
324	0.00%	0.00%	100.00%	100%	0.00%	100.00%	100%
332	0.00%	−42.96%	142.96%	100%	0.00%	100.00%	100%
341	0.00%	0.00%	100.00%	100%	0.00%	100.00%	100%
342	0.00%	0.00%	100.00%	100%	0.00%	100.00%	100%
351	0.00%	98.52%	1.48%	100%	0.00%	100.00%	100%
352	0.00%	−27.39%	127.39%	100%	0.00%	100.00%	100%
361	0.00%	0.00%	100.00%	100%	0.00%	100.00%	100%
362	0.00%	0.00%	100.00%	100%	0.00%	100.00%	100%
369	1.86%	1.02%	97.12%	100%	0.00%	100.00%	100%
371	0.00%	19.73%	80.27%	100%	0.00%	100.00%	100%
372	0.00%	0.00%	100.00%	100%	0.00%	100.00%	100%
381	0.00%	17.00%	83.00%	100%	0.00%	100.00%	100%
382	0.00%	−11.68%	111.68%	100%	0.00%	100.00%	100%
383	0.00%	0.00%	100.00%	100%	0.00%	100.00%	100%
384	0.00%	0.00%	100.00%	100%	0.00%	100.00%	100%
385	0.00%	0.00%	100.00%	100%	0.00%	100.00%	100%
390	13.67%	29.20%	57.13%	100%	0.00%	100.00%	100%

Source: Authors' calculations Industrial Census and Survey, Department of Statistics (Jordan)

On the other hand, there are few sectors that experienced negative productivity growth, namely, the food industry, leather products, manufacturing metal and pottery. These sectors are dominated by a small and medium scale industry and lack economies of scale. Operational costs for these industries are not high, hence they managed to stay in the market even with low productivity rates.

The main concern in this section is how much each group – that is the new entrants, survivors and exitors – contributes to enhancing or reducing productivity. From the table above and utilizing the accounting methodology described earlier, it can be seen that clearly the incumbent plants are on average more productive than entrants and exitors over the period 2000–2004. This is the "within effect" which refers to factors internal to firms such as organizational change, and the introduction of new technologies.

New entrants play a minor role in enhancing productivity. In some subsectors they are less productive than the exiting plants in the early years, but become more productive in the later years. They also exhibit the highest positive productivity change during the early years.

This was the case in most of the subsectors under investigation. However, the main contribution to the achieved productivity came from survivors (within effect) who seem to move towards the production frontier as they spent more time in the market. At this stage, one cannot determine the reasons behind these dynamics, because institutional arrangements concerning all sectors are similar.

Productivity dynamics also varied over time and across sectors. During some years when there was a high rate of entry into specific subsectors, new entrants seemed to contribute positively to the total growth. In the absence of new entrants or exitors, the total productivity change was attributed to the survivors.

2.5.4 Econometric Analysis

2.5.4.1 Determinants of Growth

The above approach is used only for comparison purposes. Being strictly an accounting approach, it does not measure precisely the impact of entry and exit on productivity growth. On the one hand, the distinction between the 4 effects ("within", "between" and entry and exit) is not necessarily clear since entry and exit can also induce "internal restructuring" by survivors and reallocation of market shares among firms. On the other hand, "present" competition (i.e., abstracting from entry and exit) can also induce "internal restructuring" and reallocation of market shares. To adequately assess the impact of entry and exit on productivity, the following regression was calculated[3]:

$$\Delta\log(Y_{it}) = \eta_0 + \eta_1 \times \Delta\log(K_{it}) + \eta_2 \times \Delta\log(L_{it}) + \eta_3 \times \log(C_{it}) + \eta_4 \times (9) + \eta_5 \times \log(EX_{it}) + \xi_{it}$$

Aggregated firm level data is used.

It emerges from the results that rate output growth is highly dependent on labor and capital. Both coefficients are significant and they hold the expected positive signs suggesting that growth to some extent is resource based rather than productivity driven. In order to emphasize the impact of entry and exit on productivity changes, several regressions are utilized; the first run using present value of the entry and exit demonstrates that entry rate holds negative sign. This might be so because its influence is more likely to appear later. While exit rate hold negative signs but was not statistically significant, it seems that under this model both exit and entry play marginal role in determining the level of output (Table 2.14).

High concentration, which resembles the market structure, seems to contribute to an increase in survival rate. This simply means that high concentration rate is associated with high output growth. The same logic applies as far as the tariff rate is concerned. Higher tariff rates that represent, to some extent, the state of competition, seems to be attractive and conducive to business survival. This is consistent with earlier findings (Saif and Barakat 2008) which demonstrate that the manufacturing sector in Jordan is highly concentrated and incumbent industries are keen to maintain their interests by sustaining high level of tariffs and through highly concentrated markets.

Table 2.14 Regression results for the following model: $\Delta\log(Y_{it}) = \eta_0 + \eta_1 \times \Delta\log(K_{it}) + \eta_2 \times \Delta\log(L_{it}) + \eta_3 \times \log(C_{it}) + \eta_4 \times \log(EN_{it})$ +(9) $\eta_6 \times \log(EX_{it}) + \xi_{it}$

Variable	Coefficient
Constant	0.206 (2.486)**
Coefficient of the change in the natural logarithm of capital	0.476 (2.668)**
Coefficient of the change in the natural logarithm of labor	1.178 (2.389)**
Coefficient of the change in the natural logarithm of the concentration ratio	0.235 (5.347)***
Coefficient of tariff rate	0.137 (3.705)***
Coefficient of entry rate	−0.124 (−1.959)*
Coefficient of exit rate	−0.003 (−0.083)
Coefficient of determination R^2	0.679
Adjusted Coefficient of Determination	0.530
Number of cross-sections	11
Period	2000–2004

Source: Authors' calculations, Industrial Census and Survey, Department of Statistics (Jordan)
Values in parentheses indicate *t*-statistic
***, **, and * denote that the coefficient is significant at 1, 5, and 10 respectively
$\Delta\log(Y_{it})$ = change in the natural logarithm of outputs, $\Delta\log(K_{it})$ = change in the natural logarithm of capital, $\Delta\log(L_{it})$ = change in the natural logarithm of labor, $\log(CON_{it})$ = the natural logarithm of concentration ratio, $(Tarif_{it})$ = tariff rate, $\log(EN_{it})$ = the natural logarithm of entry rate, and $\log(EX_{it})$ = the natural logarithm of exit rate

Overall, variables explain more than 50% of variations in the dependent variables and the main message through this is that output growth is highly dependent on labor and capital. That growth is resource based more than productivity driven.

Utilizing lag variables has not changed the conclusion; most of the variables held the same signs with the same level of significance, lag variables for entry were used, or whether, variables were entered to capture the nonobservable effects, such as the mark-up.

2.5.4.2 Analysis of Entry

This section aims at analyzing determinants of entry at firm level. In order to do so, the following equation was utilized. It included both observable and nonobservable factors[4].

$$\text{Entry rate}_{i,t} = \alpha_0 + \alpha_1 \times \text{average size of entrants}_{i,t} + \alpha_2 \times \text{industry characteritci}_{,t} + \alpha_3 \times \text{institutional environment}_{i,t} + \alpha_4 \times \text{exit rate}_{i,t\mu i,t} \quad (2.3)$$

To include specific variables about industry characteristics and institutional environment, the above (2.3) can be rewritten as follows:

$$\text{Entry rate}_{i,t} = \alpha_0 + \alpha_1 \times \text{average size of entrants}_{i,t} + \alpha_2 \times \text{profit margin}_{i,t} + \alpha_3 \times \text{concentration ratio}_{i,t} + \alpha_4 \times \text{growth rate}_{i,t} + \alpha_5 \times \text{average productivity}_{i,t} + \alpha_6 \times \text{wage rate}_{i,t} + \alpha_7 \times \text{capital intensity}_{i,t}$$

The regression utilizing the pooled data methods was used in order to identify the main determinants of the entry rate over the period under investigation. Though the correlation coefficient was low, however, most of the independent variables found to be significant and holding the expected sign. The most significant factor that seems to influence the decision to enter any market was profit margin. The more profitable the sector is. the more attractive it is for new comers. Similarly, entry rate was found to be positively correlated with the average values added, which is the measure for productivity (Table 2.15).

These findings suggest that decision to enter the market is rational on the side of the new comers since it is consistent with the conventional wisdom that places profitability and high productivity as the main drivers of new investments. High productivity implicitly means that the overall business environment is conducive and also the available labor force in general is skillful and adequate.

As far as institutional barriers are concerned, it was revealed that concentration for example found to be negatively correlated with entry rate. In other words, highly concentrated sectors seem to erect barriers to new entry, or it may be the case that these sectors are closed to new entrants due to the nature of some of these sectors. Therefore, even while these sectors are highly profitable and secured, in practice, it is extremely difficult to enter such sectors. In other less concentrated sectors, other unobservable factors such as profitability, exposure to competition and productivity, were found to play a more significant role.

Table 2.15 Regression results for the following model: Entry rate$_{i,t}$ = α_0 + α_1 + average size of entrants$_{i,t}$ + α_2 + profit margin$_{i,t}$ + α_3 + concentration ratio$_{i,t}$ + α_4 × growth rate$_{i,t}$ + α_5 + average productivity$_{i,t}$ + α_6 × wage rate$_{i,t}$ + α_7 × capital intensity$_{i,t}$ + α_8 * Tarif$_{i,t}$ + α_9 × exit rate$_{i,t}$ + $\mu_{i,t}$

Variable	Coefficient
Constant	0.008 (1.274)
Coefficient of the average size of entrants	0.000 (2.141)**
Coefficient of the profit margin	0.000 (1.828)*
Coefficient of the concentration ratio	−0.011 (−3.143)***
Coefficient of the growth rate	−0.007 (−1.988)**
Coefficient of the average productivity	0.001 (2.643)***
Coefficient of the wage rate	−0.003 (−4.212)***
Coefficient of the capital intensity	−0.000 (−2.914)***
Coefficient of the tariff	0.045(1.500)
Coefficient of the exit rate	0.041 (1.671)*
Coefficient of determination R^2	0.097627
Adjusted coefficient of determination	0.020280
Number of cross-sections	23
Period	2000–2004

Source: Authors' calculations, Industrial Census and Survey, Department of Statistics (Jordan)
Values in parentheses indicate *t*-statistic
***, **, and * denote that the coefficient is significant at 1, 5, and 10 respectively

The other factor that negatively influences the decision to enter is the wage rate. Higher wage rates, which mean a higher cost, seems to be an important factor before entering a new market. This is not surprising in a country that relies heavily on imported labor and where there is a serious problem regarding finding the right caliber to fill in new vacancies. This is serious problem in the manufacturing sector which strives to survive an era of trade liberalization at a time when surrounding potential competitors, Syria, Egypt, are enjoying a much lower wage rate. It emerges in the first section that there are few restrictions regarding acquiring foreign laborers.

Along with the wage, higher capital intensity, where capital is mostly imported, holds a negative sign suggesting that higher capital intensity does not encourage new comers. Capital intensive industry means higher sunk costs and hence, decision to enter becomes more difficult as our results have suggested.

Other institutional barriers such as investment regulations, labor regulations and other trade and nontrade barriers (discussed in Sect. 2.1) seem to be less significant in deciding whether to enter the market or not. Tariff rates were utilized as one of the factors that might have an influence on the decision to enter, but the coefficient turns out to be significant. Other institutional variables that have been discussed earlier do not discriminate against any sector and hence, it is expected that their impact across sectors is similar to a great extent.

Overall, most of the variables hold the expected sign and decision to enter a certain market is based on a combination of factors that is consistent with the traditional threats associated with doing business, namely, profitability, cost of labor and capital, and productivity rather than the institutional or the exit rate.

2.5.4.3 Analysis of Exit

The other side of the story is related to firm that exit the market. This section analyse determinant of exit through the following equation:

$$\begin{aligned} \text{Exit rate}_{i,t} = \beta_0 &+ \beta_1 \times \text{average size of exitors}_{i,t} + \beta_2 \times \text{average age of exitors}_{i,t} + \\ &\beta_3 \times \text{industry's characteristics}_{i,t} + \beta_4 \times \text{institutional environment}_{i,t} + \\ &\beta_5 \times \text{entry rate}_{i,t} + \upsilon_{i,t} \end{aligned} \quad (2.4)$$

To include specific variables about industry characteristics and institutional environment, the above equation can be rewritten as follows:

$$\begin{aligned} \text{Exit rate}_{i,t} = \; &\beta_0 + \beta_1 \times \text{average size of exitors}_{i,t} + \beta_2 \times \text{average age of exitors}_{i,t} + \\ &\beta_3 \times \text{profit margin}_{i,t} + \beta_4 \times \text{concentration}_{i,t} + \beta_5 \times \text{growth}_{i,t} + \beta_6 \times \\ &\text{average productivity}_{i,t} + \beta_7 \times \text{wage rate}_{i,t} + \beta_8 \times \text{capital intensity}_{i,t} + \\ &\beta_9 \times \text{tarif}_{i,t} + \beta_{10} \times \text{entry rate}_{i,t} + \beta_{i,t} \end{aligned}$$

Variables employed in the regression explain nearly 35% of the variation in the dependent variables as indicated by the correlation coefficient. Profit margin seems to be the most important factor in deciding whether to stay or to exit from the market. Coefficient of profit margin negatively and significantly correlates with the exit rate. Interestingly, it also seems that lower productivity also pushes inefficient firms out of the market, though the coefficient of average value added for exitors, which holds the expected sign, was not statistically insignificant (Table 2.16).

Wage rate, which is a major concern, holds the expected negative sign and was significant. This suggests that higher wage rate, especially when associated with low value added growth, may significantly contribute to push firms out of the market.

This is quite consistent with the findings in the accounting exercise when it was found that survivors are the most productive, while exitors are the least, in terms of labor productivity.

Table 2.16 Regression results for the following model: Exit $\text{rate}_{i,t} = \beta_0 + \beta_1 \times \text{average size of exitors}_{i,t} + \beta_2 \times \text{average age of exitors}_{i,t} + \beta_3 \times \text{profit margin}_{i,t} + \beta_4 \times \text{concentration}_{i,t} + \beta_5 \times \text{growth}_{i,t} + \beta_6 \times \text{average productivity}_{i,t} + \beta_7 \times \text{wage rate}_{i,t} + \beta_8 \times \text{capital intensity}_{i,t} + \beta_9 \times \text{tarif}_{i,t} + \beta_{10} \times \text{entry rate}_{i,t} + \upsilon_{i,t}$

Variable	Coefficient
Constant	0.198 (4.503)***
Coefficient of the average size of exitors	−0.000 (−3.165)***
Coefficient of the average age of exitors	−0.001 (−0.656)
Coefficient of the profit margin	−0.000 (−1.892)*
Coefficient of concentration	0.046 (1.458)
Coefficient of growth	0.127 (2.726)***
Coefficient of the average productivity	−0.003 (−0.595)
Coefficient of the wage rate	−0.032 (−2.282)**
Coefficient of the capital intensity	0.002 (1.196)
Coefficient of the tariff	0.542 (10.958)***
Coefficient of the entry rate	0.348 (0.740)
Coefficient of determination R^2	0.454413
Adjusted coefficient of determination	0.351473
Number of cross-sections	23
Period	2000–2004

Source: Authors' calculations, Industrial Census and Survey, Department of Statistics (Jordan)
Values in parentheses indicate *t*-statistic
***, **, and * denote that the coefficient is significant at 1, 5, and 10 respectively

It is still the case that there is no significant relationship between exitors and entrants. Clearly, the decision to exit from a certain market has little to do with the number of entrants. Other unobservable factors seem to be more significant, especially those related to direct cost, such as wage and profit.

Average size of the firms does not seem to be significant in deciding to exit the market. Exitors vary in terms of size and could be small firms belonging to the small and medium scale industries or could be large firms that belong to a different category. What matters, is the financial performance and the level of productivity.

Also, capital intensity seems to play a minor role in deciding whether to stay or to exit from the market. What is puzzling though, is the positive and significant relationship with the tariff rate which was insignificant as far as the entry rate is concerned. While concentration rate was insignificant as far as the exit rate is concerned, seems that even protected industries may exit market when other factors are not contributing to the survival of the firms.

Other institutional factors are less significant and it seems that the main factors deciding exit and entry rate are related to firm's behavior and its management rather than the external factors (business environment) or other political factors concerning the overall stability.

Overall growth, entry and exit in the manufacturing sector seem to follow certain logic and behaved in a predicted manner. Results found to be consistent with the conventional wisdom as far as conducting business is concerned. There were some data limitations concerning firms that employ between 10 and 19 employees. Level data of firms is not available because annual surveys do not include all these companies. In order to estimate entry and exit within this group, a number of assumptions were made.

It is for these reasons, that we limited the regression analysis to firms that employed 20 or more employees, while we utilized data regarding firms 10–19 in the descriptive side of the analysis.

2.6 Conclusion

The manufacturing sector is an important sector in the Jordanian economy, contributing both to creating jobs and generating added value. The structure of the sector is such that it comprises many small firms that contribute little to the overall output and value added.

Reviewing the institutional arrangements and regulations governing the sector reveals that, there are some impediments that hinder the sector's performance. However, there are barely any measures that distinguish among sectors. Hence, variation in performance is sector-specific and the dynamic of entry and exit relates more to the structure of the sectors more than anything else.

Analyzing the market dynamics of entry and exit revealed some important facts. Entry and exit over the period 1999–2004 was stable and no pattern was inferred since exit and entry were not associated with major economic events in the country over the period under investigation.

Very few firms exited the market after 1 or 2 years. Most of them seem to spend several years before exiting the market.

The mean size, measured by the number of employees, for entrants is similar and sometimes found to be higher than for the survivors. This means that in order to be able to compete and later to survive in the market, average employee size must be close to the mean of the survivors.

Firms, which managed to survive, began to expand their size, reflecting their rising share in the market and their confidence. This also suggests that economies of scale are important for such firms. Increase in the number of employees was gradual and consistent over the 5 year period that was covered. At a subsector level exit, entry and survivor rates vary to some extent.

There is no clear pattern between entry and exit. An estimation of the correlation between entry and exit was implemented in order to determine if there was any significant relation between these two variables. Findings suggest that there were no significant correlation between exit and entry. The correlation between entry and exit was found to be negative suggesting that as more firms exit the market, entrepreneurs would find it less attractive to enter into the same sector.

Regarding productivity issues, average productivity per employee for new entrants increased over the following years. This rise can be traced back to the productivity gains received from the advantages of an increasing firm size as well as an upward sloping learning curve. It seems also that competition from other companies forced the manufacturing companies to be more productive and efficient. As more time elapsed and firms managed to pass the critical first few years, their productivity exhibited an upward trend.

The overall trend in productivity was negative for most of the years preceding the firms' exit from the market. Productivity deterioration was clear just 1 year before exiting the market which suggests that firms spend some years striving to survive. They only exit when they can no longer stay in the market.

This was the case in most of the subsectors under investigation. However, the main contribution to the achieved productivity came from survivors (within effect) who seemed to move towards the production frontier as they spent more time in the market.

It emerged out of the regression, that growth is related to factors such as capital and labor. Entry rate was found to be positively contributing to growth, while exit was less significant. For entry and exit, it seems that the most decisive factors are those related to profitability and wage level more than to the overall institutional barriers or business environment. Moreover firm size concentration and tariff were found to be less significant.

Regarding entry determinants, it emerges that the decision to enter a certain market depends on a combination of factors that is consistent with the traditional threats associated with doing business, namely, profitability, cost of labor and capital, and productivity, rather than the institutional or the exit rate. The same applies to the dynamics of the exit rate when it was found that institutional factors are less significant, and it seems that the main factors deciding exit and entry rate are related more to the firm's behavior and its management than the external factors (business environment) or other political factor concerning the overall stability.

Finally, findings suggest that there was no significant relationship between exitors and entrants. Clearly, the decision to exit from a certain market has little to do with the number of entrants. Other unobservable factors seem to be more significant especially those related to direct cost such wage and profit.

2.7 Notes

1. CBJ Annual Report, preliminary estimates for 2004–2006.
2. For the purposes of this study, SMEs are those establishments that have between 1 and 19 employees.
3. The number of observation=55 (11 industry×4 years). The sample denotes cross section and time series.
4. The sample is a cross-section and times series. Estimation method is pooled data regression.

References

Central Bank of Jordan (1999–2007) Monthly statistical bulletin, several bulletins

Central Bank of Jordan Annual Report (2006) Accessed http://www.cbj.gov.jo/uploads/chapter2/pdf

Department of Statistics (2004) Press release

Department of Statistics (2007) Statistical yearbook 2006

Saif I, DeBartolo (2007) The impact of displaced Iraqis on the Jordanian economy. Center for Strategic Studies, University of Jordan, Amman

Saif I (2005) The socio economic implications of the qualified industrial zones in Jordan. Center for Strategic Studies, University of Jordan

Saif I, Barakat N (2008) Competition and competition policy and economic policy and economic efficiency in Jordan. In Sekkat Kh (ed) Competition and efficiency in the Arab world, Palgrave Macmillan, New York

World Bank (2007) Resolving Jordan's labor market paradox of concurrent economic growth and high unemployment

Chapter 3
Industrial Dynamics and Productivity in Morocco: A Quantitative Assessment

Lahcen Achy and Khalid Sekkat

3.1 Introduction

Since the early 1980s, the Moroccan authorities have decided to switch from a model of a relatively closed import substitution economy with a large public sector to free trade and a market oriented economy. Price liberalization policy has been one of the main components of the Structural Adjustment program (SAP). Most prices of goods and services were freed in order to promote competition and allow market mechanisms to have a greater role in allocating and pricing factors, goods and services. The country speeded up the process of economic reforms during the 1990s. The new strategy is thought to set the economy on a path of higher efficiency as a result of the intense competition, and thus foster growth and development.

Twenty-five years after the starting of the comprehensive program of economic reforms, the economy is, however, still highly specialized in comparison to many other developing countries (LDCs) and this specialization is increasing over time. Few industries (Textile, wearing apparel, food products and chemicals) represent around 70% of total manufacturing employment. In these industries, productivity is decreasing markedly (except for chemicals) and mark-ups are relatively high. The issue is the most worrying, as the lack of competitive pressure is found to be associated with low efficiency and concerns the most important industries in terms of employment. There seems, therefore, to be a clear issue of industry dynamisms in the Moroccan manufacturing sector (Achy and Sekkat 2008).

Comparing these observations to recent empirical evidence across a number of LDCs shows that the persistence of inefficiency, despite reforms, is specific to few of them (including Morocco) and is, therefore, worrying. The analysis of a set of 25 liberalization episodes by Wacziarg and Wallack (2004) shows that while liberalization induced little inter-sectoral labor reallocation (i.e., decrease in specialization), it led to important intra-sectoral reallocations towards more productive firms.[1]

L. Achy (✉)
INSEA, Rabat, Morocco
e-mail: lachy@ulb.ac.be

K. Sekkat (ed.), *Market Dynamics and Productivity in Developing Countries: Economic Reforms in the Middle East and North Africa*, DOI 10.1007/978-1-4419-1037-0_3,

Aw et al. (2000) find that exposure to trade forces the exit of the least efficient producers in Korea and Taiwan, while Pavcnik (2002) finds that market share reallocations contributed significantly to productivity growth following trade liberalization in Chile. Hoekman and Winters (2005) report that studies using firm-level data conclude that major impacts of trade reforms are natural selection among firms and reductions in X-inefficiency: less efficient firms in a sector are forced to downsize, improve efficiency or exit, while more productive (efficient) firms expand their market shares.

The fact that the process of trade liberalization in Morocco has not induced a similar productivity gain as in other emerging countries, suggests that other reforms such as domestic regulation also play an important role for intra-sectoral reallocation. For instance, Revenga (1997) suggests that the small market responses found in developing countries may reflect restrictive labor market regulation. Harrison and Hanson (1999) argue that imperfect product markets may also be a relevant factor underlying the observed limited impacts of trade liberalization. Borjas and Ramey (1995) suggest that capital or financial market distortions or inefficiencies will affect the ability of firms to expand or to enter. These variables may even be more important than the labor market. Finally, studies on the determinants of investment (e.g., Mauro 1995; Wei 2000) suggest that the institutional framework of a country could also have marked impacts on entry and exit.

The present chapter examines whether the above documented processes by which economic liberalization affects productivity have taken place in Morocco. It addresses three specific questions. First, how much important is the dynamic of firms' entry and exit in Morocco? Second, what are the economic, policy and institutional factors that affect such a dynamic? Third, does the process of firms' entry and exit improve the manufacturing sector's productivity?

The rest of the chapter is divided into five sections. Section 3.2 provides a deep discussion of the main changes in regulations and policies that might affect dynamic of firms' entry and exit in Morocco. Section 3.3 presents our dataset and its main characteristics. Section 3.4 analyses the determinants of firms' entry and exit in Morocco while Sect. 3.5 is devoted to the impact of firms' entry and exit on productivity. Finally, Sect. 3.6 concludes.

3.2 The Institutional Environment for Business

3.2.1 Overview

There is a vast body of economic literature showing that business regulations are essential for investment, trade, and ultimately economic growth. Business regulations cover a whole range of laws, formal and informal rules governing business conduct in the economy. These include rules for entry in and exit from business, labor and tax regulations, degree of contract enforcement, cost and efficiency of dispute settlement mechanisms and so forth.

Over the last two decades, Moroccan authorities have made significant efforts to reform and streamline various business regulations, in order to create an environment conducive to investment and growth. These efforts often took place as a component of foreign investment attractiveness package and more recently under the pressure exerted by "international rankings" such as "doing business" ranking conducted by the World Bank.

The implementation of regulatory reforms faced resistance and has been sometimes politically contentious because of their impact on the initial distribution of power and rents among various administrative departments. Still, many improvements have been recorded, such as the reduction in the number of procedures required to start a business, availability of information on services provided by administrative departments for firms, simplification of customs procedures and the diminution of delays in trading across borders.

Despite these efforts, various indicators reveal that business environment in Morocco continues to represent a serious handicap for investment, both domestic and foreign.

Part of the explanation is related to the restrictive nature of legal and regulatory provisions. The cost of firing an employee, for instance, was found to be too high under the Moroccan labor code compared to international standards (World Bank 2006). Corporate tax, although reduced in 2008 from 35 to 30%, is still above its level in Europe or in other competing countries. The average corporate tax rate in Eastern Europe and Central Asia is 20% (Pricewaterhouse Coopers 2008). Similarly, Turkey, which has a Free Trade Agreement with Morocco, has lowered its corporate tax rate from 30 to 20 since 2006. Marginal taxes on personal income, which reach 42% in Morocco, are also very high and represent according to the World Bank (2006) a severe constraint to employing human capital in Morocco.

The second part of the explanation is related to the degree of enforcement of the existing regulations. Regardless of the quality of business regulations, what really matter for investors are the barriers and constraints they effectively face on the ground. For instance, competition law was expected to enter into force in July 2001; however, so far there has been no effective implementation of its provisions. In the same vein, commercial courts have been created, but judges have not been adequately trained to settle disputes and enforce contracts.

The rest of this section deals with various business regulations relevant to the purpose of entry and exit dynamics in the Moroccan manufacturing sector in Morocco.

3.2.2 *Corporate Regulations*

Business in Morocco can be conducted under various legal forms. In addition to individual companies, two additional forms are frequently encountered: "Joint stock companies[2]" and "Limited liability companies (LLC).[3]"

Joint Stock Companies (SA) must have a minimum of five shareholders and a minimum capital of MAD 300,000 (roughly US$ 37,000 in 2007), if the company is non-listed on the stock market and MAD 3 millions (US$ 370,000) otherwise. The capital must be entirely subscribed and at least 25% paid up. The rest must be paid up within 3 years from the date of its registration. The company can be 100% held by foreign companies or individuals.

Regarding LLC, they can be created even with a single shareholder, and a minimum capital of MAD 10,000 (US$1250). They may be 100% owned by foreign companies or individuals.

A majority of manufacturing firms in Morocco (58%) are LLC. Individual firms represent 24% and joint stock companies 15%. The rest of the firms (3%) have other marginal legal forms such as cooperatives.

The legal structure of an LLC is rather simple and its management easier. It offers the possibility of incorporating an individual LLC which is new under the Moroccan law. This legal status is also flexible, as an LLC can be transformed into a joint stock company if shareholders need a more sophisticated structure. Under the LLC, the manager's liability is civil and criminal, but penalties are less severe compared to the directors and the president of the board in joint stock companies.

3.2.3 Labor Market Regulations

Restrictive labor market regulations are often highlighted among major impediments to business growth and may lead to a large informal manufacturing sector. The degree of restrictiveness of the labor market regulations is examined by reviewing the main provisions of the Moroccan labor code adopted in 2003 and entered into force in 2004.

The Moroccan labor code stipulates that labor contract may be oral or written. The term of the contract can be fixed or indefinite. However, companies can enter into fixed term contracts for 1 year, renewable only once, after which the contract is converted by law into an indefinite period contract. Companies must register all their employees with the social security department (CNSS) from the beginning of their contract. The Moroccan labor code sets a minimum monthly wage (referred to as SMIG) that is revised regularly to preserve purchasing power of workers. However, minimum wage in Morocco seems to evolve very irregularly, and without any close link with the consumer price index variation or labor market conditions. For instance, minimum wages were frozen from 1996 to July 2000, and increased by as much as 10% in July 2000. This irregular pattern of the minimum wage in Morocco can be attributed to the fact that, in practice, it is highly driven by political cycles, and trade unions' pressures.

As far as layoff of employees is concerned, it can only occur in the case of serious offense. Firing costs per year are paid on the basis of seniority. Dismissal without well founded cause may result in the payment of damages. The labor code has fixed the indemnity to 1.5 months of salary per year worked with a maximum of 36 months. Finally, employers wishing to close their business must first receive an authorization from the local authority represented by the governor.

3.2.4 Trade Policy and Regulations

Protective trade policy implemented before 1983 created anti-export bias and generated rent-seeking situations in the manufacturing sector. Frequent and unpredictable tariff revisions were mainly driven by government financial and balance of payment distresses. They reflect discretionary power enjoyed by public authorities in setting trade policy. Trade liberalization was a key component of the SAP in which Morocco embarked in 1983. The Foreign Trade Law promulgated in 1992 (law 13/89) consolidated trade liberalization process and adapted Morocco's legislation to principles and provisions of the General Agreement on Tariffs and Trade (GATT).

The general trend of Morocco's trade policy is one of liberalization according to its WTO commitments. Morocco has therefore kept on reducing its external tariffs. Yet, the observed level of tariffs remains high and even seems to have increased over the late 1990s. This was the outcome of converting quantitative restrictions into equivalent tariffs in 1996, and the inclusion of the fiscal levy on imports (PFI) into tariff rates in 2000 (WTO 2003).

Morocco grants preferential treatment for imports originating in countries members of regional or bilateral trade agreements to which it takes part, on a reciprocal basis. These are for example, the United Maghreb Arab countries (UMA), the Arab Free-trade Area (GAFTA), the Association Agreement with the EU, the Free-trade Agreement with EFTA, and bilateral free-trade agreements with countries in the region such as Egypt, Jordan and Tunisia. Morocco also grants such treatment under trade and tariff agreements and the Global System of Trade Preferences (GSTP). However, to be eligible for preferential treatment, goods must be covered by a certificate of origin. They also must be directly shipped to Morocco from the country of origin.

Moroccan standards and technical specifications are generally optional. However, they become compulsory for reasons related to health, security, hygiene and environmental protection. In such cases, they apply without discrimination to imported and domestic goods. Imports are subject to a conformity certificate issued by the Ministry of trade and industry. Mandatory standards currently apply to some iron and steel products, gas products, electrical equipment, textile products, domestic appliances, and toys. Morocco has not signed any mutual recognition agreement and does not automatically accept foreign certification; the current regulatory framework, which is under revision, may address this issue.

Table 3.1. reports data on tariff rates computed as simple averages at two digit level. It indicates the average tariff for the whole manufacturing sector declined from roughly 68% in the early nineties to 27.6% in 2005. The trend recorded by the level of protection in Morocco reflects the process of tariff dismantling implemented under multilateral commitments (WTO) as reported rates are granted on an

Table 3.1 Morocco's MFN simple average tariffs

Code	Industry	1993	2001	2005
15	Food and beverage	84.68	51.59	47.36
16	Tobacco	22.50	25.00	25.00
17	Textile	92.55	42.48	41.10
18	Wearing	99.64	49.99	49.80
19	Footwear	77.92	45.33	44.53
20	Wood	73.88	41.51	41.03
21	Paper	87.03	45.32	42.81
22	Printing	55.17	29.18	24.61
24	Chemicals	54.28	26.74	20.97
25	Plastic	83.19	44.83	42.54
26	Other non-metallic mineral products	66.91	36.92	33.22
27	Metallurgy	33.69	24.63	14.35
28	Other fabricated metal products	72.76	33.92	33.46
29	Machinery and equipments	52.76	13.02	9.19
30	Office machine	63.09	10.73	5.45
31	Other electrical equipment	72.58	29.19	24.93
32	Television, radio receivers etc	58.65	7.02	6.86
33	Medical and other precision equipments	62.51	7.32	6.13
34	Cars	64.38	27.70	25.55
35	Manufacture of other transport equipment	59.69	22.60	20.95
36	Other manufacturing	87.20	29.10	19.29
	All manufacturing sector	67.86	30.67	27.58

Source: Data compiled by the authors from TRAINS Database, UNCTAD 2006

MFN basis. Under regional and bilateral agreements (with the EU, GAFTA members or Agadir members) tariffs are even lower.

However, the average tariff rate for the manufacturing sector dissimulates large differences among industries. The highest tariffs are recorded in labor intensive industries, such as wearing and apparel (49.8%), footwear (44.53%), textiles (41.1%) or in food and beverages industries (47.36%), which make these industries less exposed to import competition. On the other hand, capital intensive and technology-based industries, such as "medical and other precision equipments industry," "machinery equipment" tend to benefit from substantially lower rates (less than 10%).

3.2.5 Exchange Rate Policy

Morocco reformed its foreign exchange system in the late 1980s and early 1990s by, gradually, unifying and liberalizing foreign exchange markets. Morocco has established current account convertibility since 1993, but still imposes restrictions on capital account convertibility for residents, and fewer restrictions are imposed on inflows than on outflows. Non residents are allowed to hold accounts in foreign and domestic currencies, but residents' accounts are subject to more regulation than non-residents' accounts.

The Central bank law that entered into force in February 2006 contributed to clarify the roles of the Bank Al Maghrib (BAM) in relation to those of the Ministry of Finance (MOF) in the area of exchange rate policy. As a consequence, the MOF and the BAM are holding joint monthly meetings to investigate issues related to the exchange rate regime, the deepening of exchange and financial markets, and foreign exchange regulations.

The main objective of exchange rate policy in Morocco has been to stabilize the Real Effective Exchange Rate (REER) vis-à-vis the main trading partners. This objective is sought, in nominal term, by pegging the MAD to a basket of currencies and, in real terms, via budgetary and monetary policies aiming at curbing inflation. In the past, the exchange rate was determined on the basis of a currency basket including Morocco's major trading partners, weighted by their importance in Morocco's foreign trade and the pattern of currencies settlement. The composition was kept secret by the central bank. More recently, more transparency has been introduced in the exchange rate setting mechanism by disclosing the composition of the currency basket. The latter is 80% composed by the euro and 20 by the US dollar.

Our estimates of the real effective exchange rate suggest that the Moroccan Dirham exhibited some level of overvaluation over the nineties, particularly starting from 1994. The level of overvaluation has even increased following the adoption of a single currency in Europe. The Moroccan government faced a critical issue since the Moroccan Dirham appeared to be undervalued against the dollar, but overvalued compared to the Euro. In April 2001, the currency composition of the basket was revised by attributing more weight to the Euro. This revision has not entirely eliminated the overvaluation but reduced its magnitude as shown in the Table 3.2.

3.2.6 Competition Policy

Morocco adopted a competition law in July 2001. The law applies to all natural persons or corporations whether their headquarters are established or not in Morocco, provided, that their operations or behaviors have an effect on competition in the Moroccan market or in a substantial part of it. The law covers all activities of production, distribution and services. It also applies to public entities, which engage in commercial activities as economic agents, but does not apply to the sovereign acts of the state itself. The competition law defines provisions that govern freedom of prices and rules to protect competition. It determines the rules to deal with anti-competitive practices, abuse of dominant position and economic concentrations. However, there are, exemptions when anti-competitive practices are the result of implementing legal or regulatory provisions, or in case their authors can

Table 3.2 Bilateral and reel effective exchange rate

	Bilateral nominal exchange rate (DH/US $)	Real effective exchange rate (trade weighted)
1990	8.24	100.00
1991	8.71	103.12
1992	8.54	103.81
1993	9.30	106.77
1994	9.20	110.07
1995	8.54	113.69
1996	8.72	114.67
1997	9.53	115.57
1998	9.60	118.50
1999	9.80	119.56
2000	10.56	123.10
2001	11.61	118.09
2002	10.97	117.62
2003	9.57	115.23
2004	8.87	114.23
2005	8.86	110.57

Source: Authors' computation from exchange rate data provided by IMF and trade data provided by Foreign exchange office

justify that their effect on economic progress are sufficiently high to compensate for restrictions on competition, and that they allow consumers to get a fair share of profit, without eliminating competition in a substantial part of the market.

There are two major authorities in the field of competition: The Prime Minister and the Competition Council. The Prime Minister, through the "*Department of General Affairs*," is the Administrative Authority in charge of competition policy implementation. However, so far there has been no effective implementation of the law's provisions. The department in charge of competition has received a number of complaints related to anti-competitive practices, but no concrete actions have been taken already.

3.3 Data and Descriptive Statistics

3.3.1 Data Source

The database used originates from the yearly survey conducted by the Ministry of Industry and Trade. This survey covers all manufacturing firms with at least ten employees or with an annual turnover that exceeds 100,000 MAD (Between US $ 9000 and 12,000 depending on the exchange rate). It collects firm level data on a set of variables such as turnover, output, value added, exports, investment, gross labor cost, and the number of permanent and temporary employees.

Table 3.3 Share of firms with more than ten employees and their contribution in the manufacturing sector in Morocco

	Total (1)	Firms with more than ten employees on average (2)	% (2)/(1)
Year 1995			
Number of firms	6,176	4,128	67%
Employment	371,420	356,479	96%
Production	142.9	135.7	95%
Exports	35.0	34.8	99%
Investments	8.0	7.6	95%
Year 2000			
Number of firms	7,046	4,387	62%
Employment	422,932	406,036	96%
Production	164.0	153.9	94%
Exports	43.1	42.7	99%
Investments	11.1	10.7	97%
Year 2004			
Number of firms	7,737	4,478	58%
Employment	445,639	425,859	96%
Production	185.4	176.3	95%
Exports	50.7	50.1	99%
Investments	11.5	11.2	97%

Source: Authors calculations from manufacturing survey. Data on production, exports and investments are expressed in billion MAD

For the purpose of this study, *only firms that provide 10 or more jobs over their survival period* are included in our database. Three main reasons have motivated this choice. First, to ensure comparability of our results with those of the existing empirical literature that uses the same criterion. The second, turnover among very small firms tends to be very high, which would have distorted our results. Third, as shown in the Table 3.3, although firms with less than ten employees represented 33% of firms in 1996, 38% in 2000 and 42% in 2004, their contribution to the manufacturing sector tends to be extremely low. By using firms that provide ten or more jobs over their survival period, our study covers 95 of employment and production of the manufacturing sector and almost the total of its exports.

3.3.2 *Descriptive Analysis*

For a given year t, if a firm was present in $t-1$ but absent in $t+1$, it will be classified as an exitor. If a firm was absent in $t-1$ but present in t, it will be classified as an entrant. A firm that was absent in $t-1$ and $t+1$ (i.e., it is only present on t) is both entrant and an exitor. Finally, a firm that belongs to none of the three categories will be classified as a survivor. For comparability across sectors, we define entry and exit rates with respect to the current year's stock of establishments:

$$\text{Entry rate in } t = \frac{\text{Number of new firms from } t \text{ to } t+1}{\text{Number of firms in } t\text{; including entrants but excluding exitors}} \quad (3.1)$$

$$\text{Exit rate in } t = \frac{\text{Number of firms that exit between } t \text{ and } t+1}{\text{Number of firms in } t\text{; including entrants but excluding exitors}} \quad (3.2)$$

3.3.2.1 Entry and Exit Rates

Firm entry and exit is a part of the market selection process by which resources are reallocated within or across industries. Over the period 1996–2004, entry rates of firms in the manufactured sector in Morocco have varied between a minimum value of 3.1% in 2001 and a maximum value of 6.7% recorded in 1999 and 2000. The average entry rate over the period of time covered amounted roughly to 5% (Fig. 3.1).

Regarding the exit rate, its lowest value was 3.5% in 1999 and its highest value was 7.9% in 2000. Measured on the basis of standard deviation, entry rate has been relatively less volatile compared to exit rates with values of 1.2 and 1.5 respectively.

Over the last 5 years covered by the study, the net entry rate has been systematically negative, which probably reflects the impact of trade liberalization that places firms in a more competitive environment and forces the vulnerable ones to exit from the market.

3.3.2.2 Process of Firms' Exit

On the basis of the distribution of exiting firms by the number of their survival years, it appears that less than 25% of firms exit from the market before their fifth anniversary. In addition, more than half of the exiting firms do survive for more

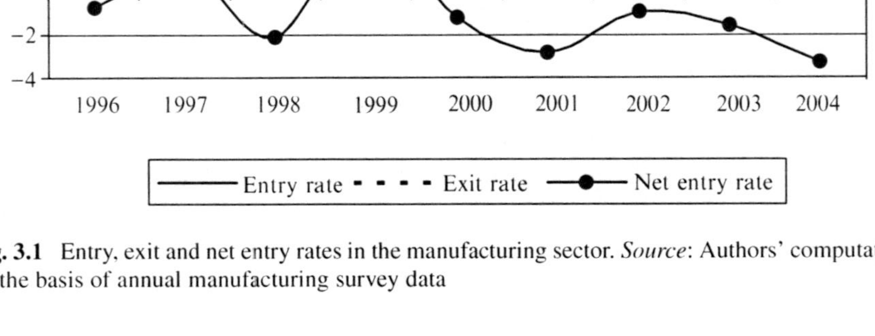

Fig. 3.1 Entry, exit and net entry rates in the manufacturing sector. *Source*: Authors' computation on the basis of annual manufacturing survey data

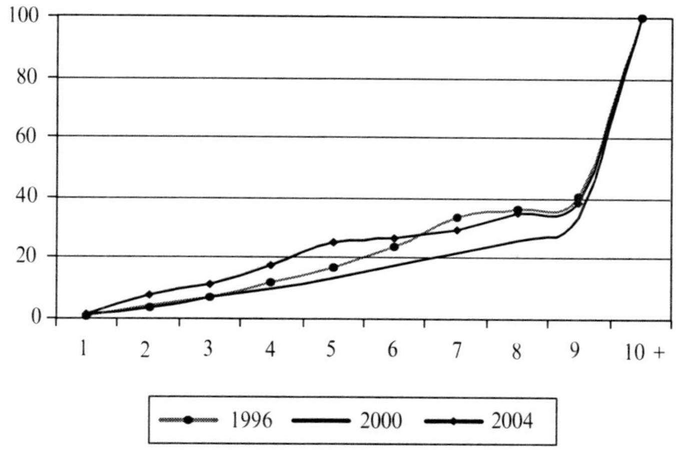

Fig. 3.2 Cumulative exitors (in %) by number of survival years. *Source*: Authors' computation on the basis of annual manufacturing survey data

than 9 years, but fail to remain in the market for longer periods. This finding seems curious compared to the literature according which the survival of entrants is low, with a large number of entrants failing within the first year (e.g., Churchill 1955; Baldwin 1995). Market in Morocco seems to have tolerated inefficient firms for a longer period of time compared to other countries (Fig. 3.2).

3.3.2.3 Entry and Exit Effects on Firms' Size

There is a relationship between firm turnover and size. Entrants tend to have a size which is lower than the average firm size found in the industry (e.g., Boeri and Cramer 1992). On the other hand, firms exiting the industry tend to have a smaller size than the average size of the industry.

For the case of Morocco, data on the manufacturing firms reveal that the average size of surviving firms is higher than the average size of firms that decide to enter the market. The difference between these two averages is statistically significant for every single year over the period 1996–2004. This finding seems to be consistent with the existing empirical evidence reported in the literature. Our computations show that while the average size of surviving firms tends to increase over the years, the average size of entrants has recorded a certain decline, particularly in 2003 and 2004.

The average size of exitors appears to be highly volatile as it ranges between 49.5 in 2004 to 83.2 in 2000. On the other hand, the difference between the average size of surviving and existing firms is only significant in four cases out of eight.

Regardless of the type of the firm (entrant, surviving or exiting), the median size is significantly lower than the average size. This result indicates that the distribution of firms is skewed to the left, in other words, small firms tend to dominate the

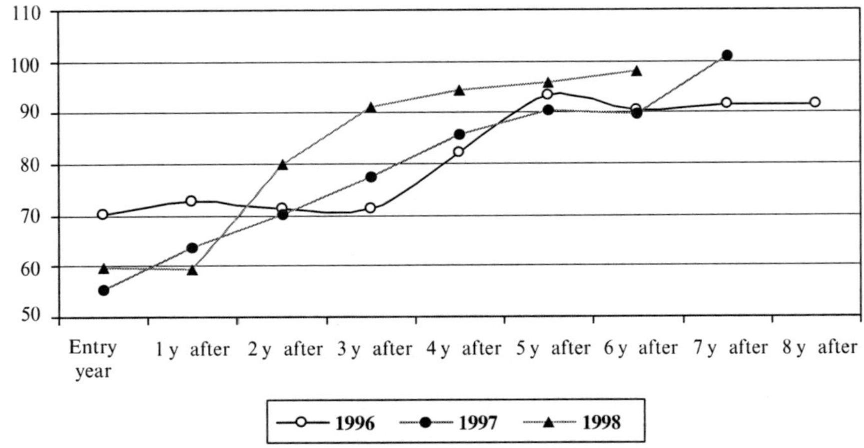

Fig. 3.3 Mean entrant's size over years of survival. *Source*: Authors' computation on the basis of annual manufacturing survey data

distribution. The median among surviving firms has been very robust over the period 1996–2004 and amounted on average to 34 employees per firm. The median size among entrants has been more volatile as it ranged from 18 employees per firm recorded in 1997 to 36.5 in 1998.

Overall, firms start business with a relatively small size and then grow progressively over the years. Figure 3.3 shows the itinerary of three cohorts of firms in terms of their average size. The figure reveals different growth patterns.

Firms that entered the market in 1996 had on average, a larger size at their birth. However, they struggled to grow over the three first years of their lives. Their average size increased significantly during their fourth and fifth year, and roughly stabilizes over the rest of the covered years. On the other hand, firms that started their business in 1997 were smaller at their birth. But their average size increased faster and become larger by their seventh birthday when compared to firms that entered in 1996.

Figure 3.4 reports the average size of three cohorts of firms over the years preceding their death. In all cases, the average size tends to decline some years before the complete exit of the firm from the market. In other words, firms facing difficulties attempt first to adjust through workers' layoff. Achy (2006) has shown that 48% of jobs destroyed in the manufacturing sector in Morocco over the period 1990–2002 were due to surviving firms. When firm's situation worsens, the decision to exit is then taken.

Entry and exit rates presented earlier are computed as averages for the whole manufacturing sector. These averages dissimulate substantial variation among industries. Figure 3.5 shows that in 2004, for instance, entry rates varied between 0 and 13% with an average of 4.6% for the whole manufacturing sector. Exit rates varied within the same range, and their average amounted to 7.9%. The same finding applies to every single year within the period covered by the study.

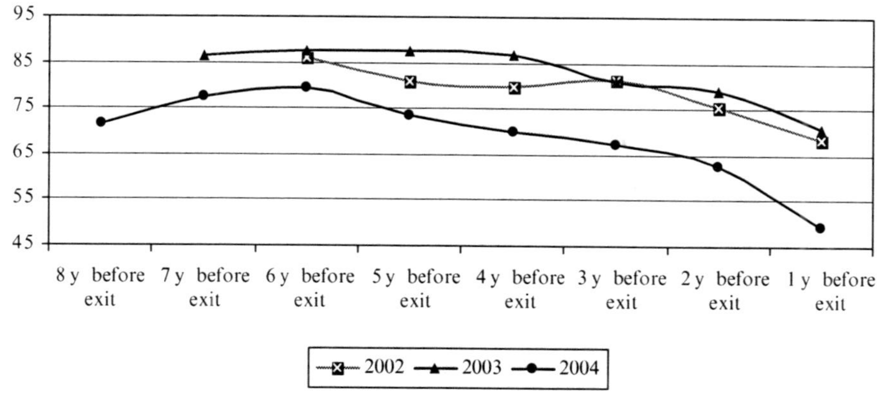

Fig. 3.4 Mean firm's size over the last years of survival. *Source*: Authors' computation on the basis of annual manufacturing survey data

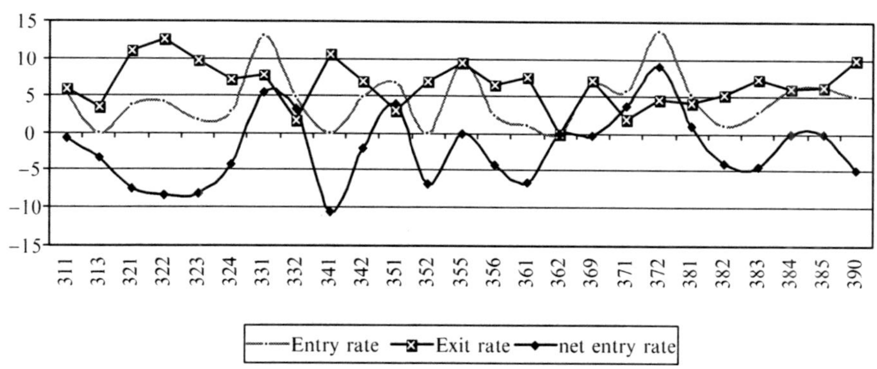

Fig. 3.5 Entry, exit and net entry rates by industry in 2004. *Source*: Authors' computation on the basis of annual manufacturing survey data

Therefore, the behavior of entry and exit rate tends to be sector specific, which is in line with the previous empirical literature that reports a strong variation of entry and exit rates across industries (Siegfried and Evans 1994; Geroski 1995; Fotopoulos and Spence 1998; Carree and Thurik 1999; Hölzl and Sögner 2004).

Achy and Sekkat (2008) has shown that irrespective of the indicators under consideration, textiles, wearing apparel (except footwear) and food products (Coded 321, 322 and 311 respectively in Fig. 3.5) emerge as the most important industries in the manufacturing sector in Morocco. Together, they represent more than 50% of the total manufacturing employment and exports and around 30% of its value added. Hence, instead of looking at each one of the 25 manufacturing industries, the rest of this section focuses on the behavior of entry and exit rates within these key industries over the period 1996–2004.

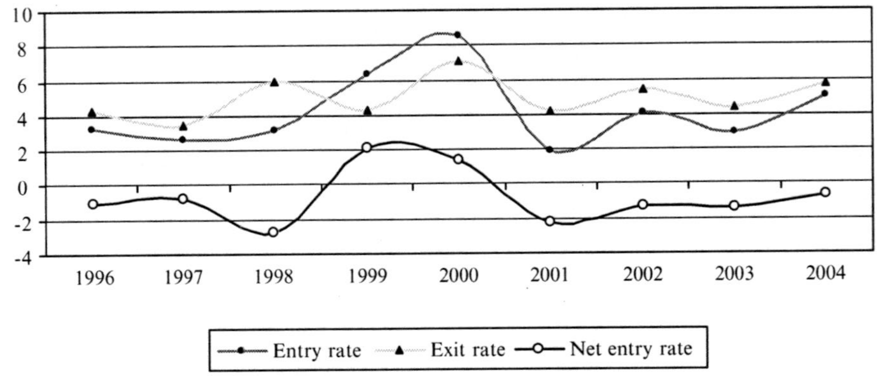

Fig. 3.6 Entry, exit and net entry rates in the sub-sector of food product. *Source*: Authors' computation on the basis of annual manufacturing survey data

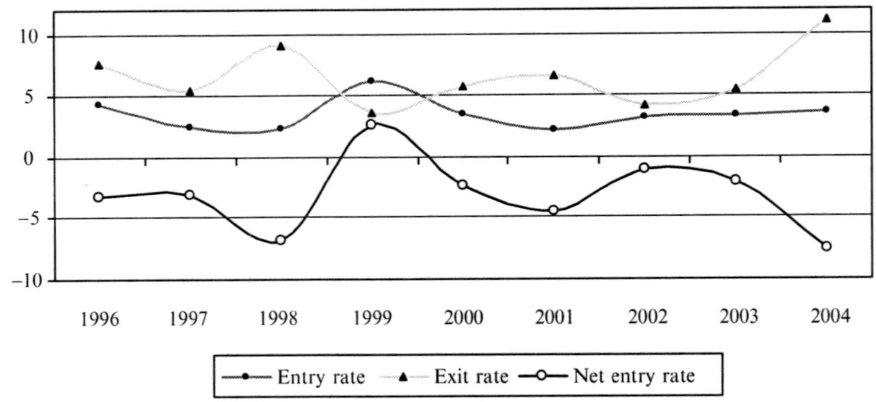

Fig. 3.7 Entry, exit and net entry rates in the sub-sector of textiles. *Source*: Authors' computation on the basis of annual manufacturing survey data

Entry rates in the food products varied between 1.9 and 8.55%. These rates tended to be relatively more volatile compared to exit rates, which varied between a minimum value of 3.5 and a maximum value of 7.1%. On the basis of the net entry rate, three clear sub periods can be distinguished. From 1996 to 1998 and from 2001 to 2004 exit rates surpassed entry rates. Conversely, for the period 1999–2000, entry rates were higher than exit rates (Fig. 3.6).

Regarding textiles, the net entry rate over the period 1996–2004 has been negative. At the exception of 1999, the flow of firms exiting has always been stronger than the flow of firms entering the textile industry. The gap between entry and exit has even widened over the last years and reaches 7.6 by the end of 2004. In addition to the East European competition, textile industry also suffered from the expected effect of dismantling of the Multi-Fiber Agreement (MFA) that occurred in 2005 (Fig. 3.7).

For the sub-sector of wearing apparel except footwear, two contrasting sub periods emerge from analyzing the behavior of entry and exit rates. Over the first sub period that lasted 4 years (1996–1999), entry rates have always been superior to exit rates. The net entry rate reached a maximum of 12.6% in 1999 compared to an exit rate of roughly 4%. However, since 2000, the net flow of firms into the sub-sector of wearing apparel except footwear has been negative. The net entry rate recorded an extremely worrying value of –8.5% in 2004 with the closure of more than 100 firms (Fig. 3.8).

Correlations between entry and exit rates among various industries have been computed for each year over the period 1996–2004 and reported in the Table 3.4 below. These correlations do not exhibit any specific pattern and tend to be globally low.

Regarding correlations between entry and exit rates for each of 25 industries covered by our study, their values are presented in Table 3.5. Theoretically, if entry and exit rates at the industry level are mostly driven by industry specific shocks,

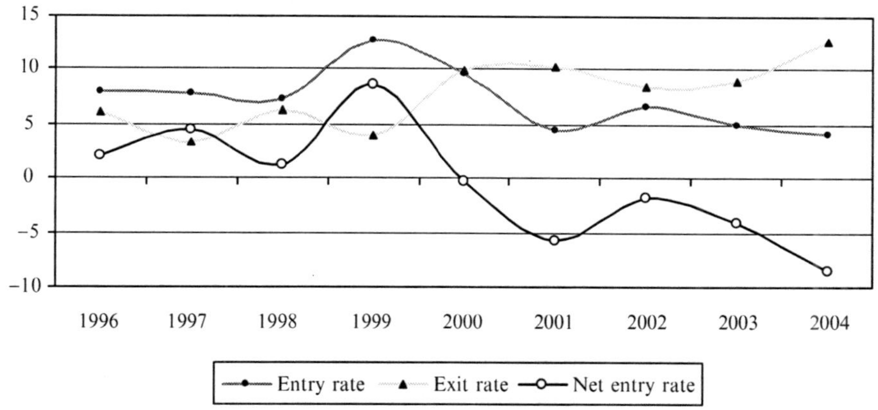

Fig. 3.8 Entry, exit and net entry rates in the sub-sector of wearing apparel except footwear. *Source*: Authors' computation on the basis of annual manufacturing survey data

Table 3.4 Correlations between entry and exit rates among industries by year

Year	Correlation
1996	0.218
1997	0.037
1998	0.346
1999	–0.234
2000	0.169
2001	–0.387
2002	0.330
2003	0.134
2004	–0.004

Source: Authors' computation on the basis of annual manufacturing survey data

then the cross-sectional correlation should be negative (Bartelsman et al. 2004). Alternatively, if entry and exit rates at the sectoral level are driven by a process of creative destruction within the industry, it is expected that entry and exit will exhibit both high entry and high exit rates. In this case, the cross-sectional correlation of entry and exit rates should be positive. According to Caves' (1998), entry and exit rates tend to be positively correlated in industries with steady states of maturity, but varying structural entry barriers. The correlation between the two is negative during the early and late phases of a product's life cycle. During the expansion phase, industries have both high entry rates and high exit rates.

In 5 manufacturing industries out of 25, entry and exit rates are positively correlated. This is particularly the case of food products, rubber and plastic products, and other chemical products. These correlations corroborate the predominance of within industries reallocations over sectoral shocks. On the other hand, entry and exit rates are negatively correlated in two industries (including wearing apparel). This finding confirms the fact that these industries are hit by industry specific shocks that lead simultaneously to high exit rates and low entry rates. Finally, in the rest of the industries, entry and exit rates are not significantly correlated.

3.4 The Determinants of Firm Entry and Exit

A series of firm, industry and country specific factors determine the intensity of entry and exit. We investigate the determinants of entry and exit in Morocco using a methodology inspired by Disney et al. (2003a) and Klapper et al. (2004) and distinguishing between the three categories of factors. The econometric model for the entry is:

$$\begin{aligned}\text{Entry rate}_{i,t} = {} & \alpha_0 + \alpha_1 \times \text{average size of entrants}_{i,t} + \alpha_2 \times \text{industry characteritcs}_{,t} \\ & + \alpha_3 \times \text{institutional environment}_{i,t} + \alpha_4 \times \text{exit rate}_{i,tt} + \mu_{i,t} \qquad (3.3)\end{aligned}$$

where i stands for industry, t stands for time, entry rate is defined in (3.1), exit rate is given by (3.2).

Firm's characteristics include average size of entrant in terms of employment or output.

Industry's characteristics include profit margin, concentration ratio, growth rate, average productivity, average wage rate and capital intensity. Profit margin determines the attractiveness for new firms to enter into the industry. It is measured using the markups computed by Achy and Sekkat (2008). The concentration is an indicator of the easiness to enter a market. It is easier to enter perfectly competitive industries in which many small firms produce standard products. The C4 or Herfindahl will be used. The change in the growth rate (acceleration) of the industry is a proxy of its life cycle. New firms prefer to enter rapidly growing industries. The other variables aimed at capturing some "natural" barriers to entry. Capital intensity may discourage entry because if the industry uses capital-intensive

Table 3.5 Correlations between entry and exit rates by industry

Code	Industry	Correlation
311	Foods products	0.672
313	Beverages	−0.112
321	Textiles	−0.319
322	Wearing apparel, except footwear	−0.655
323	Leather products	−0.392
324	Footwear, except rubber or plastic	−0.468
331	Wood and wood products, except furniture	0.330
332	Furniture, except metal	0.035
341	Paper and paper products	0.270
342	Printing and publishing	−0.012
351	Industrial chemicals	0.087
352	Other chemicals	0.543
355	Rubber products	0.546
356	Plastic products	0.417
361	Pottery, China, Earthenware	−0.570
362	Glass products	−0.180
369	Other non-metallic mineral products	0.767
371	Iron and Steel	−0.271
372	Non-ferrous metals	0.290
381	Fabricated metal products	0.174
382	Machinery, except electrical	0.268
383	Machinery, electric	0.314
384	Transport equipment	0.657
385	Professional and scientific equipment	0.152
390	Other manufactured products	0.239

Source: Authors' computation on the basis of annual manufacturing survey data

technology, the cost of the initial investment could be substantial. It can be computed as the ratio of capital to the number of employees. The average labor productivity reflects the performance of existing firms. It can also be associated with investment. In both cases, high labor productivity should discourage entrants either because investment requirements are indivisible and massive or because of the risks of severe post-entry competition. The average wage rate in an industry can be negatively correlated to the entry rate, if it reflects the demand for industry-specific skills. Finally, since entry and exit rates tend to be correlated as shown in Table 3.5 and reported in (Caves 1998), exit rate is included in (3).

Country's variables include trade barriers, exchange rate, investment and labor market regulations as well as indicators of governance (e.g., political stability, corruption, democratic accountability, bureaucratic quality). Some of the indicators are published by international institutions (e.g., ICRG, WB, and TI) with a time dimension and can be fruitfully introduced in the regression. They are complemented by information on regulations and policies presented in Sect. 3.2.

Note that the impact of some explanatory variables may depend on the value of others. For instance, the correlation between entry and exit rates is negative during the early and late phases of a product's life cycle, but it is positive during the expansion phase industries. For this reason, lags and interaction terms of explanatory variables are considered.

The model for exit is similar to entry:

$$\begin{aligned}\text{Exit Rate}_{i,t} = {} & \beta_0 + \beta_1 \times \text{average size of exitors}_{i,t} + \beta_2 \times \text{average age of exitors}_{i,t} + \\ & \beta_3 \times \text{industry's characteristics}_{i,t} + \beta_4 \times \text{institutional environment}_{i,t} + \\ & \beta_5 \times \text{entry rate}_{i,t} + \upsilon_{i,t}\end{aligned} \tag{3.4}$$

where i, t, industry's characteristics, institutional environment indicators and entry and exit rates are defined as above. Average size (age) of entrant is the average size (age) of exitors between t and $t+1$. The following signs are expected for the coefficients. Negative for profit margin (losses stimulate the decision to exit), capital intensity (sunk cots delay exit), growth rate (firms can survive in rapidly growing industries) and concentration ratio (high concentration reduces competition among firms).

Estimations of (3.3) and (3.4) were conducted using various combinations of the above explanatory variables, of interactions terms and of lags. To save on space, Tables 3.6 and 3.7 concern regressions giving the most robust results; i.e., the less sensitive to the estimation methods, presence of other control variables and missing values. Given the fact that the dependent variable can not take values below zero (there is no negative entry or exit rate), econometric theory implies that OLS estimation gives biased results and should use instead the Tobit method. However, if the sample contains no (or a very limited number of) zeros, OLS is preferred by applied econometricians. In this case, the bias is almost inexistent and OLS gives easily interpretable coefficients. Since in our sample the proportion of zeros is non negligible, we present the results with both estimation methods. Moreover, the analysis in Sect. 3.3 suggests that there was a change in the behavior of the entry and exit rates in the early 2000s. This may be related to an expected change in labor regulations (see Sect. 3.2) or to the adoption of competition law (see Sect. 3.2). Whatever the reason, this suggests that conducting estimation on the whole sample on the one hand and on a sub-sample covering only the 2000s may be instructive.

Tables 3.6 and 3.7 show that the results are slightly better for the exit than for the entry equation. The quality of fit is markedly higher when estimation is conducted over the 2000s only. The results are almost not affected by the estimation method. Focusing on the Tobit results and the 2000s sub-sample, entry is affected significantly and negatively by the Real Effective Exchange Rate (REER). An increase in the REER means an appreciation of the dirham and, hence, a loss of competitiveness of Moroccan firms with respect to foreigners both on the domestic and international markets. This dissuades firms from entering. The coefficient of the lagged entry rate is positive and significant. This implies that if entry is feasible into a given market (less barrier to entry or expanding demand), there will be more and more entry. Interestingly, the coefficient is almost twice higher during the

Table 3.6 Determinants of entry rate (dependent variable = log ((entrants/survivors) × 100+1))

	Estimates			
	OLS		Tobit	
	1997–2004	2001–2004	1997–2004	2001–2004
Explanatory variables				
Constant	−1.66	16.56	−1.70	19.27
	−0.70	2.47	−0.62	2.88
Log of capital intensity	−0.07	−0.10	−0.07	−0.08
	−1.02	−0.87	−0.83	−0.77
Acceleration of demand	−0.44	−0.07	−0.49	−0.04
	−0.92	−0.12	−1.21	−0.08
Log of concentration ratio	−0.26	−0.06	−0.31	−0.11
	−2.69	−0.43	−2.59	−0.62
Log of trade protection	−0.09	0.13	−0.11	0.17
	−0.57	0.67	−0.80	0.93
Real effective exchange rate	0.03	−0.14	0.02	−0.16
	1.23	−2.32	1.04	−2.78
Log of lagged entry rate	0.19	0.36	0.23	0.44
	1.69	2.39	2.24	3.10
Adjusted R^2	0.11	0.20		
Number of observations	136	68	136	68
Percentage of zeros			12.50	16.18

Table 3.7 Determinants of exit rate (dependent variable = log ((entrants/survivors) × +1))

	Estimates			
	OLS		Tobit	
	1997–2004	2001–2004	1997–2004	2001–2004
Explanatory variables				
Constant	−3.69	5.99	−3.85	5.91
	−1.50	1.31	−1.48	1.26
Log of capital intensity	−0.10	−0.04	−0.10	−0.03
	−1.50	−0.52	−1.27	−0.46
Acceleration of demand	−0.68	−1.02	−0.73	−1.10
	−1.75	−2.36	−1.97	−3.28
Log of concentration Ratio	−0.28	−0.38	−0.31	−0.41
	−2.95	−3.20	−2.77	−3.49
Log of trade protection	−0.05	−0.15	−0.03	−0.15
	−0.31	−0.82	−0.27	−1.32
Real effective exchange rate	0.05	−0.03	0.05	−0.03
	2.14	−0.84	2.09	−0.82
Log of lagged exit rate	−0.01	−0.03	−0.01	−0.04
	−0.07	−0.18	−0.10	−0.31
Adjusted R^2	0.10	0.23		
Number of observations	136	68	136	68
Percentage of zero			8.09	2.95

2000s than over the whole period irrespective of the estimation method. One possible explanation is that the competition law enacted in 2000, although not completely enforced, facilitated entry of new firms.

Demand plays an important role in the process of firms exit. The corresponding coefficients are negative and significant. When the increase in demand is higher and higher there is less exit; firms stay in the market. When the decrease in demand is larger and larger there are more exits; firms abandon the market. This contrasts with the entry estimation results where demand acceleration (or deceleration) has no effect. A possible explanation is that for entry, firms (because of, say, new investment to establish that may be sunk) prefer to see whether the trend in demand is permanent or temporary. In contrast, a sharp deceleration in demand may put some firms into unsustainable deficits and push them to exit. This is especially the case if credit is difficult to obtain. Concentration, reflecting the intensity of competition, has a significant and negative coefficient. Firms operating in poorly competitive environment are likely to survive than those in highly competitive environment. Finally, the REER and the lagged exit rate have no effect on exit rate which also contrast with the results for entry rates.

The contrast between the results for entry rate and those for exit rate may appear striking at first sight. However, one would adopt a broader interpretation of the effect of the variables given, that the phenomenon underlying the dependent variable is firm's decision while the one behind some explanatory variables is macroeconomic or sectoral. From a firm point of view, the effect of the REER and sector demand might both reflect demand constraints while concentration and lagged entry might both reflect competition intensity. In this framework, the results of entry and exit point to the same "broad determinants": entry is encouraged by (permanent) demand's increase and intense competition while the reverse is true for exit.

3.5 Entry, Exit and Productivity

There are two commonly used measures of productivity: TFP and labor productivity. Although TFP contains more information than labor productivity (Hulten 2000), it requires a number of assumptions to construct capital stock and factors' shares that it is likely to have more measurement error.[4] We will focus on labor productivity.

3.5.1 *Accounting Analysis*

We decompose labor productivity into the contribution of "internal restructuring" (i.e., productivity growth within the surviving establishments, or the "within" effect), changes in the market shares of the survivors (i.e., productivity grows further if the shares of higher productivity establishments increase, or the "between" effect) and contribution of entry and exit. Let's define a given industry's labor productivity at time t, P_t, as its real gross output per worker. Firm j labor productivity at time t, p_{jt}, is defined in a similar way. The share of firm j in the industry, total employment at time t is γ_{jt} and Δ is the first difference operator. So one can show that:

$$\Delta P_t = \frac{\sum_{j \in \text{Survivors}} (\gamma_{jt-1} \times \Delta p_{jt}) + \sum_{j \in \text{Survivors}} (\Delta \gamma_{jt} \times \Delta p_{jt})}{\sum_{j \in \text{Survivors}} (\gamma_{jt} \times p_{jt}) - \sum_{j \in \text{Survivors}} (\gamma_{jt-1} \times p_{jt})} \tag{3.5}$$

The change in the industry wide productivity is equal to the sum of the changes in productivity within survivors (first term in (3.5)), changes in survivors' market share (second term in (3.5)), entrants' contribution (third term) and exitors' contribution (last term).

For the same reasons as in Sect. 3.4, we computed the decomposition of labor productivity for the whole period and for the sub-sample 2001–2004. These are presented in Tables 3.8 and 3.9 respectively. The results read as follows. In Table 3.8, the cell corresponding to foods products-total means that for each year between 1997 and 2004 (included), labor productivity was 4.50% higher with respect to its level in 1996. This additional productivity decomposes as follows: Contribution of entrant (5.68%) + Contribution of exitors (−10.33%) + Between effect (0.00%) + Within effect (9.15%); which gives 4.50%. Figures in Table 3.9 read in a similar way except that the additional productivity is with respect to its level in 2001.

The results pertaining to the whole period correspond to the one an analyst familiar with the manufacturing sector in Morocco expects. Labor productivity decreased in 14 sectors out of 25. Except for food, the most important industries belong to the decreasing group. The process of entry and exit resulted in a net decrease of productivity in almost all industries (20 out of 25). The reallocation of market shares among firms (between effect) plays no role. Any improvement in industries productivity was due to restructuring by survivors (within effect). However, such restructuring was enough to improve industries' productivity. Firms that exit are not necessarily less productive than survivors.

The picture emerging from Table 3.8 seems a little bit dark. However, the results in Table 3.9 mitigate greatly this vision. On average, for each year between 2002 and 2004, productivity is higher than its 2001 level in a large majority of industries (i.e., 19 out of 25) and the additional productivity is far from negligible (a minimum of 4.48% of the 2001 level each year). All the important industries in the Moroccan manufacturing sector belong to the increasing group. The process of entry and exit resulted in a net increase of productivity in almost all industries (19 out of 25). Its contribution is sizeable ranging from 15% of the additional productivity (Other non-metallic mineral products) to 150% (Non-ferrous metals). For wearing apparel (the most important in terms of employment), its contribution is almost 80%. Like in the previous table, the reallocation of market shares among firms (between effect) plays no role. In contrast, restructuring by survivors (within effect) improved

Table 3.8 Decomposition of labor productivity over the whole period

Code ISIC	Industry	Employment in 2001	Entry	Exit	Between	Within	Total	Net entry
311	Foods products	18.27	5.68	−10.33	0.00	9.15	4.50	−4.65
313	Beverages	1.17	2.71	−9.54	0.00	11.14	4.30	−6.84
321	Textiles	8.06	7.36	−12.79	0.00	1.71	−3.73	−5.43
322	Wearing apparel, except footwear	34.60	18.17	−24.60	0.00	2.78	−3.66	−6.44
323	Leather products	3.62	2.86	−14.19	0.00	−0.59	−11.92	−11.33
324	Footwear, except rubber or plastic	–	9.56	−19.06	0.00	1.45	−8.05	−9.50
331	Wood and wood products, except furniture	1.94	5.94	−20.58	0.00	12.89	−1.74	−14.64
332	Furniture, except metal	0.83	3.62	−10.90	0.00	1.66	−5.62	−7.28
341	Paper and paper products	1.63	1.20	−18.51	0.00	2.35	−14.96	−17.32
342	Printing and publishing	1.69	5.30	−9.63	0.00	2.22	−2.12	−4.34
351	Industrial chemicals	6.29	1.25	−4.56	0.00	2.84	−0.47	−3.31
352	Other chemicals	0.23	12.92	−5.37	0.00	8.47	16.02	7.55
355	Rubber products	2.51	1.16	−26.34	0.00	−5.62	−30.80	−25.18
356	Plastic products	1.10	6.43	−10.30	0.00	3.84	−0.03	−3.87
361	Pottery, China, Earthenware	0.38	7.48	−7.08	0.00	3.20	3.60	0.40
362	Glass products	5.34	1.21	−0.81	0.00	4.60	5.00	0.40
369	Other non-metallic mineral products	0.38	5.59	−17.09	0.00	11.94	0.43	−11.51
371	Iron and Steel	0.58	6.83	−5.09	0.00	1.01	2.75	1.74
372	Non-ferrous metals	4.56	12.50	−0.51	0.00	3.59	15.58	11.99
381	Fabricated metal products	0.98	6.70	−12.75	0.00	4.48	−1.57	−6.05
382	Machinery, except electrical	4.42	4.22	−8.63	0.00	5.26	0.85	−4.41
383	Machinery, electric	1.60	20.58	−7.56	0.00	2.90	15.92	13.02
384	Transport equipment	0.49	5.39	−7.16	0.00	2.77	0.99	−1.78
385	Professional and scientific equipment	0.38	4.33	−33.85	0.00	3.70	−25.82	−29.52
390	Other manufactured products	0.38	3.57	−15.38	0.00	−1.10	−12.91	−11.81

productivity in many instances. Finally, unlike in Table 3.8, exitors are less productive than survivors in many industries (13 out of 25). The contrast between the results of the two tables is striking. It suggests a sort of "self selection" process (Hausman and Rodrik 2006) by which firms try different method and strategy before finding the most profitable one and adopting it. The contrast between the results for the whole period and the 2000s period mainly reflect the disappointing results of the years 1995–1999. During the latter, firms have been involved in such process of "self selection" with poor results, but once the process led to a good selection, the reward was there. It is beyond the scope of this report to test the well founding of such explanation, but it is worth investigating.

3.5.2 *Econometric Analysis*

The above approach is used only for comparison purposes. Being strictly an accounting approach, it does not measure precisely the impact of entry and exit on productivity growth. On the one hand, the distinction between the four effects ("within," "between" and entry and exit) is not necessarily clear, since entry and exit can also induce "internal restructuring" by survivors and reallocation of market shares among firms. On the other hand, "present" competition (i.e., abstracting from entry and exit) can also induce "internal restructuring" and reallocation of market shares. To adequately assess the impact of entry and exit on productivity, we will run the following regression:

$$\begin{aligned}\Delta\log(\mathrm{Y}_{it}) = \eta_0 + \eta_1 \times \Delta\log(\mathrm{K}_{it}) + \eta_2 \times \Delta\log(\mathrm{L}_{it}) + \eta_3 \\ \cdot \log(\mathrm{C}it) + a4 \cdot \log(\mathrm{EX}it) + a5 \cdot \log(\mathrm{EX}it)\, xit \end{aligned} \tag{3.6}$$

which simply states that the change in output (Y) of a survivor i at time t depends on the change in its inputs (K, L) and on the state of present competition (C), entry (EN) and exit (EX) rates in its sector. The changes in Y, K and L are measured as the changes in real value added, capital (real net investment) and the number of workers respectively. The variables C, EN, EX are introduced separately to distinguish between the impacts of present competition, entrants and exitors respectively. Present competition (C) will be proxied using openness to trade at the sector level (which avoids simultaneity issues), concentration ratio among survivors or mark-up. To account for non-observable effects, industry and time dummies will be introduced. Since entry and exit may produce their effect only after some time, their lags will also be considered.

Equation (6) was estimated using various combinations of the above explanatory variables, of interactions terms and of lags. To save on space, Table 3.10 reports regressions giving the most robust results; i.e., the less sensitive to the estimation methods, presence of other control variables and missing values. Given the fact that some of the explanatory variables (employment and capital) are determined simultaneously with dependent variable, using the OLS estimation

Table 3.9 Decomposition of labor productivity over the period 2001–2004

Code ISIC	Industry	Employment in 2001	Entry	Exit	Between	Within	Total	Net entry
311	Foods products	18.27	9.69	–5.10	0.00	7.90	12.49	4.59
313	Beverages	1.17	4.62	–2.52	0.00	–3.23	–1.13	2.10
321	Textiles	8.06	13.58	–6.26	0.00	3.07	10.39	7.32
322	Wearing apparel, except footwear	34.60	30.23	–11.72	0.00	5.06	23.58	18.52
323	Leather products	3.62	6.24	–12.87	0.00	–3.50	–10.12	–6.62
324	Footwear, except rubber or plastic	–	19.47	–7.38	0.00	4.32	16.41	12.08
331	Wood and wood products, except furniture	1.94	7.94	–4.18	0.00	9.94	13.70	3.76
332	Furniture, except metal	0.83	5.70	–0.73	0.00	1.32	6.29	4.97
341	Paper and paper products	1.63	1.87	–11.95	0.00	2.29	–7.80	–10.08
342	Printing and publishing	1.69	9.53	–4.49	0.00	3.26	8.29	5.03
351	Industrial chemicals	6.29	2.10	–0.74	0.00	5.70	7.06	1.36
352	Other chemicals	0.23	15.61	–1.06	0.00	12.31	26.86	14.55
355	Rubber products	2.51	2.45	–9.35	0.00	–16.20	–23.09	–6.89
356	Plastic products	1.10	9.68	–4.03	0.00	4.74	10.39	5.65
361	Pottery, China, Earthenware	0.38	11.29	–2.45	0.00	7.83	16.67	8.84
362	Glass products	5.34	1.77	0.00	0.00	4.90	6.67	1.77
369	Other non-metallic mineral products	0.38	8.11	–5.60	0.00	14.47	16.98	2.51
371	Iron and steel	0.58	11.73	–1.26	0.00	3.19	13.66	10.46
372	Non-ferrous metals	4.56	15.76	–0.68	0.00	–5.00	10.08	15.08
381	Fabricated metal products	0.98	11.19	–6.16	0.00	9.56	14.58	5.02
382	Machinery, except electrical	4.42	7.61	–2.67	0.00	8.15	13.09	4.94
383	Machinery, electric	1.60	38.49	–4.77	0.00	7.51	41.23	33.72
384	Transport equipment	0.49	8.81	–3.38	0.00	–0.95	4.48	5.43
385	Professional and scientific equipment	0.38	4.78	–7.74	0.01	0.95	–2.00	–2.96
390	Other manufactured products	0.38	7.52	–9.96	0.00	0.99	–1.45	–2.45

Table 3.10 Impact of entry and exit on industry productivity (dependent variable: change in log of output)

	Estimates			
	OLS with fixed effects		GMM	
	1997–2004	2001–2004	1997–2004	2001–2004
Explanatory variables				
Change in log of employment	0.27	0.34	−0.12	−0.16
	10.79	7.01	−1.39	−1.05
Log of investment	0.03	0.05	0.01	0.01
	7.63	6.40	2.46	1.71
Concentration ratio	0.09	0.04	−0.02	−0.03
	1.24	0.27	−2.18	−1.97
Net entry	0.50	0.66	0.63	0.56
	3.01	1.71	3.89	1.64
Adjusted R^2	0.20	0.06		
Number of observations	12,790	6,576	10,293	5,302

method gives biased coefficients. To take account of such simultaneity, the GMM estimation method is used with lags of the "problematic" variables (employment and capital) as instruments. However, for comparison purpose, the OLS results (with fixed effects) are also reported. Moreover, the change in capital stock is proxied using investment and because of co-linearity, we use the net entry rate instead of entry and exit rate separately. Finally, as in Sect. 3.4, we consider possible change in the impact of the explanatory variables during 2000s. We conduct estimation on the whole sample on the one hand and on a sub-sample covering only the 2000s.

Table 3.10 suggests that if one disregards the simultaneity issue, the coefficients of employment and capital can be highly overestimated. GMM results (which accounts of the simultaneity issue) show that the results are not much different between the whole period and the 2000s period. Except for the significance level (5% for the whole period instead of 10% in the 2000s period), the impact of the explanatory variables, in particular net entry, on survivors production is almost the same. This contrasts with the results in Sect. 3.5.1, where the impacts of entry and exit rates on productivity are different between the two periods. However, the approach in that section is accounting one, and may not measure precisely the impact of entry and exit on productivity growth.

The coefficient of labor is non significant. This may reflects the fact that our measure of labor is the number of workers, and not effectively working hours. The latter is best to reflect the impact of labor on output, but is not available. Investment has a positive and significant coefficient. The coefficients of the concentration ratio is significant and negative implying that less competitive industry are also less productive. Finally, net entry exerts a positive and significant impact on productivity.

3.6 Conclusion

A growing literature shows that the process of firms' entry and exit is an important driver of industry productivity improvement. This chapter examines whether such a process has taken place in Morocco and to what extent it improves productivity; a major weakness of Moroccan industries. The analysis used the database of the yearly survey conducted by the Ministry of Industry and Trade over the period 1995–2004. This survey covers all manufacturing firms with at least ten employees or with an annual turnover that exceeds MAD 100 000.

The analysis of the regulatory framework in the country may explain that there was a change in the behavior of the entry and exit rates in the early 2000s. Hence, the analysis is conducted both over the whole period and on a sub-sample covering only the 2000s. The consistency and the quality of the results are markedly better when estimation is conducted over the 2000s only. This suggests that the change in the country's regulatory framework might have allowed market forces to play through the dynamic of firms' entry and exit and its impact on productivity. In addition, entry is found to be positively affected by demand's increase and intense competition, while the reverse is true for exit.

The decomposition of labor productivity into the contribution of internal restructuring by survivors; changes in the market shares among survivors, entrants and exitors show that the process of entry and exit resulted in a net increase of productivity in almost all industries (19 out of 25). Its contribution is sizeable. The reallocation of market shares among firms plays no role while restructuring by survivors improved productivity in many instances. Finally, exitors are less productive than survivors in many industries (13 out of 25). The positive effect of the process of entry and exit on productivity is confirmed by an econometric analysis. Even if one controls for the impact of labor, capital, and the state of present competition, estimation shows that net entry exerts a positive and significant impact on productivity.

3.7 Notes

1. Bernard and Jensen (1999) found that intra-industry reallocations to higher productivity exporters explain up to 20% of productivity growth in US manufacturing.
2. Known as Sociétés Anonymes (SA) organized by the decree No. 17/95 enacted in 1996.
3. Known as Sociétés à Responsabilité Limitée (SARL) organized by the decree No. 5/96 enacted in 1997.
4. Moreover, Disney et al. (2003a, 2003b) argued that labor productivity gives a better reflection of how markets select establishments of different productivity.

References

Achy L (2006) Job creation and job destruction in the manufacturing sector in Morocco. Cahiers du Plan, 8

Achy L, Sekkat K (2008) Competition, efficiency and competition policy in Morocco. In: Khalid Sekkat (ed) Competition and efficiency in the Arab world. Palgrave-McMillan, Basingstoke, Hampshire, pp 123–158

Aw BY, Chung D, Roberts M (2000) Productivity and turnover in the export market: micro-level evidence from the republic of Korea and Taiwan (China). World Bank Econ Rev 14:65–90

Baldwin J (1995) The dynamics of industrial competition. Cambridge University Press, Cambridge

Bartelsman E, Haltiwanger J, Scarpetta S (2004) Microeconomic evidence of creative destruction in industrial and developing countries. Tinbergen Institute Discussion Paper (TI 2004-114/3)

Bernard A, Jensen J (1999) Exporting and productivity, NBER Working Paper No. 7135. National Bureau of Economic Research, Cambridge, MA

Boeri T, Cramer U (1992) Employment Growth, Incumbents and Entrants: Evidence from Germany. Int J Ind Organ 10:545–565

Borjas GJ, Ramey VA (1995) Foreign competition, market power, and wage inequality. Q J Econ 110:1075–1110

Carree M, Thurik A (1999) The carrying capacity and entry and exit flows in retailing. Int J Ind Organ 17:985–1007

Caves RE (1998) Industrial organization and new findings on the turnover and mobility of firms. J Econ Lit 36(8):1947–1982

Churchill B (1955) Age and life expectancy of business firms. Surv Curr Bus 35(12):15–19

Disney R, Haskel J, Heden Y (2003a) Exit entry and establishment survival in UK manufacturing. J Ind Econ 51:93–115

Disney R, Haskel J, Heden Y (2003b) Restructuring and productivity growth in UK manufacturing. Econ J 113(489):666–694

Fotopoulos G, Spence N (1998) Entry and exit from manufacturing industries: symmetry, turbulence and simultaneity – some empirical evidence from Greek manufacturing industries 1982–1988. Appl Econ 30:245–262

Geroski P (1995) What do we know about entry. Int J Ind Organ 13:421–441

Harrison A, Hanson G (1999) Who gains from trade reform? Some remaining puzzles. J Dev Econ 59:125–154

Hausman R, Rodrik D (2006) Economic development as self-discovery. J Dev Econ 72(2003):603–633

Hoekman B, Winters A (2005) Trade and employment: stylized facts and research findings. ECES Working Paper No. 102 May 2005

Hölzl W, Sögner L (2004) Entry and exit dynamics in Austrian manufacturing. Vienna University of Economics & Business Administration, Working Paper in Growth and Employment in Europe: Sustainability and Competitiveness, No. 36, June 2004

Hulten CR (2000) Total factor productivity: a short biography. NBER working paper 7471

Klapper L, Laeven L, Rajan R (2004) Business environment and firm entry: evidence from international data. NBER Working Paper No. 10380

Mauro P. (1995), "Corruption and Growth", *Quarterly Journal of Economics*, vol 110 n° 3, p.681-712, August.

Pavcnik N (2002) Trade liberalization, exit and productivity improvements: evidence from Chilean plants. Rev Econ Stud 69(1):245–276

Pricewaterhouse Coopers (2008) Paying taxes: the global picture (joint study with the World Bank)

Revenga A (1997) Employment and wage effects of trade liberalization: the case of Mexican manufacturing. J Labor Econ 15(3):S20–S43 Part 2

Siegfried JJ, Evans LB (1994) Empirical studies of entry and exit: a survey of evidence. Rev Ind Organ 9:121–155
Wacziarg R, Wallack JS (2004) Trade liberalization and intersectoral labor movements. J Int Econ 64:411–439
Wei S-J (2000) How taxing is corruption on international investors? Rev Econ Stat 82(1):1–11
World Bank (2006) Country economic memorandum. Morocco
World Trade Organization (2003) Trade policy review. Morocco

Chapter 4
Entry, Exit, and Productivity in Tunisian Manufacturing Industries

Riadh Ben Jelili and Mohamed Goaied

4.1 Introduction

For a number of MENA economies, the barriers to entrepreneurship manifest by the unfriendly environment for start-ups and relatively high regulatory and administrative burdens are estimated to be among the highest in the world. Potential investors and existing firms in those countries face a complex regulations and licensing requirements which are often unclear or inconsistent with international norms. Policy, regulatory and institutional distortions, as well as constraints and barriers to efficient private sector investment, operations and exit, are then prevalent throughout the region. Complexity and the rents created by economic distortions breed administrative discretion and corruption. The bureaucratic burden is often especially heavy for small and medium enterprises. Higher levels of government rent seeking and/or bureaucratic obstacles to legal firm entry will lead to a greater bifurcation of firm sizes – very small informal firms, relatively large formal firms and an absence of medium sized formal firms.

However, almost all countries in the MENA region entered the new millennium with large unemployment rates. In this context, decision makers emphasize the role of efficient markets which could lead to higher firm creation rates and thereby, to lower unemployment rates. Aside to direct employment effects, high firm creation rates are supposed to have a positive impact on the technical and organizational change of economies because new firms are on average, better equipped with the latest technical and organizational knowledge. The structural change of the economy goes hand in hand with high firm creation which is believed to be an important channel of GDP growth.

Indeed, in addition to expanding the range of products, entry can first create more competition, lower prices for consumers, and may lead to better technology adoption. Changes in the status of existing firms from informal to formal may also have important effects on GDP growth. Indeed, it is likely that informal firms have

R. Ben Jelili (✉)
Arab Planning Institute, P.O.Box: 5834 Safat 13059 State of Kuwait
e-mail: riadh@api.org.kw

K. Sekkat (ed.), *Market Dynamics and Productivity in Developing Countries: Economic Reforms in the Middle East and North Africa*, DOI 10.1007/978-1-4419-1037-0_4,

less secure property rights and thus lower than optimal investment and productivity growth, leading to lower profits and value added. Starting a firm with expansive potential is finally an option for educated and high-skilled workers. In presence of labor market frictions, this additional option can be seen as reducing the probability of ending up in a low-wage job and hence, increases the incentives for education.

The structure of this chapter is as follows. The first section deals with regulations, upgrading program and business environment in Tunisia. Data used to analyze patterns of entry and exit in Tunisian manufacturing industries and their impact on firm's performance are presented in Sect. 4.2. The main shortcomings of the data sources constructed for this purpose will also be discussed, and some descriptive statistics based on the entry–exit data sets will be presented in order to highlight, according to the literature, some stylized facts about entry and exit. The determinants of entry and exit process are discussed in Sect. 4.3. This section focuses on the implications that the interdependence between aggregate entry and exit has for the analysis of manufacturing industry dynamics in Tunisia. The purpose of the forth section is to investigate whether entry and exit of firms affect performance and labor productivity.

4.2 Regulations, Upgrading Program and Business Environment in Tunisia

The ability to start a firm is limited by several factors including the burden of complying with regulations governing business activity. Excessive governmental regulations can provide an incentive to operate in the informal sector, or may prevent some entrepreneurs from operating at all. Based on the data from 85 countries, Djankov et al. (2002) find that the countries with more open access to political power, greater constraints on the executive, and greater political rights have less burdensome regulation of entry than do the countries with less representative, less limited, and less free governments. They also find that "stricter" regulation of entry is associated with sharply higher levels of corruption, and a greater relative size of the unofficial economy.

In a more recent paper Djankov et al. (2006) create an index of the burden of regulation based on average country rankings in the World Bank's "Doing Business" indicators. They find that countries that are in the highest (best) quartile of this index grow 2.3 percentage points faster than countries in the lowest (worst) quartile. This effect is more than twice the effect on GDP growth of going from the second quartile to the highest quartile in terms of primary school enrollment. The authors stress that initiative such as a "one-stop shop" for business registration could accelerate GDP growth.

It also arises from the preceding papers that the magnitude of the effect of lower registration costs on firm creations is an empirical issue. Indeed, if the main reason that firms choose to be informal is the desire to evade taxes, making registration procedures more efficient would likely have little impact. It is also possible that entrepreneurs are able to avoid the excessive regulations through bribes, thus effectively reducing the impact of regulation. Finally, it is possible that the most important constraint on firm creation in developing countries is the availability of credit or other complementary inputs.

4.2.1 Tunisian Institutional Context

Through a combination of colonial heritage and 1950s development philosophy, Tunisia has historically had a highly centralized economic system controlled by the government particularly since 1961. The post-independence government pushed towards a centrally planned system, although one moderately open to the outside economy. The government ran the banking system, transportation, and some of the major industries. It controlled import and export of most goods and fixed their prices at levels unrelated to either internal or world markets. It also supported the industrial sector by investing directly in some existing industrial projects.

In May 1964, the National Assembly enacted the expropriation of all foreign-owned lands, to establish 300 state co-operative farms. By 1969, the collectivization rate achieved 90% in the agriculture sector alone. The government also promoted the institution of co-operatives in other economic sectors: wholesale and retail trade, industry, banking, in addition to the already controlled transports, power and mines sectors.[1]

The cooperative experiment only ran for few years (1964–1969) before encountering unbeatable difficulties. The central planned development strategy came to a halt in September 1969. Beginning in the seventies, a new economic policy was put in place, consisting in the promotion of the private sector while continuing to support an expanding public sector. Trade policy continued to strongly protect Tunisian manufacturing, but important incentives were also granted to the off-shore sector, thus attracting significant domestic and foreign investment to exporting activities, mainly to textiles, and resulting in a significant expansion of manufacturing exports.

The new emphasis in the Tunisian economic planning was on labor intensive manufacturing industry, financed by private investors. The new political regime pursued the creation of new institutions that would promote the private sector, such as the Investment Promotion Agency (API), the Industrial Real Estate Agency (AFI), the Centre for export Promotion (CEPEX), and the Fund for Industrial Promotion and Investment (FOPRODI), with the aim to streamline and simplify industrial policy.

The first law offering incentives to foreign investors for the establishment of manufacturing industries was promulgated in 1972 (law 72-38). This law granted to approved industrial projects a wide range of tax concessions and duty-free import of capital equipment, raw materials and semi-processed goods. The new units were to produce mainly for export, and this reduced further the linkages with the Tunisian economic base. Under this law, foreign investors were exempted from corporate income tax during the first 10 years of operation and, amongst other benefits, they were permitted to repatriate profits free of tax.

Offshore industrialization was promoted under the decree 73-19, by which API was also established and charged to promote new investment opportunities and to streamline investment procedures by introducing potential investors to the legislative mechanisms. More than 500 foreign firms established their production units under law 72-38 between 1973 and 1978.

FOPRODI was created in 1974 with three important objectives:

1. Increasing entrepreneurship by promoting new entrepreneurs in SMEs (defined as firms with capital of up to one million Tunisian Dinars).
2. Helping decentralize manufacturing activities in a country in which these activities had been highly concentrated in the coastal region in general and its three principal cities (Tunis, Sfax, and Sousse) in particular.
3. Lowering country's persistently high official unemployment rate (of about 16%).

A second industrial investment law was introduced in 1974 (law 74-74), which sought to relate incentives more closely to employment creation. The law was also intended to encourage Tunisian private investment, which had previously been less favored than foreign one.

The constitution of industrial zones is also subject to open competition since 1973, when the government founded the AFI in charge of facilitating the establishment and equipment of such zones.

However, the return to a market economy announced by the government was less decisive than is appeared to be. Tunisia still maintained extensive price subsidization, the financial sector was entirely administered by the government, and the economy was protected through very high customs rights and import restrictions.

By the end of the 1970s, Tunisia appeared to be over-dependent on oil revenues, having extended its foreign borrowings and showing no stable productive base, capable of absorbing excess labor force and of exporting a diversified and competitive range of goods. In particular, the lack of basic state investment in infrastructure had blocked growth and deterred private investment.

The sixth development plan (1982–1986) was an austerity plan, designed to introduce the economic adjustments necessary to prepare Tunisia for an era of reduced income from petroleum. Investment was directed towards non-oil industries, severe controls were maintained on external debt and balance of payments, cuts in public investment and consumption were decided, also though wage freezes and import restrictions.

Beginning in 1987, the government embarked on a structural adjustment program (SAP) which envisaged significant readjustments in the essential instruments of the economic and financial policy, especially in the fields of taxation, price determination, foreign trade, public utilities and income policy. One of the targets of the program was the reallocation of tasks between the economic players, to be realized through the total or partial cession of some public utilities to the benefit of banks, parent companies or private individuals.

The SAP strategy was carried out under the Seventh (1987–1991) and the Eighth (1992–1996) Development Plans. While the first Plan was intended to achieve macro-economic stability and to introduce the initial measures of structural liberalization, in terms of sectoral, financial and trade reforms, the main orientation of the second Plan was to increase efficiency and promote market mechanisms through legislative framework which would encourage foreign investment, accelerate privatization, develop the stock market, and deepen integration with the European market.

The readjustment of the industrial policy was obvious in the new investment code, Law 87-51, intended to unify and simplify the investment laws of 1972 and 1981. The new Code granted several tax and financial incentives, especially to wholly exporting industries and was aimed at promoting a major liberalization of the Tunisian industrial sector. At the same time, the prior approval of manufacturing investment by the API was removed (since 1987), the three industrial support agencies were merged into a single Industrial Promotion Agency, and investment undertaking has been greatly facilitated through the establishment of a one-stop shop, where all the administrative and legal services involved in the opening of a business are gathered. In the case of FDI, there are no restrictions on investment in off-shore activities, but the prior approval is still needed for all investment in activities serving the domestic market. Domestic price deregulation was enacted in 1991 and a shift from a positive list to a negative list regime was introduced in trade policy in 1994.

This reform has shortened the delays involved in setting up a company. A unified investment incentive code was also put in place in 1993, replacing sectoral codes with fiscal and financial incentives varying across economic activities. The new code set incentives based on the cross-cutting objectives of exports, regional development and acquisition of new technology. The code, designed to unify the existing sectoral codes in a "Code Unique," regulates all productive sectors, except projects relating to mining, energy production, finance and foreign trade, which are governed by specific laws.

Thanks to this new legislation, investment in agriculture, manufacturing industries (excluding the mechanical weaving of rugs and carpets, weapons manufacture, the recycling processing of waste and garbage), agribusiness, certain totally exporting services and services related to industry, and public works requires no previous authorization, but a simple declaration to the competent authority. The incentive system includes schemes very favorable to investment, a 10-year tax holiday and total exemption from import duties and the value added tax for totally exporting projects and generous income tax exemption measures on reinvested income.

The Code distinguishes between two categories of investment, offshore, in which foreign capital accounts for at least 66% of equity, and at least 80% of the production is designed to export, and on-shore, in which foreign equity is limited to 49% in non-industrial projects, while industrial projects can reach 100% of foreign equity. Additional incentives are provided to off-shore industries or totally exporting industries.

With respect to small and medium enterprises (SMEs), the Code enlists particular incentives under articles 46bis and 47. SMEs in agriculture, industry and services can benefit from an equity participation of the State and a grant covering part of the expenditures incurred for studies and technical assistance; both benefits are granted through the FOPRODI.

In 1992, Tunisia approved of a law for geographically bounded free trade zones, and the zones of Bizerte (60 km north of Tunis) and Zarzis (450 km south of Tunis) were created. They were installed in order to offer an even more favorable environment for foreign investors. The free trade zone at Zarzis, operational since 1995, is specialized in services of the oil sector, and the other one at Bizerte, includes industry and construction, ship repair and demolition activities, as well as several services. The land is state-owned, but managed by a private company. The geographic aspect as well as the infrastructure and proximity to the markets give both Bizerte and Zarzis a great potential to attract foreign investment into the zones.

Some flexibility has also been brought to the labor market since 1994, through two important reforms involving firing and the limited duration contract. Prior to this law, compensation was left completely to the judge's decision, which created a lot of uncertainty for both employees and employers. This law set a scale limiting compensation between 1 and 2 months per year worked and to a maximum of 3 years of salary. The limited duration work contract has been generalized since 1996, regardless of the nature of the work involved. According to a law enacted in 1996, an employer can conclude with an employee, a work contract for a limited duration, provided that the total period of work does not exceed 4 years, including renewals. At the end of the 4 year-period, the employer has to either fire the employee or grant him the permanent worker status. These reforms of labor legislation allow both a great deal of employment flexibility and minimum job security and compensation in case of firing.

In February 1999, the government created the Fonds d'Incitation à l'Innovation dans les Technologies de l'Information (FITI) to support small-scale investments by the private sector in information technologies. The government cofinances up to 49% or a maximum of 200,000 TD for information technology projects, if the following conditions are met: the project is approved by, and presented to, FITI by a venture capital firm (SICAR), and the SICAR commits to provide at least 30% of the startup capital of the project; the investor provides at least 2% of the startup capital; and FITI's cofinancing is not higher than the share of the SICAR in the startup capital.

More recently (November 2003), the Tunisian government launched the Industrial Modernization Program[2] (PMI), financed by a European Union donation to prepare the country economy enters the free trade area planned by the association agreement accord with the European Union, for which final establishment is set to 2008. The program has strived to speed up the rate of setting up enterprises and to diversify the industrial base. Investment is supported by using modern management methods that are underpinned by innovation and through new information and communication technologies. Innovation plays a key role in this context, since it allows Tunisian companies to position themselves better in relation to other emerging countries. The PMI also provides a technical assistance of a more institutional kind in Metrology, Standardization, Industrial Property and the access of SMEs to financing.

4.2.2 Tunisian Upgrading (Mise à Niveau) Program

The external outlook for Tunisia changed dramatically in the mid-1990s with the Association Agreement with the EU and the phase out of the Multi-Fiber Arrangements (MFA). Their implementations will result in a very large fall in effective protection for domestic industries and in increased competition on export markets. To date, the private sector has assumed a wait-and-see attitude, as indicated by a weak investment performance, particularly in the manufacturing sector while sentiment remains positive. However, opportunistic investments have occurred to take advantage of temporary distortions in effective protection caused by the phased implementation of the EU agreement.

A key government initiative to meet the twin competitive challenges of the EU agreement and the phasing out of the MFA has been a large program of *Mise à Niveau*, which includes investment incentives for selected producers in sectors that either have had strong export performance in the recent past (textiles and garments, and mechanical and electrical products) or that are judged to have good potential (agro-processing), to help manufacturing industry adapt and upgrade its methods and practices of organization, management, innovation, training, technology, distribution, marketing, communications, and research and development.

The *Mise à Niveau Program* (PMN), implemented since 1995, includes a number of projects destined to enterprises and to their environment to allow the productive system to compete at an international level. It is addressed to the private sector enterprises which have a margin of growth, an expanding market and, above all, which express the intention to upgrade themselves. The target of this program is to restructure 4,000 firms in 10 years, given that enterprises can take advantage of the program more than once, if they have promising plans and produce good results.

The program is divided into two phases:

1. The first one covering the period 1995–2000, is aimed at reinforcing Tunisian firms ability to face international competition.
2. The second one, covering the period 2001–2005, aims to consolidate the process of economic upgrading, extending it to trade and services.

To participate in the program, an enterprise must submit a detailed application and demonstrate strong growth potential, a good market and promising products at existing quality/price ratios that can be improved. Size, industry, and location are supposedly not a factor determining acceptance in the program; however, the program has sectoral targets for participation that reveal an export oriented bias in favor of the textile and clothing, and the mechanical and electrical subsectors.

By March 2007, 3,735 firms have joined the program; of these 9 have been rejected and 2,489 have received the approval for their plans from the steering committee involving a total planned investment of 3881 million TD (about 2982 million US$), of which 20% was allocated to food processing business, 20% to textiles and clothing, 19% to building materials, ceramics and glass products, 16% to mechanical, electric and electronics, 7% to chemicals, 4% to leather, and the remaining 14% to unclassified activities. The remaining 1,237 dossiers were still at the diagnostic level (cf. Table 4.1).

Over time, the program has increased its focus on SMEs. The average size of investments in the PMN declined from 3 million TD in 1996 to 1.6 million in 2007 (March). In addition, the share of enterprises with less than 100 employees rose from 29% of total enterprises participating in the program in 1996, to almost 2/3 in 2007 (March).

Enterprises that are in financial difficulties are excluded from the PMN, but are provided assistance in resolving these problems under the law 95-34 of April 17, 1995. The law creates a Monitoring Committee called "*Commission de suivi des entreprises économiques*" charged to collect information on the activities of enterprises and to provide information to the President of First Instance Court, who is responsible for administering the bankruptcy law, warning of enterprises in difficulty, and proposing restructuring plans. There is also a Bureau of assistance to enterprises whose activities involve three phases of assistance. The first two phases are administrative and try to help enterprises reach an agreement with their creditors to continue their operations and, thus, avoid failure. The third phase is judicial and seeks to help enterprises to get recapitalized after bankruptcy. No financial support is provided for the enterprises, but when they are successfully restructured, they are eligible for support under the PMN.

The government has recently established a PMN for services tied to industry. These include the key services that are important in improving the productivity and competitiveness of the industrial sector. The service PMN covers business services, engineering, informatics, training, agricultural consultants. Other important services, such as financial services, telecommunications, electricity, and transportation, are already being upgraded under other programs. It is expected to function like the PMN for manufacturing enterprises, with similar approval procedures and funding from the Fonds de Développement de la Competitivité (FODEC).

4.2.3 Business Environment in Tunisia

4.2.3.1 Starting a Business

Reductions in start-up costs can take two forms. One is to reduce the bureaucratic hurdles that increase the start-up costs for new firms. The second is to provide institutions for venture capital as well as public financial support for new firms.

Table 4.1 Participation to the Mise à Niveau Program – March 2007

	Food processing	Leather and shoes	Chemical	Wood, cork, furniture and diverse	Building materials, ceramics and glass	Mechanical, metal works, electric and electronics	Textiles and clothing	Total
Approved	327	191	137	336	124	303	1,071	2,489
Investment amount million dinars	787	150	264	526	756	630	768	3,881
Share of investment by sector (%)	20	4	7	14	19	16	20	100
Immaterial Investment	85	36	34	62	48	100	152	517
Share of immaterial investment (%)	11	24	13	12	6	16	20	13
Precede granted	105	24	36	77	76	94	137	549
Dossiers at the diagnostic level	201	74	68	189	115	175	415	1,237
Dossiers refused	3	–	1	–	–	5	–	9
Total adhesion	531	265	206	525	239	483	1,486	3,735

Source: Programme de mise à niveau, Ministère de l'Industrie; de l'Energie et des Petites et Moyennes Entreprises. http://www.pmn.nat.tn/www/fr/REPAR_SECT.ASP

Business registration is relatively fast and efficient in Tunisia when compared with countries at similar levels of economic development. It takes ten procedures (10.3 in MENA) and only 11 days (40.9 days in MENA) to start up a business. By contrast, in Hungary, although the number of procedures is only six, it takes about 38 days to start up a business.

The one-stop shop of the API, which was certified ISO 9002 in June 2000, has undoubtedly facilitated business registration and starts up in the manufacturing sector. It informs prospective entrepreneurs on the procedures for statistical and tax registration, assists with on-line registration, provides 24 h responses to business related queries and maintains a detailed database on the registered companies.

However, prior authorizations relating to environment, labor and sectoral regulations are still relatively numerous and impinge on the establishment of new businesses in non manufacturing sectors. Delays are also reported in securing finance, land and in obtaining the construction permit. If these are added up, the effective period to start up a business in Tunisia may exceed 2 years.

4.2.3.2 Hiring and Firing Rules

In Tunisia, hiring rules are flexible but termination regulations are rigid and too protective when compared with its peers. Surveys of managers show that employment regulation is seen to be a bottleneck to improving efficiency, and thus productivity of investment.

Indeed, Tunisia compares favorably with other countries in the MENA and OECD regions in terms of flexibility in hiring. The legal conditions of employment – covering flexibility in working time requirements, mandatory payment for non-working days, and minimum wage legislation – also compare favorably with the selected peers. Labor reforms in Tunisia have introduced flexibility in hiring. The 1996 revision of the labor code introduced fixed-term contracts, covering by 2001 about 15% of the labor force. According to the Labor Code, businesses can hire workers on part-time or fixed term contracts for any job, without specifying maximum duration of the contract.

However, there are areas where regulatory reform could introduce more flexibility. Tunisia restricts the use of fixed contracts, and the use of temporary help agency workers is not allowed for example.

Flexibility of firing encompasses grounds for dismissal, procedures for dismissal, notice periods, and severance payments. Compared with other countries in the region, Tunisian termination rules seem to be rigid and too protective.

Dismissals for economic reasons are still heavily regulated. Companies must notify the labor inspector of planned dismissals in writing 1 month ahead, indicating the reasons and the workers affected. The inspector may propose alternatives to layoffs. If these proposals are not accepted by the employer, the case goes to the regional tripartite committee of labor inspector, employer organization, and labor union (*commission du contrôle des licenciements*). The committee decides by a majority vote (if the inspector and union reject the proposal, no dismissal is possible). It may also suggest retraining, reduced hours, or early retirement. Only 14% of dismissals end up being accepted. As a result, annual layoffs are less than 1% of the workforce, compared with more than 10% in the average OCDE country. Yet, the unemployment rate remains persistently high, above the OECD average.

As a result, private enterprises in Tunisia find it hard to restructure, and small firms often find solutions outside the legal framework. In Tunisia, an estimated 38% of business activity takes place in the informal sector. International evidence shows that heavy labor market regulation encourages entrepreneurs to operate in the informal economy. This is also likely to hamper private investment. Indeed, firms in the informal sector do not operate at full capacity, while their counterparts in the formal sector suffer from unfair competition, and may thus not expand capacity at potential.

4.2.3.3 Credit Facilities

In Tunisia, there exists a public credit bureau (*Centrale de Risques*) established in 1958, which is supervised by the Central Bank of Tunisia. The length of historical data collected is 10 years, on a total of 56,000 credit reports. However, it records only loans above a minimum size of 13 605USD, indicating a focus on monitoring systemic risk. Fewer regulatory restrictions on credit information sharing will benefit small firms' access to finance the most. In terms of the scope of credit information distribution, only positive data is made available in Tunisia – that is, total loans outstanding, assets and personal information. Access to credit information is limited to the creditor's own customers. Thus, weaknesses in design makes Tunisia's public credit registry a less valuable tool for lenders than in similar countries. Access of lenders to credit information is also hampered by the absence of private credit registries.

In deciding whether to extend credit and at what interest rate, lenders need to know what share of debt they can recover if the borrower defaults. Collateral laws enable firms to use their assets as security to generate capital and strengthen the incentives of debtors to repay their loans. By providing creditors with the right to an asset on default, collateral also reduces a lender's costs of screening loan applicants.

However, over-collateralization restricts access to credit by the private sector, particularly for small firms. The value of collateral depends largely on the ease of creating and enforcing security agreements. The value of collateral also depends on the efficiency of the insolvency regime, as creditors are concerned about recovering collateral if a firm goes bankrupt. Bankruptcy laws define who controls the insolvency process, who has rights to the property of a bankrupt firm and with what priority, and the efficiency of realizing the rights. In Tunisia, there are no legal protections along any of these dimensions. This leads creditors to either increase the price of loans to adjust for the additional risk or decrease the amount of loans.

4.2.3.4 Enforcing Contracts

In Tunisia, there are no requirements to appoint a lawyer or initiate a protest procedure before a public notary. The creditor files a claim in a court, and the court issues a summons to the debtor. The recovery of overdue small debts is normally achieved by means of a special procedure called "*injonction de payer*" before a general-jurisdiction judge. Provided that the debt has proven an established, the judge grants the injunction to pay. The debtor cannot oppose the order. Therefore, the civil lawsuit excludes the usual stages of service of process, opposition, hearing and gathering of the evidence. This simplified procedure for small debt recovery, which does not mandate legal representation, helps reduce the legal costs which amount to 17% of the total enforcement cost.

4.2.3.5 Closing a Business

In Tunisia, the bankruptcy process is short. It takes 1.3 years, shorter than in countries in the MENA region and in OECD. Moreover, the bankruptcy process is not as costly as it is in peer countries. It represents about 7% of estate, compared to 12.1% in the MENA region.

The Tunisian jurisdiction, like many other jurisdictions of French-legal origin, has attempted to reach the goals of insolvency by giving broader powers to the court. But evidence shows that expanding court powers in bankruptcy proceedings do not have the desired effects.

Involving creditors and other stakeholders in the insolvency process is important to preserve absolute priority of creditors' claims. In Tunisia, the bankruptcy report is filed only with the court and is not accessible to creditors. Such a report would inform the creditors and provide a higher chance of maintaining absolute priority. Another set of judicial procedures defines the powers of various stakeholders in formulating and adopting a rehabilitation plan. The Tunisian bankruptcy law mandates the formulation of a plan by the court, without the effective participation of creditors or management. Adopting a rehabilitation plan without considering their views does not help achieve the insolvency goal of preserving the value of creditor's claims.

4.3 Firm Demographics Data in Tunisia: Some Stylized Facts

The purpose of this section is to describe the data used to analyse patterns of entry and exit in Tunisian manufacturing industries. Some descriptive statistics based on the entry–exit data sets will be presented in order to highlight, according to the literature, some stylised facts about entry and exit.

4.3.1 Data Sources

Two sources of information are used to build manufacturing entry and exit database. The first comes from administrative files including the National Repertory of firms in Tunisia, which is based on continuous report of fiscal affiliation of firms. The main advantage of administrative data set rest in the full coverage of the business registers of firms' population in the Tunisian Manufacturing sector. Nevertheless, this data set has also some important weaknesses such as the accuracy of information of exitors by year and for each industry, and the lack of information on the characteristics of entrants/exitors, except industry affiliation.

To circumvent these weaknesses, an additional source of administrative file related to the quarterly register of employees taken from the Tunisian National Social Security Fund (CNSS) is used; it constitutes a valuable database of private firm affiliates. At the Tunisian National Institute of Statistics (INS), this second source is merged with firms' fiscal register.[3] The database constituted will serve as a basis for computing series on the number of entering (new), exiting (out of business) and total firms with ten workers or more, by year and by industry over the period 1996–2004.

4.3.2 Characteristics of Entry and Exit Process of Firms

A considered manufacturing firm is assumed in business, if it has a positive number of employees. The entry–exit data set contains three basic variables:

- T_{it}: Total Numbers of firms active in the *i*th industry at the end of period *t*.
- E_{it}: Number of new firms that entered the *i*th industry in year *t*.
- X_{it}: Number of firms that exited the *i*th industry in year *t*.

For comparability across sectors, entry and exit rates are defined with respect to the current year's stock of establishments:

- Entry rate in $t = \dfrac{E_{it}}{T_{it-1}}$
- Exit rate in $t = \dfrac{X_{it}}{T_{it-1}}$
- Turnover = Entry rate + exit rate
- Net entry rate = Entry rate − exit rate

Fact 1: Sizeable firm turnover in all manufacturing industries

Our data confirm a relative high firm churning in all sectors. In Fig. 4.1, we present average annual entry and exit rates over the period 1996–2004, for the considered 15 manufacturing industries. Total firm turnover involves 4–12% of all firms in most manufacturing industries and more than 12% in three sectors: 31.4% in textile industries, 14.4% in wood products and 12.4% in leather and footwear industries.

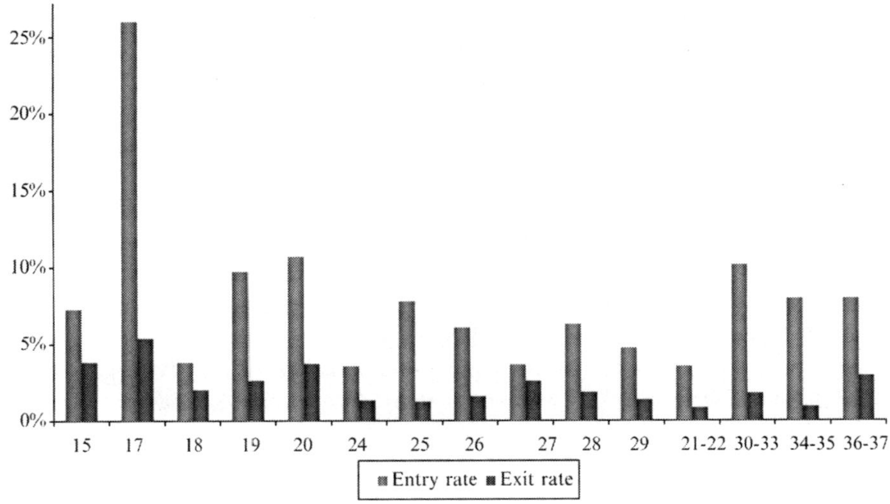

Fig. 4.1 Firm turnover rate in manufacturing industries, mean 1996–2004

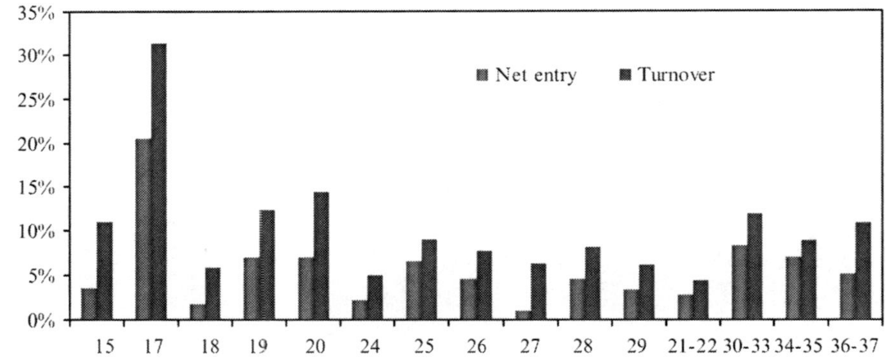

Fig. 4.2 Average net entry by sectors, 1996–2004

Over the sample period (1996–2004), we have an annual average exit rate of 2.3%, which is comparable to exit rates found in other developing regions. For instance, Clerides et al. (1998) report annual average exit rates for Colombia of 1.7%, for Morocco of 3.7% and for Mexico of 1.5%. The entry rate in our sample is much higher, on average 8% per year. This compares to entry rates of 2.7%, 4.9% and 4.8% reported for Colombia, Morocco and Mexico respectively. The higher entry rates in the Tunisian economy are not that surprising, taking into account that the entry of new firms was an important component of the restructuring process concerning the manufacturing industries since 1995.

The data confirm previous findings that, in all sectors, net entry is far less important than the gross flows of entry and exit that generate it (cf. Fig. 4.2 and Table 4.2). This suggests that the entry of new firms in the market is largely

Table 4.2 Firm turnover rate in manufacturing industries, mean 1996–2004

Code	Industry	Entry rate	Exit rate	Turnover
15	Food industries	0.073	0.038	0.111
17	Textile industries	0.260	0.054	0.314
18	Clothing and lining industries	0.038	0.020	0.058
19	Leather and footwear industries	0.097	0.026	0.124
20	Wood products	0.107	0.037	0.144
24	Chemical industries	0.036	0.013	0.049
25	Plastics material and rubber industries	0.078	0.012	0.091
26	Mineral non metallic products	0.061	0.016	0.077
27	Metallurgy	0.037	0.026	0.063
28	Fabricated metal products	0.063	0.018	0.081
29	Machinery and equipment	0.047	0.014	0.061
21–22	Paper and cardboard industries, printing and related support activities	0.036	0.008	0.044
30–33	Electrical equipment, radio and TV and other communications equipment, Measuring and medical instruments	0.101	0.018	0.119
34–35	Motor vehicle manufacturing, other transportation equipment	0.080	0.009	0.089
36–37	Miscellaneous manufacturing	0.080	0.029	0.109

Source: Authors' calculation based on INS data

driven by a search process rather than augmenting the number of competitors in the market.

Fact 2: Firm turnover is principally driven by small and medium sized firms

An important step in the analysis of creative destruction consists of looking at the distribution of firm by size across industries. Size is a crucial dimension in the analysis of firm entry and exit for several reasons. Small firms seem to be affected by greater mixing, but also have greater potential for expansion. Thus, a distribution of firms skewed towards small units may imply higher entry and exit, but also greater post entry growth of successful firms. Alternatively, it may point to a sectoral specialization of the given country towards newer industries, where mixing tends to be larger and more firms experiment with different technologies.

However, any observed difference in one single indicator, like firm size, cannot, as such, be taken to indicate differences in the magnitude or characteristics of creative destruction. The distribution of firm by size is likely to be influenced by the overall dimension of the internal market as well as the business environment in which firms operate that can discourage firm expansion. So, the analysis of firm size should be taken as one of the important aspects that, together with the others on firm demographics, will enable to identify a coherent story about cross-sectoral differences in creative destruction.

Size seems to be an important dimension in the analysis of firm entry and exit in Tunisian manufacturing industries. Not surprisingly, small firms (fewer than 60 employees in average) account for more than 75% of total firm turnover

Table 4.3 Average workers per exiting firm

Code	Average size	1996	1997	1998	1999	2000	2001	2002	2003	2004
15	Food industries	25	21	26	16	33	19	19	15	13
17	Textile industries	51	85	53	51	60	66	40	63	41
18	Clothing and lining industries	59	68	54	43	63	80	56	99	111
19	Leather and footwear industries	45	39	65	10	100	42	42	25	24
20	Wood products	13	37	27	25	36	62	43	96	14
24	Chemical industries	26	32	–	21	59	15	53	14	22
25	Plastics material and rubber Industries	11	–	12	33	13	25	–	23	–
26	Mineral non metallic products	15	24	87	30	21	69	15	15	109
27	Metallurgy	–	126	13	31	25	14	48	–	–
28	Fabricated metal products	21	21	42	29	31	26	49	42	13
29	Machinery and equipment	15	63	88	22	17	18	13	–	70
21–22	Paper and cardboard industries, printing and related support activities	29	–	13	44	–	–	43	–	24
30–33	Electrical equipment, radio and TV and other communications equipment, measuring and medical instruments	–	19	127	47	224	52	70	114	17
34–35	Motor vehicle manufacturing, other transportation equipment	–	–	–	16	53	–	–	18	–
36–37	Miscellaneous manufacturing	30	17	27	40	45	23	125	159	30
	All industries	28	46	49	30	56	39	47	57	41

Source: Authors' calculation based on INS data

Table 4.4 Average workers per firm entrants

Code	Average size	1996	1997	1998	1999	2000	2001	2002	2003	2004
15	Food industries	30	27	32	22	23	23	27	23	27
17	Textile industries	53	59	51	51	51	41	61	45	53
18	Clothing and lining industries	64	77	68	75	93	72	134	79	42
19	Leather and footwear industries	50	99	93	41	65	26	53	70	75
20	Wood products	18	21	17	26	20	22	27	30	21
24	Chemical industries	53	39	14	56	32	23	23	18	50
25	Plastics material and rubber Industries	27	25	47	31	42	27	22	36	23
26	Mineral non metallic products	69	33	49	49	42	31	26	23	18
27	Metallurgy	25	15	12	20	153	31		127	
28	Fabricated metal products	30	33	20	21	18	18	22	19	50
29	Machinery and equipment	15	36	33	22	21	31	16	68	36
21–22	Paper and cardboard industries, printing and related support activities	25	18	39	33	29	19	21	16	18
30–33	Electrical equipment, radio and TV and other communications equipment, measuring and medical instruments	71	146	113	66	155	56	101	46	37
34–35	Motor vehicle manufacturing, other transportation equipment	11	62	215	75	374	64	13	150	81
36–37	Miscellaneous manufacturing	50	31	70	39	24	33	37	16	31
	All industries	39	48	58	42	76	34	41	51	40

Source: Authors' calculation based on INS data

Table 4.5 Average workers per active firm

Code	Average size	1996	1997	1998	1999	2000	2001	2002	2003	2004
15	Food industries	47	54	54	65	55	49	50	50	50
17	Textile industries	87	66	44	115	119	120	111	96	84
18	Clothing and lining industries	85	97	99	78	59	57	62	76	92
19	Leather and footwear industries	60	66	63	63	66	72	76	77	74
20	Wood products	33	32	40	73	42	42	44	38	33
24	Chemical industries	113	89	79	78	80	80	85	58	67
25	Plastics material and rubber Industries	60	57	57	61	60	59	66	63	60
26	Mineral non metallic products	83	75	73	58	78	72	79	77	74
27	Metallurgy	125	114	111	123	129	132	104	92	85
28	Fabricated metal products	54	55	51	268	54	50	46	43	45
29	Machinery and equipment	65	46	46	63	42	44	53	53	48
21–22	Paper and cardboard industries, printing and related support activities	59	58	61	42	48	45	51	49	49
30–33	Electrical equipment, radio and TV and other communications equipment, Measuring and medical instruments	112	147	131	140	145	135	141	153	158
34–35	Motor vehicle manufacturing, other transportation equipment	113	118	147	120	93	86	89	89	97
36–37	Miscellaneous manufacturing	72	65	54	20	85	96	97	97	82
	All industries	78	76	74	91	77	76	77	74	73

Source: Authors' calculation based on INS data

Table 4.6 Average size of exitors and entrants, 1996–2004

Code	Exitors			Entrants		
	Average size	Share in total exit (%)	Average exit rate (%)	Average size	Share in total entry (%)	Average entry rate (%)
15	21	20.7	3.8	26	12.9	7.3
17	57	26.4	5.4	52	36.6	26.0
18	70	20.9	2.0	78	12.6	3.8
19	43	5.5	2.6	63	6.3	9.7
20	39	2.7	3.7	22	2.7	10.7
24	30	2.1	1.3	34	2.0	3.6
25	20	1.4	1.2	31	3.0	7.8
26	43	4.5	1.6	38	5.5	6.1
27	43	1.1	2.6	55	0.5	3.7
28	30	4.0	1.8	25	4.5	6.3
29	38	1.3	1.4	31	1.4	4.7
21–22	31	1.3	0.8	24	1.8	3.6
30–33	84	2.9	1.8	88	5.0	10.1
34–35	29	0.4	0.9	116	1.1	8.0
36–37	55	4.7	2.9	37	4.1	8.0
All industries	44	100	2.3	48	100	8.0

Source: Authors' calculation based on INS data

(cf. Tables 4.3–4.6) and firm turnover tend generally to decline with average size. However, this is not completely true for measuring and medical instruments industries, where relatively high turnover (11.9%) and medium average size (84) are jointly observed. This suggests a possible role of the business environment that reduces firm dynamics among medium-sized businesses.

It is also interesting to look at the dispersion of firm by size within each sub-sector. Table 4.7 presents average within coefficient of variation of firm size, normalized by the overall manufacturing sector coefficient of variation[4]. If technological factors were predominant in determining the heterogeneity of firm size across sectors, the values should be concentrated around one. If, on the contrary, the size differences were explained mainly by sectoral factors inducing a consistent bias within sectors, then we would expect the sub-sectors with an overall value above (below) the average to be characterized by values generally above (below) one in the sub-sectors.

Textile (17), Chemical (24), Mineral non metallic products (26) and Fabricated Metal Products (28) industries display greater within-industry dispersion in firm size. This is due to the fact that in particular, in textile industries small businesses coexist with large multi-plant enterprises.

The relatively high turnover rates amongst small-medium sectors suggest that the process of entry and exit involves a proportionally low number of workers. For most sectors, new firms are only 32–63%, the average size of incumbents

Table 4.7 Within-industry coefficient of variation of firm size

Sectors	1997	1998	1999	2000	2001	2002	2003	Average
15	1.15	0.94	1.05	1.06	0.98	0.79	0.83	0.97
17	1.30	1.36	1.29	1.24	1.06	0.93	0.90	1.16
18	0.58	0.59	0.59	0.65	0.69	0.67	0.59	0.62
19	0.82	0.78	0.95	1.15	0.98	0.91	0.92	0.93
20	0.64	0.74	0.61	0.64	0.64	0.56	0.72	0.65
24	0.80	1.13	1.15	1.24	1.25	1.14	0.99	1.10
25	0.84	0.81	0.84	0.86	0.77	0.89	0.84	0.84
26	0.90	0.88	1.08	1.68	1.37	1.17	0.80	1.13
27	0.56	0.64	0.76	0.25	0.62	0.93	0.75	0.64
28	0.83	1.17	1.18	0.89	1.19	1.42	1.06	1.10
29	1.46	0.95	1.30	1.01	0.94	1.03	0.75	1.06
21–22	0.98	1.05	1.02	1.00	0.96	1.00	0.97	1.00
30–33	1.18	1.20	1.21	0.75	0.75	0.75	0.75	0.94
34–35	0.92	0.88	0.90	0.87	0.91	0.92	0.95	0.91
36–37	0.83	0.85	0.68	0.73	0.70	0.63	1.25	0.81

Source: Authors' calculation based on INS data

Table 4.8 Average size of entrants and exitors in proportion of incumbents average size, 1996–2004

	Average size/Incumbents average size (%)	
Sectors	Entrants	Exitors
15	49.3	39.3
17	55.1	60.5
18	99.9	89.7
19	92.6	63.4
20	53.8	94.1
24	41.9	37.2
25	51.4	32.3
26	50.7	57.3
27	48.4	38.0
28	34.4	40.9
29	60.4	74.7
21–22	47.3	59.6
30–33	62.6	59.6
34–35	109.7	27.4
36–37	49.5	74.0

Source: Authors' calculation based on INS data

(cf. Table 4.8). The relatively low entry and exit costs may increase incentives to start up relatively small businesses in Tunisian manufacturing industries.

Fact 3: The creative destruction process is the predominant factor driving entry and exit in many manufacturing industries

It is interesting to compare entry and exit rates across sectors to test two competing conjectures: one hypothesis is that entry and exit rates at the sectoral level are mostly driven by sectoral shocks. Sectors with positive profit shocks will have high entry and sectors with negative profit shocks will have high exit. If sectoral profit shocks are the predominant source of variation, then the cross-sectional correlation between entry and exit rates should be negative. Alternatively, entry and exit rates at the sectoral level might be driven by the within sector creative destruction process. A sector with a high dispersion of idiosyncratic shocks and/or low barriers to entry and exit will exhibit both high entry and high exit rates. If the creative destruction process is the predominant factor driving entry and exit, then the cross-sectional correlation of entry and exit should be positive.

As indicated in Table 4.9, there is a high correlation of industry-level entry rates with exit rate (coefficient of correlation 0.75 for all industries), suggesting that firm turnover not only account for the life cycle of different industries, but also for a continuous process of reallocation of resources in which new businesses (firms) displace obsolete units. The correlation is particularly high in Fabricated Metal Products (0.83), Clothing and Lining (0.81), Wood Products (0.75) and Textile Industries (0.60). Conversely, weaker correlation of entry and exit rates across industries is observed in five industries: Paper and Cardboard, Printing and related support activities (0.001), Chemical (−0.07), Motor vehicle manufacturing and other transportation equipment (−0.09), Food Industries (0.20) and Plastics material and rubber Industries (−0.25); this weaker correlation seems to

Table 4.9 Correlation between entry and exit rate, 1996–2004

Code	Industry	Correlation between entry and exit rate
15	Food industries	0.203
17	Textile industries	0.601
18	Clothing and lining industries	0.807
19	Leather and footwear industries	0.342
20	Wood products	0.745
24	Chemical Industries	−0.066
25	Plastics material and rubber Industries	−0.226
26	Mineral non metallic products	0.390
27	Metallurgy	0.548
28	Fabricated metal products	0.831
29	Machinery and equipment	0.376
21–22	Paper and cardboard industries, printing and related support activities	0.001
30–33	Electrical equipment, radio and TV and other communications equipment, Measuring and medical instruments	0.246
34–35	Motor vehicle manufacturing, other transportation equipment	−0.091
36–37	Miscellaneous manufacturing	−0.499
	All industries	0.749

Source: Authors' calculation based on INS data

be largely due to the systemic changes in which some over-populated industries shrank while expanded.

4.4 Determinants of Entry and Exit

The theoretical and empirical literature addressing the dynamics of entry and exit is considerable and uses a variety of terms to refer to it, such as turnover, turbulence, mobility, and market selection intensity. In the present section, the term turnover is used to refer to the sum of entry and exit rates in a specific industry. Turnover as a market selection process restructures industries, relocates their confines and changes the foundations of competition. It is not surprising, therefore, to find so many papers investigating the reasons behind the inflows and outflows of firms. Yet, the only studies that are of interest in this section are those that analyse the determinants of the rates of entry and exit in manufacturing industries. It focuses on the implications that the interdependence between aggregate entry and exit has for the analysis of manufacturing industry dynamics in Tunisia.

4.4.1 Theoretical Background

Studies of entry and exit have shown that the factors underlying these phenomena are very diverse, being related with industry-specific and firm-specific causes, as well as with changes in the macroeconomic and political environment. Turnover is therefore fed by a variety of factors occurring at the firm, market and macroeconomic levels, which can be either momentary or persistent over time.

Various studies suggest that different stages of the cycle yield different regularities in entry and exit rates. A series of empirical studies has shown that entry rates are higher than exit rates in the earlier phases of industry life cycle (Agarwal 1997; Agarwal and Audretsch 2001; Klepper and Simons 2005). As industries age and set standards, the focus of innovative activity switches from product to process, opportunities for scale economies emerge and shakeout begins. Exit rates overtake entry rates and turnover levels decrease. The important conclusion emerging from these studies is that levels of turnover are higher in earlier stages of the industry or product life cycle.

However, the high correlation between the rates of entry and exit found in different countries and periods suggests that these are not isolated phenomena. In our context, for example, the correlation between the annual rates of entry and exit in the Tunisian manufacturing industry is 0.75. Also, as the detail of Table 4.9 shows, in most of the Tunisian manufacturing sectors, the correlations over the period of analysis defining our data set are effectively positive and significant. Modeling the empirical behavior of these variables, therefore requires some form of interrelation in the econometric specifications. Following the influential paper by Shapiro and Khemani (1987), this is usually done in two ways: via the error terms, maintaining certain symmetry in the vector of explanatory variables, i.e.

estimating a system of seemingly unrelated regressions; or via the explanatory variables, including entry and exit, i.e. estimating a simultaneous equations model. These two approaches have become a benchmark and are the starting point for our empirical investigation.

4.4.1.1 Entry, Exit, and Symmetry Hypothesis

One possible explanation for the statistical regularities around the rates of entry and exit is that their determinants are in fact the same. This would imply perfect symmetry in the vector of explanatory variables. In empirical works, however, it is common to employ a weak version in which only some of the regressors are the same and allow for correlation between the error terms of the entry and exit equations. These regressors are "common" (structural or behavioral) barriers in the sense that they affect both entry and exit.

Well-known examples of these barriers are assets that, because of their specificity and durability, become sunk costs. On the one hand, investing in such assets is a requirement for entry and, if the potential entrant effectively becomes an incumbent, the investment eventually becomes a discouragement to exit. On the other hand, these barriers to exit can also raise barriers to entry because they can alter the expectations of the potential entrants directly by increasing the discount factor of the expected benefits; and/or indirectly as a form of signaling that incumbents will behave aggressively against the entrants.

The hypothesis of symmetry is usually tested by using seemingly unrelated regressions system specifications (*SUR*). Statistically significant coefficients for the barriers to exit (respectively entry) included in the entry (respectively exit) equation would support accepting this hypothesis.

4.4.1.2 Entry, Exit, and Simultaneity Hypothesis

An alternative or complementary explanation is that entry and exit are interrelated in a Schumpeterian setting of creative destruction process. The entry of new, supposed more efficient, firms in a market causes the exit of the relatively less efficient producers and there is consequently a displacement effect. However, existing firms leave behind an emptiness of resources and sets of unsatisfied customers that are an appealing carrot for potential entrants. This may change the subjective probability of success for the potential entrants to the extent that they may indeed, decide to enter and replace those who have left. The outcome of these opposite effects is known in the literature as the revolving door phenomenon or the negative feedback model.

However, what we observe really is not necessarily a creative destruction, but simply trial and error processes. Indeed, some industries may have higher or lower rates than others, just because of their idiosyncratic characteristics. If that is the case, the relation between entry and exit is mostly due to fluctuations in demand, as in the market size model of Geroski and Mazzucato (2001). Changes in the size of the markets are finally responsible for the success or failure of many firms and for movements on the fringes of industries. Therefore, industry turnover is not necessarily due to displacement-vacuum effects.

The displacement/replacement effects would be supported by statistically significant coefficients of the entry and exit variables on the right hand side of the exit and entry equations, respectively. Otherwise, the natural churning view would be accepted.

4.4.2 Econometric Specifications and Results

Following Shapiro and Khemani (1987), the basic model of entry or exit is characterized by:

$$\text{Entry or exit} = f\left(\text{Barriers to entry/exit; incentives; interaction entry/exit; controls}\right)$$

where entry (exit) are measured typically as the number of entry (exit) or the entry (exit) rate.

Barriers to entry/Exit and/or strategic actions (*BARRIERS*) is a vector and usually represented by generally time-invariant vectors of structural characteristics of the industry (minimum efficient scale, advertising, R&D, capital intensity, sunk costs etc.) that are considered to deter entry or exit. The literature on entry barriers emphasizes that there are market conditions that allow incumbents to raise prices above costs persistently without attracting entry. The distinctive element of entry barriers is that they create an asymmetry between incumbents and potential new entrants. Barriers to entry are rents derived from incumbency which impose an entry cost to entrants, which incumbents do not have to pay.

Exit barriers in turn, make it more difficult for incumbents to exit the markets (e.g., sunk costs). A number of contributions have asserted that barriers to exit are related to barriers to entry, that is they create mobility barriers. The basic idea behind this assert is that exit barriers increase the costs of exit, and thus create a zone of inaction where entrants are less likely to enter and incumbents less likely to exit. This suggests that a simple distinction between entry and exit barriers is not easily possible. However, this type of modeling has also drawbacks. Caves (1998) for example, points out that the inclusion of concentration variables and price cost margins as separate regressors the risk of adding redundancy if one accepts the view proposed by the Structure-Conduct-Performance paradigm where structural characteristics constrain the number of firms in the market and lead to an equilibrium characterized by concentration. Structural and strategic entry barriers may also introduce a difficulty, insofar as they are different in one specific characteristic. As noted by Roberts and Thompson (2003), strategic entry barriers are essentially an ex-ante phenomenon, while structural entry barriers are both ex-ante and ex-post phenomena.

The incentives (*INCENTIVES*) vector captures changing market conditions that create opportunities for new entrants. Two typical variables commonly considered are profits and industry growth. While the effect of the latter is not unambiguously to foster entry and to reduce exit, the sign of profits as price-cost margins is more ambiguous (Caves, 1998; Roberts and Thompson 2003).

The interaction entry/exit refers to the intertemporal relationship between entry and exit. Roberts and Thompson (2003) among others provide a study of the interaction between entry and exit which can encompass a number of cases: (1) displacement, where the entry of firms leads to the exit of firms, (2) replacement, where the exit of a firm opens room for the entry of new firms, (3) demonstration, where entry leads to more entry via a demonstration effect, (4) shakeout, where wave of entry is followed by a wave of exit, this leads to a revolving door hypothesis, where the simultaneous entry of firms leads to the subsequent exit of the same firms.

Beside industry characteristics, variables related to firm or sector specific characteristics can also be included (*CONTROLS*). This is usually done in order to study the post-entry performance of new firms.

Bearing in mind these considerations, the following relations between entry and exit were estimated where in all models the dependent variables are the natural logs of the gross rates of entry and exit, calculated after adding 1 to the number of entries and exits in each sector *i* and period *t* to avoid the indeterminacy caused by zero entry and exit:
Model 1: Symmetry

$$\mathrm{Ln}\left(Entry_{i,t}+1\right)= f(BARRIERS_{i,t};INCENTIVES_{i,t};CONTROLS)+\lambda_i+u_{i,t}$$

$$\mathrm{Ln}\left(Exit_{i,t}+1\right)= g(BARRIERS_{i,t};INCENTIVES_{i,t};CONTROLS)+\mu_i+v_{i,t}$$

Model 2: Simultaneity

$$\begin{aligned}\mathrm{Ln}\left(Entry_{i,t}+1\right)= f(&BARRIERS_{i,t};INCENTIVES_{i,t};CONTROLS;\\&\mathrm{Ln}(Exit_{i,t}+1))+\lambda_i+u_{i,t}\end{aligned}$$

$$\begin{aligned}\mathrm{Ln}\left(Entry_{i,t}+1\right)= g(&BARRIERS_{i,t};INCENTIVES_{i,t};CONTROLS;\\&\mathrm{Ln}(Entry_{i,t}+1))+u_i+\upsilon_{i,t}\end{aligned}$$

The considered explanatory variables are as follows:

- Structural barriers and strategic actions (*BARRIERS*):
- Entry barriers include market structure and capital requirements. These are approximated, respectively, by an index of concentration *CR4* and the average gross investment accounted in the sector *GROSSI*.

Exit barriers are reduced to sunk costs, which we proxy with the average investment per worker *SUNKC*.

- Incentives (*INCENTIVES*):
- Incentives are approximated by the export propensity *EXPROP* corresponding to the value of exports as a proportion of manufacturers' value added, the rate of profit at the industry level *PROFIT* approximated by the proportion of gross operating surplus, calculated from the value added at factor cost less the labor factor costs, to value added, the labor productivity *LPROD* defined as the ratio of real value added to total employees and the industry labor growth rate *LABORGR*.
- Sector specific characteristics (*CONTROLS*):
- Sectoral characteristics considered are the coefficient of variation of labor size *CVSIZE* and production *CVPROD*, measured as the ratio of the standard deviation of labor size and production to the mean of labor size and production respectively.

Tables 4.***10*** and 4.11 show the results under the symmetry hypothesis (Model 1). If we focus on the statistically significant estimates for the whole sector, we find that in general, the signs are in conformity with the predictions. According to these estimates, industry concentration index and capital requirements constitute important

Table 4.10 Determinants of entry rate

	Model 1[a]	Model 2[a]
Constant	0.17	0.14
	(3.28)	(4.88)
CR4	−0.26	−0.26
	(−3.4)	(−2.61)
GROSSI(-1)	−0.03	−0.03
	(−1.51)	(−1.93)
LABORGR	0.03	0.04
	(0.94)	(1.27)
PROFIT	−0.09	−0.10
	(−2.11)	(−3.43)
EXPROP	0.01	0.01
	(2.47)	(2.07)
CVSIZE	0.02	0.02
	(2.82)	(3.21)
CVPROD	0.00	0.00
	(−0.02)	(0.36)
LPROD	2.85	3.09
	(1.98)	(1.96)
LOGEXIT	–	0.69
		(3.4)
Adjusted R^2	0.69	0.71
Sample (adjusted): 1998–2003; Cross-sections included: 15		

[a]Estimation method: Panel least squares; White cross-section standard errors and covariance (d.f. corrected); Effects specification: cross-section fixed (dummy variables) and period fixed (dummy variables); *t*-statistics in parenthesis

Table 4.11 Determinants of exit rate

	Model 1[a]	Model 2[a]
Constant	0.04	0.03
	(2.19)	(2.24)
SUNKC	–4.94	–5.38
	(–2.17)	(–2.46)
LABORGR	–0.01	–0.01
	(–1.36)	(–2.16)
PROFIT	0.00	0.01
	(0.17)	(0.63)
EXPROP	0.00	0.00
	(0.35)	(–0.23)
CVSIZE	0.00	0.00
	(0.57)	(0.2)
CVPROD	–0.01	–0.01
	(–2.45)	(–2.52)
LPROD	0.49	0.20
	(1.47)	(0.69)
LOGENTRY	–	0.10
		(3.71)
Adjusted R^2	0.53	0.56
Sample (adjusted): 1998–2003 Cross-sections included: 15		

[a]Estimation method: Panel least squares; White cross-section standard errors and covariance (d.f. corrected); Effects specification: cross-section fixed (dummy variables) and period fixed (dummy variables); *t*-statistics in parenthesis

barriers to entry. As for exits, sunk costs approximated by the average investment per worker, act as barrier. However, we find no evidence of symmetry in the vector of explanatory variables.

A barrier, which gives major advantages for the incumbents, is the realization of scale economies which act as a barrier for the entrants principally via an absolute capital requirement effect (past GROSSI and SUNKC). Absolute capital requirements effect arises from the large investment outlays necessary to build an appropriate sized plant. The size of the disadvantage so created depends on the absolute size of minimum efficient plants. The imperfections in capital markets, which affect the availability of finances (credit) for investments, add to the disadvantage of the entrants. Dixit (1981) has discussed the use of investment as an entry barrier. This materializes when capital expenditures once made, become irreversible or sunk in the next period. Then an established firm might be able to commit to producing an output that it could not sustain at equilibrium if its first period expenditure were irreversible. Sunk expenditure lowers the incumbent's marginal cost for any output below the full capacity level, which, in turn discourages the firm from cutting output in response to entry. Dixit also shows that potential entry may encourage an incumbent firm to invest more in irreversible capital which has the effect of increasing the incumbent's post entry equilibrium output, while lowering the entrant's post entry equilibrium output and price. Sunk costs are a barrier that permits the incumbents to act strategically and forces the entrant to operate at a large scale in order to make profits. Capital investment can be an effective entry deterrent in the above model even if the potential entrant has the same cost function as the incumbent or even if the entrant has lower cost. This is because the extent to which costs are sunk plays an important strategic role in permitting the established firm to commit to a level of output that it would maintain if entry were to occur. The established firm's technology with its sunk capital cost is a mechanism by which the firm can sustain the aggressive market share.

Entry is positively associated with export orientation, market size dispersion and labor productivity. It is negatively associated to profit rate. It seems that the defense of high rents gives incumbents an incentive for ex-post retaliation. Knowledge, about this probably leads to a situation where high profits do not lead to new entry. Labor growth rate and production dispersion within firms deterred exit.

Tables 4.***10*** and 4.***11*** show also the results under the simultaneity hypothesis. Model 2 as cited by Evans and Siegfried (1992) is "*looking for an explanation of residual entry, over and above that which is determined by exit, and residual exit, exceeding that which is determined by entry*." The estimates support the existence of displacement replacement effects and do not reveal any hint of symmetry in any explanatory variables.

From the goodness-of-fit measures (in the bottom rows of Tables 3.1 and 3.2), the explanatory power of the model is relatively high with an adjusted R squared ranging between 53 and 71%. The statistical significance of the interaction effect between entry and exit suggests that Model 2 is indeed the best specification. Accordingly, the estimates from this model should be considered as the basis for the comparisons with other studies.[5]

4.5 Turnover, Economic Performance, and Productivity

The theory attached to firms' turnover goes back to Schumpeter. His theory is that growth, innovation and business dynamics are inherently connected and the economy develops through a process of competition and selection. Firms gain an advantage through innovation. In this way, they achieve excess profit which encourages imitation and entry. As a result, profits drop and the firms are stimulated to innovate again. As not all firms have the abilities to innovate, selection occurs. From this point of view, the entry of new firms is essential because entrants bring with them new ideas, methods and products. The exit of some firms is equally important, because the majority of these firms show bad performances and do no longer contribute to the growth of the economy. Furthermore, exit of firms creates room for new entries. Accordingly, Schumpeter states that a high level of turnover of firms contributes to economic growth because of its contribution to selection and innovation.

The purpose of this forth section is to investigate using a panel of manufacturing industry data for the years 1996 up to and including 2004 whether entry and exit of firms affect performance and labor productivity.

4.5.1 Impact of Entry and Exit Rates on Economic Performance

Many studies dealing with the impact of firm entry and exit on economic performance, focus on the relationship between firm entry and exit and productivity growth. Scarpetta et al. (2002) studied several OECD countries; the empirical results show significant differences in the contributions of entry to aggregate productivity. For the European countries, firm entry has a positive contribution to growth, but the effect is small, whereas in US, firm entry has a negative impact on growth. However, the results are unanimous for the impact of the firm exit, in the sense that the exit of low productivity firms has a positive impact on aggregate growth. The authors argue that the results may differ according to whether the economic performance indicator is measured by TFP or Labor productivity. Besides, Cincera and Galgau (2005) argues that the entry and exit of firms has an impact on both the level and the growth rate of total factor productivity.

In the present study, we concentrate on the main findings on the impact of the entry and exit rates on economic performance as measured by the growth of output. Consequently, we will run an extended Cobb–Douglas function, defined as follows:

$$\ln(Y_{it}) = \alpha_0 + \alpha_1 \ln(K_{it}) + \alpha_2 \ln(L_{it}) + \sum_{p=1}^{2} \lambda_p \ln(E_{it-p} + 1) + \sum_{q=1}^{2} \beta_q \ln(X_{it-q} + 1) + \varepsilon_{it} \tag{4.1}$$

where $i = 1 \ldots 15$, $t = 1997–2005$.

Y, K, and L represent respectively value added, capital and labor in the considered industry. Entry rate, E, and exit rate, X, are assumed to affect the production process instantaneously and with lagged components. Hence, the dynamics of entry and exit on the production process will be considered by introducing entry and exit rates to the production function, according to a distributed lag model. An alternative specification to be tested is to introduce into the production equation, production, capital and labor variables in first differences rather in levels. Hence, we will have:

$$\Delta \ln(Y_{it}) = \alpha n_0 + \alpha_1 \Delta \ln(K_{it}) + \alpha_2 \Delta \ln(L_{it}) + \sum_{p=1}^{2} \theta_p \ln(E_{it-p} + 1) + \sum_{q=1}^{2} \mu_q \ln(X_{it-q} + 1) + \varepsilon_{it} \tag{4.2}$$

The two alternative specifications presented above, are tested using a panel data of 15 manufacturing industries covering the period 1995–2004. Specification (2) has been tested using proxies for value added, capital and labor extracted from the annual firm surveys covering the period 1997–2003. Thus, we use for each sector and for each year medians values of firm value added, capital and labor. Several specifications have been tested whether output and inputs variables in the production function have been introduced in levels or in differences and whether the heterogeneity across industries is supposed to be fixed or random. Our favorite results for the impact of firm entry and exit on output growth are reported in Table 4.12.[6]

We observe a negative impact of an increase in the current firm entry rate, which is significant at the 10% confidence level, with a 1% increase in the current entry rate leading to a decrease by 1.04%.[7] However, we do not find a significant relationship between firm entry lagged by 1 and 2 years respectively. Besides, the coefficients of the exit rates are not significant for all the specifications. An exception concerns, results of specification (1) where we find that the exit rate lagged by 1 year has a positive impact on the production process.

The general policy implications that we can draw from the empirical analysis are not clear and do not support any economic considerations that influence entry and exit in

Table 4.12 Impact of entry and exit on economic performance; dependent variable lnY

	Specification (1)	Specification (2)	
	Fixed effect model	Fixed effect model	Random effect model
Constant	2.95	–	–0.026
	(4.64)		(–0.11)
Labor	0.37	0.93	0.93
	(4.97)	(5.4)	(6.11)
Capital	0.24	0.28	0.29
	(4.44)	(2.6)	(3.10)
Entry	–0.74	–1.22	–1.04
	(–1.93)	(–1.62)	(–1.63)
Entry(–1)	–0.55	0.75	0.67
	(–1.79)	(–0.95)	(1.15)
Entry(–2)	–0.04	–	–
	(–0.14)		
Exit	1.09	2.39	1.02
	(1.17)	(1.15)	(0.65)
Exit(–1)	2.15	2.20	0.72
	(2.31)	(1.11)	(1.53)
Exit(–2)	1.49	–	–
	(1.57)		
Obs	105	90	90
R^2	0.58	0.67	0.60
Haussman specification test		$x^2(6)=1.6$	p-Value 0.95

Note: Robust t-statistics in brackets fonts below the corresponding coefficients.
Specification (1) and (2) indicate that value added, capital and labor variables are introduced alternatively in levels or differences into the production function.

order to improve economic performance.[8] The results obtained are not robust and stress the limits of the present study, which are due to data availability and measurement errors. Besides, estimation results may be plagued by problems of reverse causality.

4.5.2 Labor Productivity and Firm Turnovers

This section focuses on the dynamics of labor productivity in the manufacturing sector during the 1996–2004 period, the period for which the data are readily available. We analyze labor productivity, and not total factor productivity (TFP), because of two equally important reasons. First, labor productivity is an important macroeconomic indicator of earning capacity, and a reference statistical information closely followed by the public and policy-makers alike. Second, the data on capital stocks required to study TFP are not of the same good quality as the other data and exist for only a proportion of the firms in the sample seriously limiting the scope of the analysis.

Figure 4.3 and Table 4.13 show the basic aggregate patterns using the INS aggregate data for the period 1984–2004.

Table 4.13 reveals that value-added grew rapidly between 1996 and 2004 (7% in average). Capital investment also grew at a relatively fast pace (6% in average). However, growth in worker-year and value-added per worker-year has been modest and quite erratic during this period, at an average rate of 2% and 5% per year respectively.

As mentioned above, the purpose of this part is to investigate whether entry and exit of firms affects labor productivity. A model for labor productivity is developed and estimated using a panel of 15 manufacturing sectors data for the years 1996 up to and including 2004. Table 4.14 presents averages of labor productivity.

To investigate the impact of firm dynamics (turnover) on productivity, the following equation for labor productivity is estimated:

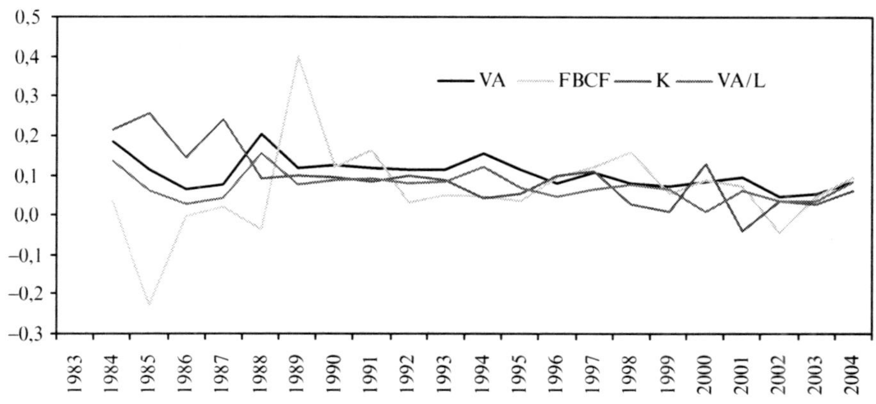

Fig. 4.3 Manufacturing sector, 1984–2004 growth rates (%)

Table 4.13 Manufacturing sector, 1984–2004 growth rates (%)

Period	Worker-years	Value added	Investment	Stock of capital	Value added per worker
1984	0.04	0.19	0.03	0.21	0.13
1985	0.05	0.11	−0.23	0.26	0.06
1986	0.04	0.07	0.00	0.14	0.03
1987	0.03	0.07	0.02	0.24	0.04
1988	0.04	0.20	−0.04	0.09	0.16
1989	0.04	0.12	0.40	0.10	0.07
1990	0.03	0.12	0.12	0.09	0.09
1991	0.02	0.12	0.16	0.08	0.09
1992	0.03	0.11	0.03	0.10	0.08
1993	0.03	0.11	0.05	0.09	0.08
1994	0.03	0.15	0.05	0.04	0.12
1995	0.04	0.11	0.04	0.05	0.07
1996	0.03	0.08	0.10	0.10	0.04
1997	0.04	0.10	0.12	0.11	0.07
1998	0.00	0.08	0.16	0.03	0.08
1999	0.01	0.07	0.05	0.01	0.07
2000	0.07	0.08	0.09	0.13	0.01
2001	0.03	0.10	0.07	−0.04	0.06
2002	0.01	0.05	−0.05	0.04	0.03
2003	0.02	0.05	0.05	0.03	0.03
2004	0.00	0.08	0.09	0.06	0.08
1984–2004	0.03	0.10	0.05	0.09	0.07
1996–2004	0.02	0.07	0.06	0.04	0.05

Source: Authors' calculation based on INS and IEQ aggregated data

$$Labor\ \mathrm{Pr}oductivity_{it} = \alpha_0 + \alpha_1 Dummy(\Delta L_{it} > 0) + \sum_{j=0}^{1} \beta_j TURNOVER_{i,t-j} + \varepsilon_{it} \quad (3)$$

Firm downsizing, i.e., a reduction in the size of the firm's labor force, is often rationalized as an integral part of a process of structural change that will eventually result in productivity gains. It is interesting then to try and confront this notion with our data.

We regressed labor productivity between 1996 and 2004 on a dummy variable Dummy(ΔL > 0) equal to one for firms that increased their number of worker-years during the period, and zero for those that did not and on present and lagged *TURNOVER* (as well as industry and temporal dummies). Table 4.***15*** presents this result.

The estimated coefficient of the dummy variable indicates that, within the same industry, firms that increased their labor force experienced 2 constant Dinars lower productivity growth than firms that decreased their workers.[9] These results also tell us that firm turnovers contribute positively and significantly to the increase of labor productivity.

Table 4.14 Labor productivity across industries (in 1,000 Dinars), 1997–2004

SECTOR	Mean	Std. Dev.	Max	Min.	Obs.
Food industries	1.81	0.20	2.07	1.47	8
Textile industries	0.44	0.31	1.02	0.25	8
Clothing and lining industries	0.81	0.22	1.15	0.57	8
Leather and footwear industries	1.06	0.08	1.18	0.97	8
Wood products	5.95	1.21	7.61	3.56	8
Chemical industries	2.74	0.46	3.62	2.19	8
Plastics material and rubber industries	1.46	0.07	1.56	1.33	8
Mineral non metallic products	1.37	0.14	1.70	1.22	8
Metallurgy	1.47	0.10	1.64	1.35	8
Fabricated metal products	1.12	0.09	1.28	0.98	8
Machinery and equipment	0.38	0.05	0.48	0.28	8
Paper and cardboard industries, printing and related support activities	1.12	0.14	1.28	0.94	8
Electrical equipment, radio and TV and other communications equipment, Measuring and medical instruments	0.85	0.05	0.93	0.78	8
Motor vehicle manufacturing, other transportation equipment	1.96	0.44	2.37	1.24	8
Miscellaneous manufacturing	0.37	0.07	0.49	0.30	8
All	1.53	1.39	7.61	0.25	120

Table 4.15 Labor productivity and turnover

Variable	Coefficient[a]
CONST	0.01
	(9.26)
Dummy(DL>0)	−0.002
	(−2.83)
TURNOVER	0.019
	(3.69)
TURNOVER(−1)	0.02
	(2.25)
Adjusted R^2	0.94
Sample (adjusted): 1997–2004; Cross-sections included: 15	

[a]Estimation method: Panel least squares; White cross-section standard errors and covariance (d.f. corrected); Effects specification: Cross-section fixed (dummy variables) and period fixed (dummy variables); t-statistics in parenthesis

One problem with modeling the consequences of turnover is the possibility of simultaneity: on the one hand, economic growth encourages entry, entry in turn has consequences for exits and, on the other hand, entries and exits affect economic growth. In ideal circumstances, this entire process should be modeled.

We chose a simple approach in this study which can be refined later. Nevertheless, this approach has provided reliable indications that turnover does affect labor productivity.

4.6 Conclusion

While there has been a profusion of theoretical work on entry and exit of firms, there is comparatively little empirical work in the area even for developed countries (Disney et al. 2003). Firm entry and exit is a part of the market selection process, by which resources are reallocated within or across industries. The process of entry and exit influences economic performance through firms' internal restructuring, reallocation of resources among firms and changes in market shares of incumbents. It also induces the introduction of new technologies, thereby improving economic performance. Unfortunately, shortage in firm demographics data in Tunisia and its coverage enables researchers to draw concrete inferences on firm dynamics and poses an important obstacle to analyzing births and deaths of enterprises. This data shortage necessitates the need for more effort to be done on data collection and dissemination for better understanding of the within-firm growth and market dynamics.

The major contribution of the study presented in this chapter is to circumvent this data shortage by merging, for the first time in Tunisia, administrative files based on continuous report of fiscal affiliation of firms with the register of firm affiliates at the National Social Security Fund (CNSS) in order to compute series on the number of entering (new), exiting (out of business) and total private firms with ten workers or more, by year and by industry over the 1996–2004 period.

First, the empirical findings of the chapter establish three basic stylized facts: a relative high firm churning in all Tunisian manufacturing sectors, firm turnover is principally driven by small and medium-sized firms and the creative destruction process is the predominant factor driving entry and exit in many manufacturing industries.

By developing a comprehensive picture of the magnitude, characteristics and effectiveness of the creative destruction process, the paper provides policy makers with a better understanding of the market's selection process at the sectoral level. While heterogeneity in productivity is a common finding in firm-level micro data, the easy entry and exit of firms is necessary if these micro differences are to be exploited in a way that contributes to aggregate productivity growth. The combination of heterogeneity in productivity and easy entry and exit of firms is found to characterize the manufacturing sector in Tunisia. Accordingly, obstacles to free entry and exit slow the reallocation process and are likely to slow (labor) productivity growth.

Second, focusing on the implications that the interdependence between aggregate entry and exit has for the analysis of manufacturing industry dynamics in Tunisia, the empirical investigations revealed that:

- Industry concentration index and capital requirements constitute important barriers to entry. As for exits, sunk costs approximated by the average investment per worker, act as barrier. However, no evidence of symmetry in the vector of explanatory variables is established.

- Entry is positively associated with export orientation, market size dispersion and labor productivity. It is negatively associated to profit rate. It seems that the defense of high rents gives incumbents an incentive for ex-post retaliation. Knowledge about this probably leads to a situation where high profits do not lead to new entry. Labor growth rate and production dispersion within firms deterred exit.
- Estimates also support the existence of displacement, replacement effects and do not reveal any hint of symmetry in any explanatory variables.

Finally, firm turnovers contribute positively and significantly to the increase of labor productivity.

4.7 Notes

1. For more details see Morrisson and Talbi (1996), Murphy (1999), and Di Tommaso et al. (2001).
2. http://www.pmi.tn/en/index.php
3. In fact, the National Repertory of firm in Tunisia is a continuous updated register of entry, exit and active firms based on a mix of two administrative files: The fiscal annual register coming from the general direction of fiscal control and the National quarterly register of employees taken from the CNSS.
4. The coefficient of variation is used because the dispersion of size across industries is not in general independent from the average size: sectors with larger size also tend to display higher standard deviations.
5. Even though the above methodology provides us reasonably good estimates of the height of the overall barriers to entry and exit it suffers from inaccuracies introduced by the use of the kinds of variables that proxy barriers. Moreover, the data available for cross section examination by itself is capable of inducing biases in the measure. Thus it can only be considered as a first step in analysing the extent of barriers. Added to this is the possibility of inter-industry variations in erecting barriers. As entry and exit are discrete and involve a time lag to respond to incentives, which differ across industries, a more suitable method will be to examine a panel of firms across industry groups.
6. Several specifications have also been tested assuming that entry and exit rates are endogenous. The results obtained are not significant and will not be reported.
7. Economic analysis on the impact of the entry and exit rates on output growth concern the results reported in column 2 and 3 of Table 5.1.
8. Our results are in contradiction with the main findings of Cincera and Galgau (2005) who find appositive correlation between entry and the growth of production.
9. The result remains unchanged after controlling for changes in the capital stock by introducing a dummy variable equal 1 for firms that increased their real investment.

References

Agarwal R (1997) Survival of firms over the product life cycle. South Econ J 3:571–584

Agarwal R, Audretsch DB (2001) Does entry size matter? The impact of life cycle and technology on firm survival. J Ind Econ 49:21–43

Cincera M, Galgau O (2005) Impact of market entry and exit on EU productivity and growth performance. European Commission Economic Papers No. 222

Clerides SK, Lach S, Tybout JR (1998) Is learning-by-exporting important? Micro-dynamic evidence from Colombia, Morocco, and Mexico. Q J Econ 113(3):903–947

Di Tommaso MR, Lanzoni E, Rubini L (2001) Support to SMEs in the Arab region: the case of Tunisia. UNIDO/UNDP, UNIDO Italia

Disney R, Haskel J, Heden Y (2003) Restructuring and productivity growth in UK manufacturing. Econ J 113(489):666–694

Dixit A (1981) The role of investment in entry deterrence'. Econ J 90:95–106

Djankov S, La Porta R, Lopez-De-Silanes F, Shleifer A (2002) The regulation of entry. Q J Econ CXVII (1):1–37

Djankov S, McLiesh C, Ramalho R (2006) Regulation and growth. Econ Lett 92(3):395–401

Evans LB, Siegfried JJ (1992) Entry and exit in United States manufacturing industries from 1977 to 1982. In: Audretsch DB, Sigfried JJ (eds) Empirical studies in honour of Leonard W. Weiss. Kluwer, Boston, pp 253–273

Geroski PA, Mazzucato J (2001) Modelling the dynamics of industry populations. Int J Ind Organ 19:1003–1022

Klepper S, Simons KL (2005) Industry shakeouts and technological change. Int J Ind Organ 23:23–43

Morrisson C, Talbi B (1996) La croissance de l'économie tunisienne en longue période. OCDE, Paris

Murphy EC (1999) Economic and political change in Tunisia: from Bourguiba to Ben Ali. MacMillan Press, Houndmills

Roberts BM, Thompson S (2003) Entry and exit in a transition economy: the case of Poland. Rev Ind Organ 22:225–243

Scarpetta S, Hemmings P, Tressel T, Woo J (2002) The role of policy and institutions for productivity and firm dynamics: evidence from micro and industry data. Economic Working Paper 15, OECD, Paris

Shapiro D, Khemani RS (1987) The determinants of entry and exit reconsidered. Int J Ind Organ 5:15–26

Chapter 5
Entry, Exit and Productivity in Turkish Manufacturing Industries

Teoman Pamukçu, Khalid Sekkat, and Erol Taymaz

5.1 Introduction

Turkey pursued an import-substitution based development strategy over the period 1960–1980, just as many other developing countries did during this period. This period came to an abrupt end following the severe balance of payments crisis in the late seventies. She then introduced a number of structural reforms in the year 1980 which led gradually to greater trade openness, liberalization of input and product markets, financial liberalization and finally liberalization of the capital account. Emphasis during the early years of the program was on encouraging exports through various direct and indirect incentives (through export tax rebates, preferential export credits, foreign exchange allocations and duty-free access to imports).

Some steps were taken towards elimination of import barriers during the period 1980–1983 and radical reforms were implemented after 1984 in order to liberalize import regime. First, quantitative restrictions on imports were rapidly phased out, and these changes in quantitative restrictions have resulted in considerable elimination of trade barriers. Second, significant reductions in tariff rates, especially on imports of intermediate and capital goods were implemented in the late 1980s and early 1990s. Although tariffs on certain goods (for example, consumer goods) were increased temporarily after the elimination of quantitative restrictions, this did not lead to an increase in the overall nominal protection rates, because imports of the low share of these goods in total imports before 1984.

A major change in the foreign trade regime in Turkey was triggered by the Customs Union Agreement signed between the EU and Turkey, which came into effect in 1996. As a result, Turkey liberalized its tariffs and adopted EU's Common External Tariff for industrial products and industrial components of processed agricultural products. The agreement also embraces a number of deep integration elements such as the

T. Pamukçu (✉) and E. Taymaz
The Middle East Technical University, Egypt

K. Sekkat
The Economic Research Forum, Egypt

K. Sekkat (ed.), *Market Dynamics and Productivity in Developing Countries, Economic Reforms in the Middle East and North Africa*, DOI 10.1007/978-1-4419-1037-0_5,

harmonization of Turkey's Competition Policy Legislation to that of the EU, the adoption of the Community's Commercial policy towards third countries, and of the EU Acquis regarding the standardization of industrial products.

A number of studies investigated the implications of the trade reforms of the post-1980 period and of the Customs Union Agreement for the performance of the Turkish economy, especially for the manufacturing sector: issues analyzed include the impact of these developments on innovation decision of Turkish firms, productivity of the manufacturing sector, the diffusion of foreign technology brought by foreign companies to domestic firms and on the development of informal activities in the Turkish economy[1].

The dynamics of entry and exit of firms in the aftermath of these far reaching reforms have not been examined thoroughly. However, one channel thorough which these reforms can influence economic performance in the Turkish economy is through their impact on the entry and exit rates of firms and, in the second stage by the effect firm demography (survivors, entrants, exitors) can exert on productivity of firms. Our aim in this report is to analyze this issue for the Turkish manufacturing sector using firm-level and sector-level data and appropriate econometric techniques.

In the second section of this chapter, the dataset that is used in this report will be presented and examined in detail: Data will be presented in order to analyze characteristics of the Turkish manufacturing sector in the nineties. Afterwards, information concerning the database of the Turkish Institute of Statistics, and its annual survey of the manufacturing industry – which is the source of the data used in our study – will be presented.

Section 5.3 of this chapter will be devoted to the analysis of the determinants of entry and exit of firms in the Turkish manufacturing industry during the period 1992–2001. First, a descriptive analysis of the data by firm status (survivor, entrant, exitor) will be carried out in order to present the main characteristics of our data set. Second, equation for entry and exit rates, respectively will be specified, estimated by alternative econometric methods, and findings will be discussed in the light of economic theory and available empirical evidence.

In the fourth section of our chapter, we will first examine links between entry and exit of firms on the one hand, and their productivity by firm status on the other hand. This descriptive analysis will be completed by a decomposition method that measures the contribution of four different factors by firm status on industry level productivity change.

In the fifth section, the aforementioned accounting-based decomposition of industry level productivity will be completed by an econometric analysis aimed at measuring the impact of sector-level entry and exit rates on firm-level productivity growth in the Turkish manufacturing sector over the period 1992–2001. An equation including other important determinants of firm-level productivity will be estimated in order to sort out possible effects of entry and exit.

Finally, in the last section, a summary of main findings will be carried out and suggestions will be made for future research.

5.2 Data and Descriptive Statistics

The main data source is the Longitudinal Database of the Statistical Institute of Turkey (Turkstat)[2]. Turkstat conducts *Annual Surveys of Manufacturing Industries* (ASMI) at private establishments with 10 or more employees and at all public establishments.

The evolution of the relative importance of nine industries within the manufacturing sector over the period 1995–2001 is presented in Tables 5.1–5.4, in terms of the distribution of employment, value added and number of firms.

It turns out that food-beverage-tobacco (ISIC 31) and textile-wearing apparel-leather products (ISIC 32) have together accounted for half of the manufacturing sector in terms of the aforementioned variables-and their share is relatively stable. Note that the share of the second sector is the double of the share of the second sector as far as employment and number of firms are concerned, but not in terms of value added. These figures point to the importance of labor intensive and low (medium) technology activities in the Turkish manufacturing sector by the late nineties.

Another major sector is fabricated metal products, machinery and equipment sector (ISIC 38). This sector is more heterogeneous compared to the two previous sectors: indeed, it contains low, medium as well as high technology sectors – manufacture of fabricated metal products (381), manufacture of transport equipments (384), and manufacture of professional and scientific instruments (385), respectively. The share of this sector is relatively stable over the period 1995–2001: it accounts on average for 20% of all the three variables included in Tables 5.1–5.3.

Finally, another major sector is ISIC 35 (chemical, petroleum, coal, rubber and plastic products). Although its share in manufacturing employment and number of firms is much lower than the three previous sectors, its weight in sector-level value added increased from 19.1% in 1995 to 30.3% in 2001. This divergent evolution is likely to be explained mainly by the existence presence of a few very capital-intensive state firms in petrochemicals.

Table 5.4 summarizes information on the size distribution of firms in the Turkish manufacturing sector for the year 1996 and the share of different size classes – seven in total – in terms of number of establishments and employees, wage bill, and value added.

Firms belonging to the first two categories represented 65% of the total number of firms, but accounted only for 16% of all employees, 7% of the wage bill, and 7.1% of the value added in the manufacturing sector in the year 1996. This observation is not modified if the third size category is included in the analysis: it then turns out that 80% of firms in the Turkish manufacturing firms accounted for 26.4% of employees, 12.3% of the wage bill, and 13.3% of the value added created in 1996. On the other hand, firms with more than 500 employees account for slightly more than 50% of payments made to employees and value added, 37.5% of the number of employees whereas they represent 3.5% of all firms with more than ten employees.

Data provided in Table 5.4 points to the massive presence of small and medium size enterprises in the formal manufacturing sector in Turkey, and at the same time,

Table 5.1 Distribution of employment in the Turkish manufacturing sector (%)

	1995	1996	1997	1998	1999	2000	2001
ISIC[a]							
31	17.5	16.7	15.6	15.4	16.0	15.5	15.2
32	33.4	35.0	35.5	34.7	33.6	34.7	33.6
33	2.2	2.2	2.3	2.4	2.4	2.5	2.3
34	3.5	3.5	3.2	3.0	3.0	3.0	2.9
35	8.9	8.8	8.9	9.1	9.6	9.2	9.4
36	7.0	6.6	6.5	6.6	7.0	6.6	6.3
37	6.7	5.8	5.7	5.6	5.5	5.4	5.1
38	20.0	20.4	21.5	22.2	21.8	22.0	21.6
39	0.6	0.6	0.6	0.7	0.7	0.8	0.9

[a]31: Food, beverages and tobacco; 32: Textile, wearing apparel and leather industries, 33: Wood and wood products, including furniture; 34: Paper and paper products, printing and publishing; 35: Chemicals and chemical, petroleum, coal, rubber and plastic products; 36: Non-metallic products; 37: Basic metal industries; 38: Fabricated metal products, machinery and equipment; 39: Other manufacturing industries

Source: Own calculations from TurkStat's ASMI database

Table 5.2 Distribution of value added in the Turkish manufacturing sector (%)

	1995	1996	1997	1998	1999	2000	2001
ISIC							
31	17.6	17.5	14.1	13.8	15.5	17.2	16.9
32	19.6	20.3	20.6	17.9	15.8	16.5	18.0
33	1.3	1.4	1.5	1.3	1.4	1.5	0.94
34	3.8	4.2	3.6	2.8	3.0	3.0	2.6
35	19.1	17.5	16.9	28.8	31.7	26.9	30.3
36	8.0	7.6	8.1	7.0	7.3	6.9	6.2
37	7.7	7.2	9.1	6.1	5.3	5.4	5.5
38	22.5	23.9	25.7	21.9	19.7	21.9	18.6
39	0.3	0.4	0.5	0.3	0.4	0.7	1.0

Source: Own calculations from TurkStat's ASMI database

Table 5.3 Distribution of number of firms in the Turkish manufacturing sector (%)

	1995	1996	1997	1998	1999	2000	2001
ISIC							
31	17.5	17.2	16.3	15.7	15.8	15.4	15.2
32	30.8	31.6	31.8	31.0	30.2	30.5	31.1
33	4.0	3.9	4.3	4.2	4.0	4.0	4.1
34	3.5	3.5	3.4	3.5	3.4	3.6	3.6
35	8.6	8.6	9.0	9.0	9.3	9.3	9.5
36	8.3	7.9	7.7	7.8	7.9	7.8	7.2
37	3.9	3.6	3.6	3.6	3.7	3.6	3.6
38	22.3	22.6	22.9	24.4	24.6	24.8	24.6
39	1.0	1.0	1.0	1.0	1.1	1.1	1.2

Source: Own calculations from TurkStat's ASMI database

Table 5.4 Turkish manufacturing sector according to size distribution – 1996 (%)

	Number of establishment	Number of employees	Payments to employees	Value added
Size classes				
10–24	36.4	5.7	2.2	2.2
25–49	28.5	10.3	4.8	4.9
50–99	14.7	10.4	6.2	7.2
100–199	10.1	14.3	11.4	10.8
200–499	7.0	21.8	22.5	24.1
500–999	2.3	16.1	21.7	19.2
> 1,000	1.2	21.4	31.2	31.6
Total	100.0	100.0	100.0	100.0

Size is measured by the number of employees
Source: Own calculations from TurkStat's ASMI database

to their poor performance in terms of four major indicators of manufacturing activity included in this table. Causes of this situation are manifold and include factors such as poor access to capital markets, low human capital, lock-in into low-technology sectors that are open to fierce international competition based on low wages, insufficient in-firm training, and a tax and regulatory system that penalizes SME activity[3].

The Censuses of Industry and Business Establishments, which cover all establishments – i.e. at least one employee – were conducted in 1980, 1985, 1992, and 2002. Besides manufacturing sector, data collected within these censuses concern two more sectors –i.e. electricity/gas/water and construction sectors. Note that firms with less than 10 employees are surveyed on a sampling basis. The data from the 2002 Census were not available at the time of writing this paper.

For this study, we limited the sample for the post 1992 period. The data, especially on employment and production, have been carefully controlled by the Turkstat staff during the annual surveys, and the firms were contacted again if inconsistencies were detected. We also checked the data for "outliers" for ratio variables, and outliers were replaced by averages of the previous and next years' values, if the data on these years were available. Otherwise, the outliers were assigned as "missing". On average, the proportion of outliers was less than 2% of plant-year observations.

"Establishment" is the statistical unit in the database. An "establishment" (or "plant") is defined as a functional and decision-making unit that operates at a single location. All data, including the accounting data, are collected at the establishment level. An establishment is defined as "entrant" when it first appears in the database, and exit is defined similarly as exit from the database (an exit occurs in the year if the establishment is observed in the database the last time in that year). An establishment may exit from the database for reasons other than a real exit (shutdown). If an establishment gets smaller than the threshold level (10 employees) for two consecutive years, it will exit from the database. That establishment, of course, may reenter into the database if it grows. This aspect of the database is likely to cause an overestimation of the exit rate, and underestimation of the survival duration for small establishments that employ about 10 people. If the owner of the firm changes as a result of an acquisition or merger, it will not be defined as "exit" as long as the plant remains in operation

It should be pointed out here that our analysis of the determinants of entry/exit of firms as well as the impact of these two factors on firm level productivity will be carried over the period 1992–2001. The main reason this period ends in the year 2001 is that statistical units surveyed in ASMI has changed from 2001 onward. Indeed, whereas establishments were surveyed period to year 2002 "enterprises" were surveyed afterward, and an enterprise can include several establishments so that we can not match units surveyed by ASMI before 2002 with those surveyed after this year[4].

5.2.1 *Descriptive Analysis*

Table 5.5 summarizes information on the number of firms according to their status (survivor, entrant, exitor) and the share of each status in the total number of firms over the period 1992–2001.

The total number of firms during this period changed between a minimum of 10,121 in 1994 and a maximum of 12,313 in 1998. Survivors have always accounted for a large share of existing firms so that their share in total was never lower than 76.3% (1998) over this period, except for the year 1992. Accordingly, entrants and exitors have always represented a low share of all firms: their share in the total was never larger than 14%, except for the year 1992. Besides, net entry rates – entry *minus* exit rates – are much lower then gross entry rates.

Data in Table 5.6 provides information on the number of firms by entry and exit years. Table 5.6 points to two well-known facts about firm demography: firstly, young firms tend to exit the market after a relatively short period of activity and

Table 5.5 Number of firms by status and year (*plus* share in percentage of the total)

	Total	Survivors	Entrants	Exitors	Survivors in % of total	Entrants in % of total	Exitors in % of total
1992	11.196	7.013	3.486	1.251	62.6	31.1	11.2
1993	10.560	8.726	779	1,215	82.6	7.4	11.5
1994	10.121	8.716	673	784	86.1	6.6	7.7
1995	10.224	8.415	994	982	82.3	9.7	9.6
1996	10.584	8.400	1.255	1.199	79.4	11.9	11.3
1997	11.358	9.072	1.581	963	79.9	13.9	8.5
1998	12.313	9.395	1.695	1.490	76.3	13.8	12.1
1999	11.253	9.636	586	1.114	85.6	5.2	9.9
2000	11.105	9.442	734	1.025	85.0	6.6	9.2
2001	11.303	10.365	938	0.0	91.7	8.3	0.0

Source: Own calculations from TurkStat's ASMI database

Table 5.6 Exitors by number of survival years

	Entry time								
Exit time	1992	1993	1994	1995	1996	1997	1998	1999	2000
1992	554								
1993	461	160							
1994	233	95	52						
1995	206	56	145	167					
1996	204	53	47	194	270				
1997	129	33	41	51	119	258			
1998	169	51	41	70	164	222	267		
1999	149	42	29	47	68	125	163	83	
2000	128	32	23	42	54	90	142	69	96

Source: Own calculations from TurkStat's ASMI database

Table 5.7 Percentage of exitors after 1 year, 2 year and at the end of the period (as a percentage of a cohort of entrants for a given year)

	Entry year								
Exit year	1992	1993	1994	1995	1996	1997	1998	1999	2000
First year	15.9	20.5	7.7	16.8	21.5	16.3	15.8	14.2	13.1
First and second year	29.1	32.7	29.3	36.3	31.0	30.4	25.4	25.9	13.1
Whole period (cumulative)	64.1	67.0	56.2	57.4	53.8	44.0	33.7	25.9	13.1

Source: Own calculations from TurkStat's ASMI database

second, the survival of entrants is low – with a large number of entrants failing within the first year[5].

Indeed, data in Table 5.7 below shows that between 15% and 20% of all entrants each year over the period 1992–2000 live only 1 year and then exit. Furthermore, this figure rises to 25.4–36.3% if exits occurring during the second year are taken into account– except for the year 2000, for which we have only one observation. Finally, the cumulative exit rate over the whole period is 64.1% for 1992 entrants (9 years), 67.0% for 1993 entrants (8 years), 56.2% for 1994 entrants (7 years) and 57.4% for 1995 entrants (6 years), etc.

Data in Table 5.8 points to another empirical regularity relating to firm demography: both entrants and exitors have a mean or median size that is lower than the corresponding size for survivor firms[6]. Note that the size gap measured with respect to the average firm is larger than the one indicated by the median firm size until 1996 and becomes similar thereafter.

Tables 5.9 and 5.10 summarize information on the evolution of the mean/median size of entrants for different cohorts over the period 1992–2001. Note that the first column is identical to the third column in Table 5.8 – mean size of entrants.

Table 5.8 Mean and median firm size by status and year[a]

	Total mean	Survivors mean	Entrants mean	Exitors mean	Total median	Survivors median	Entrants median	Exitors median
1992	87.5	122.7	27.5	26.2	27	38	16	13
1993	92.3	105.0	33.7	28.3	30	34	15	13
1994	92.1	100.7	38.1	37.0	30	34	18	13
1995	94.8	106.8	40.8	35.4	32	36	21	17
1996	97.8	112.0	35.4	47.1	34	39	19	19
1997	99.9	112.8	48.9	44.1	36	41	22	15
1998	97.5	114.5	38.9	43.6	36	41	23	18
1999	98.5	107.6	44.6	43.3	36	39	25	19
2000	101.4	110.6	52.6	43.5	37	41	25	17
2001	96.9	101.8	41.1	–	36	37	22	–

[a]Size is measured by the number of employees
Source: Own calculations from TurkStat's ASMI database

Table 5.9 Mean entrant size[a]

	Number of years after entry									
Entry time	0	1	2	3	4	5	6	7	8	9
1992	27.5	34.1	38.4	44.9	50.5	55.6	59.7	60.3	65.7	64.4
1993	33.7	38.7	48.8	56.6	58.2	60.8	60.7	68.3	70.8	
1994	38.1	48.0	68.4	77.4	77.1	80.1	86.7	88.5		
1995	40.8	54.5	69.9	78.0	80.9	89.9	94.0			
1996	35.4	45.0	49.7	56.0	64.6	67.2				
1997	48.9	57.6	60.6	66.3	68.5					
1998	38.9	45.1	49.8	50.4						
1999	44.6	54.3	60.2							
2000	52.6	61.2								
2001	41.1									

[a]Size is measured by the number of employees. Source: Own calculations from TurkStat's ASMI database

Table 5.10 Median entrant size[a]

	Number of years after entry									
Entry time	0	1	2	3	4	5	6	7	8	9
1992	16	20	22	26	29	29	32	32	33	32
1993	15	18	23	26	29	29	27	29	32	
1994	18	21	31	35	35	36	34	33		
1995	21	27	34	35	37	39	38			
1996	19	25	29	30	33	36				
1997	22	28	30	33	33					
1998	23	27	29	29						
1999	25	31	32							
2000	25	31								
2001	22									

[a]Size is measured by the number of employees. Source: Own calculations from TurkStat's ASMI database

The increase in the mean or median size for successive cohorts may point to the progress of *surviving* firms towards the efficient scale of production– but surely this is only a conjecture and it does not preclude that many small firms exit before they reach the efficient scale of production. On the other hand, it is worth recalling that there are valid reasons for firms to enter an industry with a small size and grow rapidly after entry if certain conditions are met.[7] A comparison of figures given in Tables 5.9 and 5.10 shows that it takes more than a decade for a cohort of entrant firms – if it occurs at all – to achieve a size comparable to the average/median surviving or incumbent firm[8].

Tables 5.11 and 5.12 summarize information on the evolution of average and median size of exitors, respectively, and accordingly to the number of years preceding their exit. Data points to an inverted-U type relationship between firm size and time-to-exit: for instance, exitors that entered in 1992 (1993) reach their maximum

Table 5.11 Mean exitor size by time-to-exit[a]

	Time to exit (year)								
Entry time	0	1	2	3	4	5	6	7	8
1992	27.1	28.3	32.1	33.8	32.1	31.0	29.7	30.0	28.8
1993	33.9	33.9	39.5	44.2	39.7	34.4	35.2	41.6	
1994	36.4	35.8	46.1	32.0	33.8	30.0	32.1		
1995	44.2	41.9	48.6	48.0	39.4	35.7			
1996	30.2	32.3	33.5	36.6	31.6				
1997	35.0	36.0	40.6	54.6					
1998	27.7	29.9	31.0						
1999	34.1	27.4	32.0						

[a]Size is measured by the number of employees. Source: Own calculations from TurkStat's ASMI database

Table 5.12 Median exitor size by time-to-exit[a]

	Time to exit (year)								
Entry time	0	1	2	3	4	5	6	7	8
1992	14	16	19	20	20	19	18	18	19
1993	15	18	21	20	20	19	17	17	
1994	17	17	25	20	21	17	18		
1995	22	22	24	23	22	22			
1996	17	17	20	20	16				
1997	17	18	22	20					
1998	16	18	18						
1999	15	15	19						

[a]Size is measured by the number of employees. Source: Own calculations from TurkStat's ASMI database

Table 5.13 Number of firms by status and industry (*plus* share in percentage of the total)

Industry	Total	Survivors	Entrants	Exitors	Survivors in % of total	Entrants in % of total	Exitors in % of total
311	1.384	1.130	137	163	81.7	9.9	11.8
312	351	308	25	24	87.8	7.0	7.0
313	93	83	5	6	88.7	5.8	6.8
314	38	34	1	3	90.4	1.6	8.9
321	1.787	1.431	244	155	80.1	13.7	8.7
322	1.290	952	191	196	73.8	14.8	15.2
323	147	110	22	21	75.2	14.9	14.2
324	137	104	22	18	75.5	16.1	12.9
331	249	196	30	32	78.6	11.9	13.0
332	201	147	36	29	73.1	17.7	14.3
341	171	146	16	12	85.7	9.3	6.8
342	214	181	19	20	84.5	8.7	9.3
351	91	79	7	6	87.5	7.4	6.6
352	280	242	22	19	86.6	7.9	6.7
354	42	37	4	2	87.6	8.8	4.5
355	146	126	11	12	86.0	7.7	8.1
356	419	330	59	41	78.8	14.1	9.8
361	56	45	7	5	81.1	11.7	9.4
362	88	70	14	9	78.8	15.6	9.9
369	715	613	57	59	85.7	7.9	8.3
371	273	227	26	27	83.1	9.5	9.7
372	126	108	11	10	85.2	9.0	7.6
381	867	702	106	83	81.0	12.3	9.6
382	763	631	82	69	82.6	10.8	9.0
383	425	345	50	42	81.2	11.8	10.0
384	443	374	45	33	84.3	10.2	7.4
385	90	75	10	7	83.8	10.7	8.2
390	117	93	15	12	79.4	12.9	10.0

Source: Own calculations from TurkStat's ASMI database

average size of 33.8 (44.2) 6 (5) years later and they exit industry with an average size of 27.1 (33.9). A similar conclusion is reached using data presented in Table 5.12.

Table 5.13 provides information on the number of firms by status (survivor, entrant, exitor) at the three-digit ISIC level. Although there is a certain degree of cross-industry variation in rates pertaining to survivors, entrants and exitors, inter-sectoral variation observed over the period 1992–2001 is limited: for instance, survivor rates are comprised between 70% and 90%. Similar to data included in Table 5.5, entry and exit rates are much lower than the rate of survival, as well as the net entry rates compared to gross entry rates.

Finally, in Tables 5.14 and 5.15 we present data on correlation between entry and exit rates by year, and by industry, respectively. Out of nine correlation coefficients

Table 5.14 Correlations between entry and exit rates by year

1992	0.6603
1993	0.2411
1994	0.5705
1995	0.5378
1996	0.3984
1997	0.6651
1998	0.5252
1999	−0.1848
2000	−0.3194
2001	–

Table 5.15 Correlations between entry and exit rates by industry

ISIC	
311	0.3905
312	0.2891
313	0.1604
314	−0.2828
321	0.2869
322	−0.0298
323	0.0842
324	0.5090
331	0.1436
332	0.0988
341	0.2846
342	0.5813
351	0.4814
352	0.2276
354	0.5526
355	0.0453
356	0.2008
361	0.4092
362	0.3404
369	0.2181
371	0.4965
372	0.6983
381	0.3374
382	0.2003
383	0.5577
384	0.1592
385	0.4223
390	0.3708

included in Table 5.14, seven are positive, as well as all but one of the correlation coefficients included in Table 5.15. The positive sign of these coefficients is predicted by economic theory but does not enable us to conclude whether or not there is a causal relation between these two variables[9].

5.3 Determinants of Entry and Exit Rates in the Turkish Manufacturing Sector

5.3.1 Entry and Exit Models

The two dependent variables to be investigated here are the entry and exit rates. As explained in the previous section, entry and exit rates are defined at the ISIC 4-digit industry level.

We discuss below the determinants of entry and exit. We will use the same set of explanatory variables for entry and exit, because it is difficult to conceive a variable that has an impact, for example, on entry but not on exit.

The entry and exit models are defined as follows:

$$
\begin{aligned}
\text{Nrate}_{j,t} = {} & \alpha_0 + \alpha_1 \text{Pmargin}_{j,t} + \alpha_2 \text{Herfindahl}_{j,t} + \alpha_3 \text{Grq}_{j,t} + \alpha 4\text{Rlp}_{j,t} \\
& + \alpha_5 \text{Rlw}_{j,t} + \alpha_6 \text{Rlk}_{j,t} + \alpha_7 \text{Mtax}_{j,t} + \alpha_8 \text{grm\_dc}_{j,t} + \alpha_9 \text{grm\_ldc}_{j,t} \\
& + \alpha_{10} \text{grx\_dc}_{j,t} + \alpha_{11} \text{grx\_ldc}_{j,t} + \alpha_{12} \text{Nrate}_{j,t-1} + \alpha_{13} \text{Xrate}_{j,t-1} \\
& + \alpha_{14} \text{Ave\_entsize}_{j,t} + \mu_t + \mu_j + \mu_{j,t}
\end{aligned}
\tag{5.1}
$$

$$
\begin{aligned}
\text{Xrate}_{j,t} = {} & \delta_0 + \delta_1 \text{Pmargin}_{j,t} + \delta_2 \text{Herfindahl}_{j,t} + \delta_3 \text{Grq}_{j,t} + \delta_4 \text{Rlp}_{j,t} + \delta_5 \text{Rlw}_{j,t} \\
& + \delta_6 \text{Rlk}_{j,t} + \delta_7 \text{Mtax}_{j,t} + \delta_8 \text{grm\_dc}_{j,t} + \delta_9 \text{grm\_ldc}_{j,t} + \delta_{10} \text{grx\_dc}_{j,t} \\
& + \delta_{11} \text{grx\_ldc}_{j,t} + \delta_{12} \text{Nrate}_{j,t-1} + \delta_{13} \text{Xrate}_{j,t-1} + \delta_{14} \text{Ave\_entsize}_{j,t} \\
& + \mu_t + \mu_j + \mu_{j,t}
\end{aligned}
\tag{5.2}
$$

j and *t* are indices for sector (at ISIC 4-digit level), and time, respectively. μ_t and μ_j account for time and industry specific effects. μs are the error terms.

The variables used in both equations are as follows:

Profit margin (Pmargin) is introduced in the entry equation in order to test a basic prediction about the role of profits on sector-level entry rates, i.e., profitability in a sector will determine its attractiveness for new firms to be established in the industry. Hence, we expect a positive coefficient for this variable. It is calculated as value added minus wage bill divided by total sales.

Growth rate (Grq) in an industry is likely to exert a positive influence on the entry rates since firms will prefer to enter in rapidly growing industries that have greater business opportunities. This variable is also likely to reflect the life cycle of an industry. A positive sign is expected for the coefficient of this variable.

These first two variables are indicators of opportunities and attractivity of industries for potential new firms. Variables measuring risks and sunk costs associated with entry in a sector must be, however, introduced in regressions. Numerous entry barriers faced by firms that intend to enter in a specific industry are of special relevance here and will be measured by a host of indicators.

Capital intensity (Rlk) of a sector is highly correlated by the extent of entry barriers since the amount of initial investment to be carried out in capital-intensive industries may act a significant deterrent to potential entrants. This negative effect will be all the more important if investments are indivisible and capital markets are imperfect. Capital intensity is calculated as the logarithm of the ratio of an indicator of capital stock – constructed as the annual depreciation allowances divided by an investment deflator[10] – to the number of employees. A negative sign is expected for the coefficient of this variable.

The *degree of concentration* (Herfindahl) in an industry will influence entry rates since it will be easier for firms to enter industries with a high degree of competition and large number of small firms. The level of concentration is measured in this paper by the Herfindahl concentration index for output, which is defined as the sum of squared market shares of firms (this indicator takes values ranging from 0 to 1, and equals 1 if one firm dominates the market). We expect a negative sign for the coefficient of this variable.

Labor productivity (Rlp) at the sector level may signal the good performance of incumbent firms and discourage firms from entering, in order to avoid severe post-entry competition. This variable is measured as the ratio of real value added to the number of employees. The coefficient of this variable is expected to be negative.

The *average wage rate* (Rlw) at the sector-level will reflect the demand for sector-specific skills, once other determinants of the wage rate are taken into account in the entry equation. This last factor may discourage firms from entering in high wage sectors where they could face difficulties in hiring workers with appropriate skills. This variable is measured as the ratio of the real wage bill to the number of employees. Therefore, a negative coefficient is expected for this variable.

The following five variables are introduced in the regressions in order to capture the impact of openness to trade on entry. These are policy variables that reflect the extent to which reforms pertaining to trade regime influence entry rate of firms in the Turkish manufacturing sector.

High *tariff rates on imported goods* (Mtax) may hamper competition at the sector level by isolating firms from competitive pressures originating from imports. This may discourage entry of firms into those sectors that benefit extensively from import protection. The calculation of this variable is explained in section 5.4.2. We expect the coefficient of this variable to be negative.

Growth rates of exports to developed and developing countries' markets (grx_dc and grx_ldc, respectively) are introduced in the regression, in order to check whether an increase in these variables impacts on entry of firms. Moreover, *growth rates of imports* from developed and developing countries' markets (grm_dc and grm_ldc, respectively) are introduced to test for its possible impact on the rate of entry.

Empirical studies on exit and entry point out that these two variables are correlated. This correlation may arise because either exit and entry rates are influenced by the same structural factors or because they are causally related. This second approach means that (1) high levels of entry can lead to displacement of incumbent firms by the new entrants and force them to exit and, (2) extensive exits may clear the market and make room for further entry into a sector. As to the first approach, it points out that the observed correlation between entry and exit rates may simply be the outcome of industry turbulence which impacts upon both variables.

Whatever the mechanism involved, we introduce the *rate of exit* among explanatory variables in the entry equation. We introduce 1 year lagged entry rate and expect a positive coefficient for this variable ($Xrate_{t-1}$).

We also introduced *1 year lagged values of the entry rate* in the entry equation in order to test for the existence of a partial adjustment mechanism ($Nrate_{t-1}$).

Finally, since firm size may influence entry dynamics at the sector level, we introduced the logarithm of the *average firm size of entrants* as an explanatory variable in the entry equation (Ave_entsize).

For the exit model, we use the same set of variables but the expected signs of the explanatory variables are different. A negative sign is expected in the exit model for the following variables: *profit margin* (fall in profits may lead firms to exit), *concentration ratio* (higher concentration of output will hamper competition among firms), *growth rate* (firms can survive longer in rapidly growing industries), *capital intensity* (sunk costs associated with capital-intensive industries will reduce exit rates) and *tariff rates on imports* (firms in industries sheltered from foreign competition will delay exit).

The coefficients of other explanatory variables included in the exit equation (labor productivity, wage rate, tariff rates on imports, the growth of sector-level exports and imports, lagged exit rate, and average size of exitors) remains to be seen, i.e., this is basically an empirical issue. A positive coefficient is expected for the lagged entry rate variable.

5.3.2 Data and Estimation Method

The Turkstat database has been used in order to calculate dependent and explanatory variables. Data for 83 ISIC 4-digit level industries are used in regressions. Descriptive statistics for variables included in regressions are presented in Table 5.16.

Different estimation methods have been used in order to tackle different issues. First, different models containing different sets of explanatory variables have been estimated by the OLS method. Second, in order to take into account unobservable industry-specific effects that might render coefficient estimates inconsistent, fixed effect method was used to estimate entry and exit equations. Third, since about one-sixth of observations for the dependent variable are censored from below (entry and exit rates are non-negative by definition), a Tobit model may be used in order to estimate both models in an effort to obtain consistent estimates of coefficients. Given the panel nature of our data, we run random effect Tobit models so as to take into account unobservable industry-specific determinants of exit and entry rates. Finally, system GMM estimation method was used to correct for the endogeneity bias generated by the inclusion of a lagged dependent variable in both equations.

Table 5.16 Summary statistics of the variables overall

Variable	Mean	Variance
Grm_dc	0.12	0.50
Grm_ldc	0.19	1.04
grx_dc	0.18	0.73
grx_ldc	0.18	0.68
herfindahl	0.15	0.16
mtax	0.10	0.13
Nrate	0.11	0.12
Xrate	0.09	0.10
Ave_entsize	3.48	0.66
Ave_exsize	3.40	0.77
pmargin	0.30	0.11
Grq	0.05	0.27
Rlp	6.63	0.72
Rlw	5.10	0.61
Rlk	4.20	0.94
Xrate(t-1)	0.10	0.10
Nrate(t-1)	0.12	0.12

5.3.3 Estimation Results

5.3.3.1 Entry Rate

Estimation results for the entry equation are reported in Tables 5.17 and 5.18. For an earlier study about the determinants of entry rate in the Turkish economy, see Kaya and Ucdogruk (2002).

Results of the OLS estimation are presented in models 1–8[11]. Results for the remaining three models are presented in Table 5.18. Regressions are run alternatively with and without indicators associated with trade reforms and openness. We then introduce successively lagged values for entry and exit rates, and average firm size for entrants – only in OLS regressions.

We will examine below, the results for the random effects Tobit (RET) and System-GMM (GMM) models since these two estimation methods aim at overcoming shortcomings not addressed by the OLS or fixed-effect estimation methods – see above. However, it is difficult to choose one of them as our preferred model, since they deal with different problems – i.e. RET takes into account the fact that the dependent variable is a limited-dependent one and GMM corrects for the endogeneity generated by the inclusion of the lagged value of the dependent variable in the entry equation. Therefore, the foregoing discussion will be carried out by the examination of the results obtained by these two methods and pointing out to significant differences between them whenever necessary[12].

Table 5.17 Determinants of entry rate (1992–2001). OLS estimation[a]

	Model 1	Model 2	Model 3	Model 4	Model 5	Model 6	Model 7	Model 8
Pmargin	0.014	0.023	0.024	0.023	0.024	0.023	0.067[c]	0.059
	[0.30]	[0.49]	[0.58]	[0.58]	[0.59]	[0.56]	[1.75]	[1.63]
Herfindahl	0.010	−0.036	−0.034	−0.040	−0.041	−0.046*	0.223[a]	0.211[a]
	[0.22]	[1.35]	[1.20]	[1.50]	[1.42]	[1.71]	[5.04]	[5.07]
Grq	0.034	0.058[a]	0.074[a]	0.070[a]	0.070[a]	0.067[a]	0.030[c]	0.0265
	[1.23]	[4.70]	[5.81]	[5.54]	[5.11]	[4.99]	[1.84]	[1.61]
Rlp	0.0002	−0.003	−0.008	−0.007	−0.007	−0.006	−0.024[c]	−0.021*
	[0.01]	[0.20]	[0.64]	[0.54]	[0.53]	[0.44]	[1.93]	[1.66]
Rlw	−0.021[c]	−0.025[b]	−0.013	−0.016	−0.009	−0.011	0.009	0.05
	[1.86]	[2.32]	[1.07]	[1.36]	[0.74]	[1.03]	[0.86]	[0.43]
Rlk	−0.008	0.001	0.005	0.004	0.005	0.005	−0.009	−0.008
	[0.80]	[0.19]	[0.89]	[0.81]	[0.95]	[0.89]	[1.46]	[1.33]
Mtax		−0.0595[a]		−0.050[a]		−0.042[b]		−0.031*
		[3.23]		[2.85]		[2.46]		[1.70]
Grm_dc		−0.001		−0.003		−0.005		0.004
		[0.15]		[0.38]		[0.58]		[0.39]
Grm_ldc		0.009[b]		0.009[b]		0.0094[c]		0.007*
		[2.29]		[2.38]		[2.44]		[1.86]
Grx_dc		−0.003		−0.003		−0.004		−0.005
		[0.55]		[0.68]		[0.76]		[0.85]
Grx_ldc		0.016[b]		0.013[b]		0.014[b]		0.010
		[2.05]		[2.14]		[2.27]		[1.25]
$Xrate_{t-1}$			0.210[a]	0.194[a]	0.198[a]	0.183[a]	0.116	0.108
			[3.02]	[3.08]	[2.67]	[2.79]	[1.46]	[1.53]

Table 5.17 (continued)

	Model 1	Model 2	Model 3	Model 4	Model 5	Model 6	Model 7	Model 8
$Nrate_{t-1}$					0.116[b]	0.115[b]	0.203[a]	0.204[a]
					[2.37]	[2.42]	[3.58]	[3.68]
Ave_entsize							0.009[c]	0.010**
							[1.81]	[2.07]
#Observations	737	723	735	722	735	722	616	613
R-squared	0.19	0.25	0.27	0.30	0.29	0.32	0.40	0.42

[a]*Grm_dc* annual rate of import growth from developed countries; *Grm_ldc* annual rate of import growth from developing countries; *Grx_dc* annual rate of export growth to developed countries; *Grx_ldc* annual rate of export growth to developing countries; *Herfindahl* herfindahl index of concentration of output at the 4-digit ISIC level; *Mtax* level of import duties divided by total imports at the 4-digit ISIC level; *Nrate* Entry rate defined as the ratio of the number of entrants to the number of survivors plus the number of entrants at tine t; *Xrate* Exit rate defined as the ratio betweenthe number of exitors and the number of survivors plus the number of entrants at time t; *Ave_entsize* logarithm of the average size of entrants– measured by the number of employees; *Ave_exsize* logarithm of the average size of exitors; *Pmargin* profit rate at the sector level divided by total sales; *Grq* growth rate at the sector level; *Rlp* labor productivity at the sector level; *Rlw* average wage rate; *Rlk* Capital intensity

All regressions include industry and time dummies

t-statistics in brackets

[a]$p<0.01$, [b]$p<0.05$, [c]$p<0.1$

Table 5.18 Determinants of entry rate (1992–2001). Fixed effects, random effects Tobit and System-GMM estimation

	Fixed effects	Random effects Tobit		System-GMM		
Pmargin	Model 9a	Model 9b	Model 10a	Model 10b	Model 11a	Model 11b
	−0.025	−0.027	−0.012	−0.011	−0.0871	−0.06
Herfindahl	[0.38]	[0.40]	[0.26]	[0.24]	[0.089]	[0.083]
	−0.144[a]	−0.131[b]	−0.127[a]	−0.133[a]	−0.240[b]	−0.210[c]
Grq	[2.76]	[2.50]	[4.24]	[4.71]	[0.12]	[0.11]
	0.056[a]	0.056[a]	0.078[a]	0.0772[a]	0.0542[a]	0.0501[a]
Rlp	[4.58]	[4.48]	[5.95]	[0.013]	[0.02]	[0.018]
	0.004	0.005	0.003	0.0032	0.0339	0.0301
Rlw	[0.26]	[0.30]	[0.21]	[0.012]	[0.033]	[0.032]
	−0.017	−0.024	−0.019	−0.0210[c]	−0.049	−0.0417
Rlk	[0.96]	[1.31]	[1.61]	[0.011]	[0.03]	[0.03]
	−0.003	−0.009	0.005	0.0049	−0.0123	−0.00528
Mtax	[0.35]	[0.89]	[0.71]	[0.0064]	[0.014]	[0.013]
		−0.014		−0.0613[b]		−0.0905[b]
Grm_dc		[0.34]		[0.028]		[0.046]
		−0.007		−0.0102		−0.0116
Grm_ldc		[0.95]		[0.0084]		[0.011]
		0.009[a]		0.0107[c]		0.0101[a]
Grx_dc		[3.40]		[0.0029]		[0.0036]
		−0.004		−0.00454		−0.00168
Grx_ldc		[1.04]		[0.0045]		[0.0044]
		0.013[a]		0.0180[a]		0.0163[a]

Table 5.18 (continued)

	Fixed effects	Random effects Tobit		System-GMM		
Pmargin	Model 9a	Model 9b	Model 10a	Model 10b	Model 11a	Model 11b
$Xrate_{t-1}$		[3.07]		[0.0057]		[0.0057]
	0.128[a]	0.120[a]	0.209[a]	0.203[a]	0.113	0.102
$Nrate_{t-1}$	[4.28]	[4.02]	[6.07]	[5.99]	[0.093]	[0.078]
	–0.011	0.001	0.071[a]	0.090[b]	0.0499	0.0575
	[0.37]	[0.03]	[1.94]	[2.46]	[0.05]	[0.045]
#Observations	722	735	722	735	722	
R-squared	0.28	.	.	.	.	

All regressions include time dummies
t-statistics in brackets
[a]$p<0.01$, [b]$p<0.05$, [c]$p<0.1$

Results indicate that once the impact of other factors is accounted for, profit margin (*Prmargin*) does not influence significantly the entry rate in either model 10 or 11. This is consistent with empirical evidence that current profit margin has only a weak effect on entry because of the fact that entry decision is based on long term factors.

Coefficients associated with the indicator of the *degree of concentration* of output at the four-digit ISIC level (*Herfindahl*) are negative and significant at the 5% level in models 10a, 10b and 11a, and at the 10% level in model 11b[13]. In other words, the entry rate is lower in more concentrated industries, a finding that indicates that everything else equal a less populated industry acts as an entry barrier for new firms. Note that the magnitude of the negative effect of concentration on entry rate is more important for the GMM method than for the RET method, almost the double: a one percentage point increase in the concentration rate reduces the rate of entry by 0.13 points in model 10b and by 0.21 in model 11b.

Coefficient estimates for the *industrial growth* variable (*Grq*) are positive and statistically significant at the 1% in all models, confirming the positive influence of greater business opportunities and possibly of the industry life cycle on entry: Rapidly growing industries are likely to attract more new firms.

As to the effect of the level of *labor productivity* (*Rlp*) on the entry of firms, results indicate that it has a positive but not a statistically significant effect (at the 10% level). Therefore, both RET and GMM estimation results provide only weak evidence in favor of the contention that good performance of incumbent firms discourages new firms from entering in an industry. Apparently, incumbents' productivity has no impact on potential entrants' entry decisions.

Coefficient estimates of the *average wage level* (*Rlw*), which measures sector-specific skills new entrants should possess and master for a successful entry into an industry, are not significant at 10% in any model, except in model 10b, but then only at the 10% level. Hence, our estimation results do not provide evidence that skill-related constraints deter firm entry.

Coefficient estimates of the *capital intensity variable* (*Rlk*) are negative, but not significant at 10% in any regression, providing results somehow contrary to the expectations and empirical findings – since indivisibilities and large initial investment requirements characterizing in capital-intensive industries are likely to act as major obstacles to entry of new firms[14].

Our results show that *import duties* (*Mtax*) – indicator of trade restrictions used in our paper– do exert a negative and significant effect on entry rate in all the four models where this variable is included among the explanatory variables –i.e. models 10b and 11b. These results confirm the view that entry into sectors where firms are sheltered from foreign competition is more difficult than in less protected sectors. Everything else equal, tariff reductions that took place in the Turkish economy from the early nineties onwards must have eased entry of firms in the manufacturing sector.

The direction of foreign trade apparently plays an important role in the entry process. Growth rates of imports of goods originating in developed countries and exports toward these countries have not had a significant effect on the entry rate of firms. Coefficients associated with the growth rates of imports from and the growth rates of exports to developing countries are positive and significant at the 1% level in all models. It seems that trade with developing countries facilitates the creation of new (small) firms because of the fact that local entrepreneurs believe that the business prospects are better in sectors in which developing countries tend to specialize. Magnitudes of coefficients associated with this variable are similar in both models.

In the RET model, the coefficient of the one period lagged entry rate variable ($Nrate_{t-1}$) has a positive and significant effect at 1% and 5% levels, pointing to the existence of a partial adjustment mechanism, and persistence in entry. However, its coefficient is insignificant when fixed industry-specific effects are included (fixed effects and System-GMM models in Table 5.18), possibly because of the fact that entry conditions are industry-specific and do not change rapidly over time.

As for the exit rate variable ($Xrate_{t-1}$), it turns out that it exerts a positive effect (significant at the 1% level) on the entry rate in the RTE (and in the fixed effect model). This positive effect corroborates findings of existing studies on the entry–exit dynamics, but is not capable per se of indicating whether there is causal relationship between these two variables (vacuum-displacement effect) or whether this is the outcome of churning at the industry level. However, the coefficient of the exit rate variable becomes statistically insignificant when System-GMM method is used for estimation: This is the major difference between these two estimation methods as far as the results obtained for the entry equation are concerned.

5.3.3.2 Exit Rate

Estimation results for the entry exit are reported in Tables 5.19 and 5.20.

As in the case of entry equation, the profit margin variable has no impact on the exit rate. Its coefficient is not statistically significant in any model – theoretically at least, we might expect a positive profit rate to deter exit.

The level of concentration, as measured by the Herfindahl index, has a negative and significant effect (at 1 and 5% levels) in the case of the RTE model: a one point increase in the concentration rate reduces exit by 0.11 point in model 10a, and by 0.13 in model 10b. In the case of the GMM model, however, coefficients associated with this variable are negative but not statistically significant at the 10% level. These results indicate that the level of concentration does not have a robust impact on the exit rate.

Although rapidly growing industries attract more entrants, the market growth rate does not change the exit rate. The growth rate variable has a positive but statistically insignificant coefficient at the 10% level in both RTE and GMM models.

Labor productivity and capital intensity variables have also no strong impact on the exit rate. These two variables have positive and statistically significant coefficients only in fixed effects model, but in other models, they have insignificant coefficients without any consistent sign. Since the estimates of the fixed effects model with the lagged dependent variable are biased, we conclude that labor productivity and capital intensity do not matter much for survival.

The wage rate has a negative and significant (at the 1% level) coefficient in the RET model. These results indicate that firms in high wage industries have a lower

Table 5.19 Determinants of exit rate (1992–2001) OLS estimation[a]

	Model 1	Model 2	Model 3	Model 4	Model 5	Model 6	Model 7	Model 8
Pmargin	0.029	0.0497	0.0273	0.0478	0.0274	0.0477	0.0577	0.0562
	[0.073]	[0.077]	[0.073]	[0.077]	[0.073]	[0.077]	[0.068]	[0.065]
Herfindahl	−0.00286	−0.00035	−0.00166	−0.00513	−0.00118	−0.00493	0.449[a]	0.440[a]
	[0.054]	[0.054]	[0.057]	[0.055]	[0.057]	[0.054]	[0.11]	[0.11]
Grq	0.019	0.0168	0.0123	0.0163	0.013	0.0167	0.0095	0.021
	[0.019]	[0.022]	[0.02]	[0.022]	[0.02]	[0.022]	[0.023]	[0.025]
Rlp	0.00552	0.00996	0.00707	0.0107	0.00686	0.0106	−0.0286	−0.0264
	[0.024]	[0.023]	[0.024]	[0.023]	[0.024]	[0.024]	[0.026]	[0.026]
Rlw	−0.0474[d]	−0.0500[d]	−0.0444[d]	−0.0472[d]	−0.0439[d]	−0.0470[d]	−0.00935	−0.0112
	[0.021]	[0.02]	[0.02]	[0.02]	[0.021]	[0.02]	[0.022]	[0.021]
Rlk	0.000232	−0.00354	−0.00089	−0.00305	−0.00078	−0.00301	−0.0127	-0.0135
	[0.0071]	[0.0074]	[0.0072]	[0.0074]	[0.0073]	[0.0076]	[0.0083]	[0.0084]
Mtax		−0.0418[d]		−0.0370[d]		−0.0368[d]		-0.0274
		[0.02]		[0.02]		[0.021]		[0.024]
Grm_dc		−0.00648		−0.00759		−0.00767		−0.0237[d]
		[0.012]		[0.012]		[0.012]		[0.014]
Grm_ldc		−0.00531		−0.00506		−0.00506		−0.00124
		[0.0059]		[0.006]		[0.006]		[0.0067]
Grx_dc		−0.00689		−0.00714		−0.00713		−0.00886
		[0.0056]		[0.0056]		[0.0056]		[0.011]
Grx_ldc		0.00309		0.00366		0.00356		−2.9E05
		[0.01]		[0.01]		[0.011]		[0.02]
$Xrate_{t-1}$					0.0163	0.00564	−0.00414	−0.00528
					[0.068]	[0.071]	[0.11]	[0.11]

Table 5.19 (continued)

	Model 1	Model 2	Model 3	Model 4	Model 5	Model 6	Model 7	Model 8
$Nrate_{t-1}$			0.0667	0.0611	0.0646	0.0604	0.162[d]	0.180[d]
			[0.062]	[0.064]	[0.06]	[0.062]	[0.074]	[0.084]
Ave_exsize							0.0161[d]	0.0164[d]
							[0.0092]	[0.0093]
#Observations	654	640	653	640	653	640	543	540
R-squared	0.09	0.10	0.09	0.10	0.09	0.10	0.31	0.32

[a]*Grm_dc* annual rate of import growth from developed countries; *Grm_ldc* annual rate of import growth from developing countries; *Grx_dc* annual rate of export growth to developed countries; *Grx_ldc* annual rate of export growth to developing countries; *Herfindahl* herfindahl index of concentration of output at the 4-digit ISIC level; *Mtax* level of import duties divided by total imports at the 4-digit ISIC level; *Nrate* Entry rate defined as the ratio of the number of entrants to the number of survivors plus the number of entrants at tine t; *Xrate* Exit rate defined as the ratio betweenthe number of exitors and the number of survivors plus the number of entrants at time t; *Ave_entsize* logarithm of the average size of entrants– measured by the number of employees; *Ave_exsize* logarithm of the average size of exitors; *Pmargin* profit rate at the sector level divided by total sales; *Grq* growth rate at the sector level; *Rlp* labor productivity at the sector level; *Rlw* average wage rate; *Rlk* Capital intensity

All regressions include industry and time dummies

t-statistics in brackets

[b]$p<0.01$, [c]$p<0.05$, [d]$p<0.1$

Table 5.20 Determinants of Exit Rate (1992–2001). Fixed effects, random effects Tobit and System-GMM estimation

	Fixed effects		Random effects Tobit		System-GMM	
	Model 9a	Model 9b	Model 10a	Model 10b	Model 11a	Model 11b
Pmargin	−0.10	−0.101	−0.0103	0.00577	0.0164	−0.00279
	[0.10]	[0.10]	[0.074]	[0.074]	[0.24]	[0.18]
Herfindahl	−0.0589	−0.088	−0.113[b]	−0.128[a]	−0.434	−0.302
	[0.093]	[0.094]	[0.049]	[0.049]	[0.43]	[0.32]
Grq	−0.0340[c]	−0.0271	0.00204	0.00948	0.0397	0.0344
	[0.018]	[0.019]	[0.021]	[0.021]	[0.044]	[0.039]
Rlp	0.0700[a]	0.0727[a]	0.0312	0.0353[c]	−0.00606	0.00604
	[0.026]	[0.026]	[0.02]	[0.019]	[0.069]	[0.059]
Rlw	−0.0463[c]	−0.0453	−0.0785[a]	−0.0819[a]	−0.0581	−0.0673
	[0.026]	[0.028]	[0.019]	[0.019]	[0.066]	[0.059]
Rlk	0.0491[a]	0.0532[a]	0.00357	0.00135	0.00327	0.00258
	[0.014]	[0.015]	[0.011]	[0.011]	[0.019]	[0.02]
Mtax		−0.0307		−0.0820[c]		−0.0967
		[0.058]		[0.046]		[0.092]
Grm_dc		−0.0165		−0.0129		−0.015
		[0.012]		[0.014]		[0.011]
Grm_ldc		−0.00658[c]		−0.00851[b]		−0.00548
		[0.0035]		[0.0043]		[0.0059]
Grx_dc		−0.00286		−0.00901		−0.00197
		[0.0054]		[0.0067]		[0.0076]
Grx_ldc		0.00468		0.00579		0.0056
		[0.0058]		[0.0074]		[0.0095]
$Xrate_{t-1}$	−0.210[a]	−0.213[a]	−0.152[b]	−0.151[b]	−0.0343	−0.0672
	[0.045]	[0.046]	[0.065]	[0.066]	[0.059]	[0.049]
$Nrate_{t-1}$	−0.0375	−0.0351	0.0295	0.0417	−0.0236	−0.0392
	[0.044]	[0.045]	[0.05]	[0.05]	[0.13]	[0.15]
#Observations	653	640	653	640	653	640
R-squared	0.12	0.14				

All regressions include industry and time dummies*t*-statistics in brackets
[a]$p<0.01$, [b]$p<0.05$, [c]$p<0.1$

probability to exit. In other words, exit is easier in low wage/low skill industries. However, this finding is not confirmed by the GMM model: coefficients associated with the wage rate are negative but not significant at the 10% level.

Among the foreign trade-related variables, only the import tax rate (Mtax) seems to play a role in explaining exit. The coefficient of the import tax variable is negative in the RET model but not in the GMM model – nor in the fixed effect model. The estimate of the coefficient of the Mtax variable is likely to have higher standard deviation in fixed effects and System-GMM models, because the time-series variation in the Mtax variable is low in the 1995–2001 period. Therefore, we believe that our results provide evidence for the hypothesis that the exit rate is lower in more protected markets.

Although the lagged exit rate has a positive impact on current entry rate in the RET model, the lagged entry rate does not have any impact on current exit rate. It seems that entry does not intensify competition in the market, at least in the short run. The lagged exit rate, has a negative coefficient when industry-specific effects are taken into account, and the coefficient is negative and significant in the fixed effects and RET models. It seems that the elimination of poor performances in the last year did decrease the exit rate in the current year. However, according to the GMM model, this negative effect is not significant at the 10% level. On the other hand, it appears that one period lagged entry rates do not exert any significant effect on exit rates, suggesting that entry of new firms do not intensify competition in the market, at least in the short run.

5.4 Entry, Exit and Productivity

5.4.1 Contribution to Productivity Growth

In this section, we analyze first the productivity growth rates by survival status (survivor, entrant, and exitor). Second, we carry out an accounting-based decomposition of labor productivity in the manufacturing sector into a number of components related to the firm status (entrant, exitor or survivor).

Table 5.21 summarizes the data on average annual growth rates of labor productivity in Turkish manufacturing by survival status.

Average annual productivity growth rates follow the same pattern as industrial growth. Labor productivity shrinks considerably during the crisis years (17.3% in 1994 and 14.8% in 2001). Productivity growth rates show rather wide fluctuations, but the average for the whole period is very low (about 1%). Since the "survivors" constitute the largest part of all firms, it is not a coincidence that survivors' average productivity growth is almost the same as the "total".

The entrants' productivity growth (i.e., the average productivity growth of new firms at the first year of their lives) is also rather erratic and highly correlated with the survivors' productivity growth. Entrants seem to be very badly affected by the crisis in 1994. Those firms that were established in 1993 experienced almost 25% decline in their productivity in 1994.

Table 5.21 Productivity growth by status and year

	Total	Survivors	Entrants	Exitors
1992	0.102	0.110		0.012
1993	0.100	0.108	0.088	0.029
1994	−0.173	−0.160	−0.251	−0.328
1995	0.001	0.011	0.050	−0.110
1996	0.004	0.010	−0.002	−0.051
1997	0.100	0.103	0.123	0.065
1998	0.025	0.034	−0.033	−0.046
1999	0.064	0.078	0.100	−0.070
2000	0.011	0.015	−0.036	−0.027
2001	−0.148	−0.148	−0.086	

As may be expected, the exitors had the worst productivity growth performance. For example, the productivity of those firms that could not survive the 1994 crisis declined 33% in the last year of their operation. The average productivity growth rate for exitors is negative in almost all years, i.e., exitors are very much likely to experience a decline in their productivity towards the end of their life.

Table 5.22 presents average annual productivity growth rates for ISIC 3-digit industries for whole time period. Although there are significant inter-industry differences, productivity growth rates of survivors and entrants are positively correlated. This finding implies that survivors and entrants benefit from industry-specific opportunities. In certain industries (ISIC 313 beverage industries, 314 tobacco manufactures, 351 manufacture of industrial chemicals, 361 manufacture of pottery, china and earthenware, and 385 manufacture of professional and scientific and measuring and controlling equipment), entrants achieve, on average, higher productivity growth rates.

The pattern of productivity growth before exit is shown in Table 5.23. The data indicate that in food manufacturing (ISIC 311), exitors experienced 5.9% decline in productivity in the last year in which they exited. A year before exit, productivity decline was 2.6%, and 2 years before exit, it was 1.9%. As may be expected, there are substantial fluctuations in productivity growth rates, but the average values reveal that exitors have very poor productivity growth performance during their final years. Apparently, firms start to fail in improving productivity, and they try to survive in spite of deteriorating performance, but, at the end, they give up and exit from the market.

Labor productivity growth will be decomposed below into the contributions of four components related to the firm status: (1) a *within component* reflecting the productivity change in incumbent firms, (2) a *between effect* measuring the change in incumbent firms' market share (productivity at the industry level will increase if the market share of higher productivity surviving firms increase) and, (3) contribution of entrants and exitors to industry level productivity.

Table 5.22 Productivity growth by status and industry

Industry	Total	Survivors	Entrants	Exitors
311	−0.014	−0.010	0.002	−0.059
312	−0.034	−0.037	0.082	0.031
313	0.010	0.010	0.137	0.017
314	0.042	0.039	0.224	0.078
321	0.013	0.020	0.074	−0.080
322	0.011	0.022	0.011	−0.065
323	0.029	0.049	−0.020	−0.131
324	−0.012	0.003	−0.030	−0.155
331	0.029	0.027	−0.052	0.046
332	−0.055	−0.052	−0.025	−0.077
341	0.021	0.022	0.031	0.000
342	−0.007	0.002	0.049	−0.137
351	0.017	0.024	0.207	−0.124
352	−0.019	−0.006	−0.052	−0.234
354	−0.036	−0.032	−0.089	−0.159
355	−0.044	−0.048	0.000	0.007
356	0.017	0.026	−0.036	−0.089
361	0.035	0.035	0.167	0.039
362	0.002	0.003	−0.006	−0.016
369	0.013	0.017	0.083	−0.036
371	−0.006	−0.007	−0.039	0.003
372	−0.009	−0.002	−0.127	−0.122
381	0.033	0.036	0.027	−0.005
382	0.005	0.011	0.010	−0.076
383	0.061	0.065	0.075	0.012
384	0.006	0.011	0.042	−0.068
385	0.011	0.017	0.180	−0.069
390	−0.005	−0.007	−0.001	0.016

Table 5.24 summarizes information on the contribution of the four components to productivity change at the industry level.

Except 3 years, contribution of the *within effect* is always positive and the most important, precisely for those years where it is positive: this result points to the major contribution of incumbents on productivity growth. The contribution of the *between effect* is always negative and explains an important part of the negative growth rate of productivity at the industry level. In other words, changing market shares observed for incumbent firms reduced aggregate labor productivity over the period 1992–2001. As for the contribution of *entrants* and *exitors* to productivity growth, note that they are much lower than those recorded for the first two effects and that they are of opposite signs: entrants have always pushed up manufacturing productivity while exitors have depressed it over the period 1992–2001.

Table 5.23 Productivity growth by time-to-exit

Industry	Time to exit (year) 0	1	2	3	4	5	6	7	8
311	−0.059	−0.026	−0.019	−0.058	−0.084	−0.087	−0.061	0.045	0.048
312	0.031	0.026	−0.195	0.005	−0.277	0.034	−0.187	0.038	−0.279
313	0.017	−0.161	0.087	0.147	0.000	0.126	0.069	−0.377	0.453
314	0.078	0.360	−0.037	−0.166	−0.403	0.301	0.374	−0.157	0.133
321	−0.080	0.123	0.000	0.107	−0.009	0.072	0.131	−0.061	0.158
322	−0.065	0.005	−0.006	0.066	0.020	−0.007	0.118	0.070	0.241
323	−0.131	−0.057	−0.063	−0.064	0.177	0.027	0.225	−0.035	0.102
324	−0.155	0.022	−0.132	0.164	−0.177	−0.195	0.014	0.314	
331	0.046	−0.051	−0.020	0.062	−0.070	−0.142	−0.113	−0.064	−0.328
332	−0.077	−0.183	0.039	0.036	0.037	−0.049	−0.141	0.362	−0.243
341	0.000	−0.035	−0.248	0.358	−0.179	0.098	−0.320	0.202	0.033
342	−0.137	0.012	−0.186	0.100	−0.101	−0.205	−0.162	−0.122	0.099
351	−0.124	0.110	−0.081	−0.158	0.424	−0.191	−0.055	0.475	0.261
352	−0.234	−0.021	0.020	0.059	−0.085	−0.278	0.060	0.060	0.279
354	−0.159	−0.053	0.019	−0.547	0.067	−1.051	0.925	−0.593	
355	0.007	−0.128	−0.044	−0.013	−0.151	0.004	−0.198	−0.027	−0.188
356	−0.089	0.136	0.078	0.082	0.034	−0.069	0.061	0.087	0.363
361	0.039	−0.033	−0.213	0.403	−0.254	0.500	0.214	0.247	0.435
362	−0.016	−0.174	0.018	0.249	0.038	0.133	0.461	0.196	
369	−0.036	0.092	−0.004	−0.002	−0.052	0.049	−0.109	0.099	0.135
371	0.003	−0.097	0.126	−0.005	−0.169	0.195	−0.190	0.291	−0.163
372	−0.122	−0.044	0.569	−0.284	0.302	−0.093	0.209	0.046	0.617
381	−0.005	0.048	0.026	0.111	−0.066	0.031	0.093	0.100	0.197
382	−0.076	−0.048	0.104	0.074	−0.070	−0.127	−0.058	0.239	0.204
383	0.012	0.114	0.012	0.054	0.196	0.123	0.108	0.204	0.688
384	−0.068	0.064	0.053	0.057	−0.117	0.185	0.091	−0.045	−0.014
385	−0.069	0.222	−0.001	−0.044	−0.194	0.013	0.069	0.200	0.001
390	0.016	−0.121	−0.123	0.108	0.114	−0.621	0.169	−0.266	0.222
Average	−0.052	0.004	−0.008	0.032	−0.037	−0.044	0.064	0.055	0.138

Table 5.24 Decomposition of labor productivity change in the Turkish manufacturing sector

	Changes in labor productivity due to			
	Within	Between	Entrants	Exitors
1992	145.8	−85.0	37.5	−13.8
1993	140.4	−5.9	23.9	−17.8
1994	−37.7	−16.2	13.2	−12.7
1995	7.7	−28.2	18.8	−19.1
1996	−17.1	−30.0	22.2	−29.0
1997	104.0	−60.3	43.0	−22.1
1998	−32.6	−28.6	37.0	−30.0
1999	58.9	29.8	12.6	−23.3
2000	30.9	−17.9	30.3	−26.5
2001	13.8	−4.1	17.7	0.0

5.4.2 *Impact of Exit and Entry Rates on the Productivity Growth of Survivors*

In order to test for the effect of entry and exit rates on the productivity growth of survivors in the Turkish manufacturing industry over the period 1992–2001, a number of control variables together with the exit and entry rates have to be introduced in the regressions. Below, we present all the variables introduced in the regressions and discuss briefly how they are defined and measured.

- *Growth rate of value added:* value added, defined as output minus inputs used by the firm, has been measured as the annual logarithmic difference of real value added.[15]
- *Growth rate of capital stock* (ΔlogK)**:** since firm-level data on capital stock is not available in our database, we measure capital stock by the annual depreciation allowances**.** This variable's growth rate is calculated as its annual logarithmic difference.
- *Growth rate of labor* (ΔlogL)**:** since data on the number of hours worked by the labor force is not reliable we used the number of employees as our measure of labor and its annual logarithmic difference is introduced in the regressions
- *Import duties (Mtax):* The level of import duties (divided by total imports) at the four-digit industry level (ISIC, rev. 2) is used to analyze the effects of import protection on survival prospects. If less productive domestic firms could live longer in protected markets, the coefficient of the Mtax variable will have a negative coefficient.

There is no time-series data on tariff rates at the ISIC-4 level and the calculation of import tariff rates at the sectoral level is plagued with a number of problems[16].

There are a number of studies in which sectoral level tariff rates are calculated by using different methods. However, there are substantial differences between these calculations. After a careful examination of various studies, we concluded to use the import value and import tax revenue data provided in input-output (IO) tables complied by the Turkstat, because the IO data takes into account exemptions, provides estimates for weighted tax rates, and are consistent with national accounts. We used 1979, 1985 and 1990 IO tables to calculate sectoral level tariff rates.

Since the IO sectoral classification is somewhat more aggregated than sectors defined at the ISIC 4-digit level, we prepared a correspondence table to match IO and ISIC sectors. For 1990s (1993, 1995, 1997, 1999, and 2003), we used UNCTAD TRAINS database at the ISIC 4-digit level (the weighted average of actual tariff rates). The tariff rates for intermediate years were calculated by simple linear interpolation.

In all econometric models, we include dummy variables for time to compensate for the errors in interpolating the data. In other words, time dummies account for, to some extent, aggregate changes in tariff rates.

- The effect of foreign competition on productivity growth of survivors is also tested by four sector-specific variables: the annual growth rate of imports from developed (Grm_dc) and developing countries (Grm_ldc), and the annual growth of real exports to developed (Grx_dc) and developing countries (Grx_ldc). The source for these variables is the Turkstat foreign trade database. These variables are used in order to account for the impact of competitive pressures on domestic market and export markets on productivity changes occurring in surviving firms. A further distinction is made here according to the geographical origin of imports and the destination of exports – i.e. developed and developing countries.
- The level of concentration in the market (Herfindahl) is measured by the Herfindahl index at the four-digit ISIC level. It measures the concentration ratio among survivors.
- Finally, we introduce two variables measuring the entry and the exit rates at the sector level (Nrate and Xrate, respectively) as well as their one period lagged values. The entry rate (Nrate) is defined as the ratio of the number of entrants to the number of survivors[17] *plus* the number of entrant at time t. The exit rate (Xrate) is defined similarly as the ratio between the number of exitors and the number of survivors plus the number of entrants at time t.

Thus, the value added growth equation is defined as follows:

$$\begin{aligned}\Delta\log \mathrm{VA}_{i,t} = {} & \beta_0 + \beta_1\Delta\log \mathrm{K}_{i,t} + \beta_2\Delta\log \mathrm{L}_{i,t} + \beta_3\mathrm{Herfindahl}_{j,t} + \beta_4\mathrm{Nrate}_{j,t} \\ & + \beta_5\mathrm{Xrate}_{j,t} + \beta_6\mathrm{Mtax}_{j,t} + \beta_7\mathrm{grm\_dc}_{j,t} + \beta_8\mathrm{grm\_ldc}_{j,t} + \beta_9\mathrm{grx\_dc}_{j,t} \\ & + \beta_{10}\mathrm{grx\_ldc}_{j,t} + \beta_{11}\mathrm{Nrate}_{j,t-1} + \beta_{12}\mathrm{Xrate}_{j,t-1} + \mu_t + \mu_s + \mu_{i,t} \end{aligned} \quad (5.3)$$

i, j, and t are indices for firm, sector (at ISIC 4-digit level), and time, respectively. μ_t and μ_s are time and industry (at the ISIC 2-digit level) dummies. μs are the error terms.

Descriptive statistics for variables introduced in the productivity equation are presented in Table 5.25.

Table 5.25 Summary statistics of the variables overall

Variable	Mean	Variance
grm_dc	0.12	0.50
grm_ldc	0.19	1.04
grx_dc	0.18	0.73
grx_ldc	0.18	0.68
herfindahl	0.15	0.16
Mtax	0.10	0.13
Nrate	0.11	0.12
Xrate	0.09	0.10
Xrate(t-1)	0.10	0.10
Nrate(t-1)	0.12	0.12
LogL	9.5	10.0
LogK	14.0	14.6

Productivity growth equation was estimated by OLS in order to test for the impact of entry and exit rates after time dummies and industry-specific dummies (at the two-digit ISIC level) were added to account for nonobservable effects. Four different specifications ("models") were tested and findings are presented in Table 5.26.

Coefficients associated with our indicator of competition on the domestic market, i.e. the degree of concentration measured by the Herfindahl index (**Herfindahl**), are negative in all models included in Table 5.26, but are never significant at 10% significance level. In other words, our database do not enable us to sort out any significant effect – positive or negative – of the extent of domestic competition as measured by the Herfindahl index on productivity growth of survivors.

Estimation results pertaining to import tariff rates - import duties divided by total imports at the four-digit ISIC level - do not point to any statistically significant effect of import protection on the productivity growth of firms at the 10% level.

The first two variables measuring the extent of foreign competition, the annual growth rate of imports from developed (**Grm_dc**) and developing countries (**Grm_ldc**), both exert a positive and significant effect on firm-level productivity growth. This result indicates that from a (potential) positive procompetitive and a negative market-stealing effect, the first one dominates – which points to a beneficial effect of import liberalization process.

The reason we made a distinction according to the geographical origin of imports is because we want to test whether products imported from less developed countries have a more important crowding out effect since they are likely to be more close substitutes for domestic products. This last prediction is not confirmed by our findings: not only both indicators of import penetration have positive (and significant) coefficients, but also the impact exerted by the growth of imports from developed countries is almost five times larger than the one due to imports originating from developing countries.

As far as exports to developed (**Grx_dc**) and developing countries (**Grx_ldc**) - the other indicator of foreign competition - are concerned our findings do not reveal any

Table 5.26 Determinants of Growth of Survivors (1992–2001). Dependent variable: Growth rate of real value added

	Model 1	Model 2	Model 3	Model 4
ΔlogK	0.0877[a]	0.0875[a]	0.0876[a]	0.0876[a]
	[0.0048]	[0.0048]	[0.0048]	[0.0048]
ΔlogL	0.542[a]	0.542[a]	0.542[a]	0.542[a]
	[0.014]	[0.014]	[0.014]	[0.014]
Herfindahl	−0.00893	−0.0123	−0.048	−0.00894
	[0.063]	[0.064]	[0.063]	[0.065]
Nrate	−0.086	−0.139[c]		−0.115
	[0.077]	[0.078]		[0.081]
Xrate	−0.208[a]	−0.267[a]		−0.256[a]
	[0.078]	[0.079]		[0.080]
Mtax		−0.0354	−0.0267	−0.035
		[0.044]	[0.044]	[0.044]
grm_dc		0.0488[a]	0.0457[a]	0.0494[a]
		[0.012]	[0.012]	[0.012]
grm_ldc		0.0112[a]	0.0102[b]	0.0110[a]
		[0.0041]	[0.0041]	[0.0041]
grx_dc		−0.0143[c]	−0.0117	−0.0134
		[0.0085]	[0.0086]	[0.0086]
grx_ldc		−0.00589	−0.00569	−0.00507
		[0.0094]	[0.0094]	[0.0094]
$Nrate_{t-1}$			−0.121[b]	−0.0639
			[0.056]	[0.059]
$Xrate_{t-1}$			−0.043	−0.0015
			[0.079]	[0.079]
Constant	0.571[a]	0.569[a]	0.593[a]	0.565[a]
	[0.078]	[0.082]	[0.067]	[0.083]
#Observations	67482	67318	67319	67318
R-squared	0.06	0.06	0.06	0.06

All regressions include industry and time dummies
t-statistics between brackets
[a]$p<0.01$, [b]$p<0.05$, [c]$p<0.1$

positive or negative impact of this variable on firm-level productivity. One possible explanation for this result might be that the indicator of export-related foreign competitive pressure is constructed on highly aggregatated data – four-digit ISIC level here- and that data, at more disaggeragate level, should be used – possibly at the firm level.

The exit rate variable (**Xrate**) has a coefficient that is negative and significant at 1% level in all the models where it is included. One percent increase in the exit rate over the period 1995–2001 has reduced annual productivity growth in survivor firms by 0.21% in model 1, 0.27% in model 2, and by 0.26% in model 3. The coefficient associated with the lagged value of this variable is negative, but not significant at the 10% level, pointing to the existence of a contemporaneous effect.

As for the variable measuring entry rate (**Nrate),** its coefficient is negative but significant only at 10% level in model 2, where all the control variables are included in the productivity equation. One percent increase in the entry rate is associated with a 0.14% reduction in the productivity rate over the period 1992–2001. The coefficient of the 1 year lagged entry rate variable – significant at 5% level –conveys similar information.

The negative impact of entry rate on the growth rate of surviving firms could be an indication of market stealing effect. If more firms enter to the market, the share of incumbent firms is likely to decline, and this competitive pressure exerted by new firms can lead to a decline in the growth rate of the incumbents firms.

The contemporaneous exit rate has also a negative impact on the growth rate of surviving firms. It seems that the exit rate is a measure of market conditions. More firms exit under adverse shocks, and, under these conditions, the survivors also suffer.

5.5 Conclusion

This study is about the determinants of entry and exit in the Turkish manufacturing sector, and the effects of entry and exit on the growth rate of surviving firms. Our attention is focused on the effects of policy measures related to the opening up of the Turkish economy in the post-1980 period, which we measure with import tariffs and foreign trade. Our findings suggest that entry and exit processes are slowed down when the level of import tariffs are high. Import tariffs seem to have a negative impact on the process of creative destructions. The creative part of the process gets weaker when high import tariffs are imposed because high tariffs make entry more difficult. Moreover, the destructive part of the process is also obscured by high tariffs, i.e., the selection process does not function well, and poor performance gets a chance to survive longer under high tariffs. The direction of foreign trade is likely to be important. Trade with developing countries facilitates entry, whereas trade with developed countries does not have any positive or negative effect on entry. The exit process is not affected by foreign trade variables.

Although trade with developed countries does not have any discernible effect on entry and exit process, it is important for the growth of surviving firms. Our findings suggest that those surviving firms operating in industries with growing imports from both the developed and developing countries are likely to achieve higher growth rates.

5.6 Notes

1. For innovation, see Pamukçu (2003), Taymaz and Ozçelik (2004). For productivity, see Taymaz and Yilmaz (2007). For FDI-related productivity spillovers, see Lenger and Taymaz (2006); Pamukçu (2007). For the informal sector, Kose and Pamukçu (2005); Gonenç et al. (2007).

2. Note that "State Institute of Statistics" (SIS) was the official name of the institution before 2005.We prefer to use the new name along this study, even though our datasets come from the pre-2005 period.
3. For this last issue, see World Bank (2006) and (2007).
4. In fact, enterprises are or may be composed of several "local units" – an entity close to but not the same as an establishment. The change intervened in the ASMI after 2001 is explained by the efforts of Turkstat to collect data according to principles set by EUROSTAT.
5. See Churchill (1955) and Baldwin (1995). In other words, entry appears to be relatively easy but not survival.
6. See Audretsch and Mahmood (1995). This conclusion is not modified if we take into account all firms, and not only incumbents– see first column in Table 5.9.
7. See Audretsch and Mahmood (1995).
8. For example, mean (median) firm size in 1992 is 87.5 (27). Size of a mean (median) entrant during this same year is 27.5 (16). Nine years later, the mean (median) size of a firm of 1992 cohort equals 64.4 (32). On this issue, see Geroski (1995).
9. A causal relationship between these two variables would imply that incumbent firms are displaced by more efficient entrants or that the vacuum created by the exit of less efficient firms leads to more entrants.
10. We used this variable because of the absence of capital stock series at the four-digit ISIC level. Since capital stocks are used in quantitative analysis in order to measure *capital services*, use of "depreciation allowances" should not be misleading – provided, of course, that answers given by firms to this question in the ASMI do reflect the actual depreciation of the capital stock.
11. The OLS models include ISIC 2-digit industry dummies.
12. Both estimation methods include lagged values of exit and entry rates as explanatory variables.
13. Note that the OLS estimates for concentration need to be interpreted cautiously because concentration in an industry changes gradually overtime, and the OLS model does not account for unobserved industry specific effects that could be correlated with the concentration variable. When unobserved industry specific effects are taken into account (see models in Table 5.23), the coefficient of the concentration variable becomes negative and statistically significant.
14. This result might be due to the fact that the proxy used for capital stock – annual depreciation allowances – is an imperfect one.
15. Real value added is obtained by the double deflation method. Firm-level price indexes were not available to deflate output and input. Instead, price indexes at the four-digit level have been used separately for output and for the inputs.
16. First, one can use either simple average or weighted average of product level tariff rates. In the case of weighted average, values of imports are generally used as weights. Second, one can use either the most favored nation (MFN) rates, or (weighted) average of all rates applied to different country categories. Finally, one can simple use nominal rates, or take into account exemptions.
17. Survivors are those establishments that remain in the market at times t-1, t, and $t+1$.

References

Audretsch DB, Mahmood T (1995) New firm survival: new results using a hazard function. Rev Econ Stat 77(1):97–103

Baldwin J (1995) The dynamics of industrial competition. Cambridge University Press, Cambridge

Churchill B (1955) Age and life expectancy of business firms. Surv Curr Bus 35(12):15–19

Geroski P (1995) What do we know about entry? Int J Ind Organ 13:421–440

Gonenç R, Leibfritz W, Yilmaz G (2007) Enhancing Turkey's growth prospects by improving formal sector business conditions. Economics Department Working Papers No. 542, OECD, Paris

Kaya C, Ucdogruk Y (2002) The Dynamics of Entry and Exit in Turkish Manufacturing Industry. Middle East Technical University, Ankara, ERC Working Papers in Economics 02/02

Kose AH, Pamukçu T (2005) Economie grise. In: Vaner S (ed) La Turquie, Fayard Editions, pp. 317–350

Lenger A, Taymaz E (2006) To innovate or to transfer? A study on spillovers and foreign firms in Turkey. J Evol Econ 16:137–153

Pamukçu T (2003) Trade liberalization and innovation decisions of firms: Lessons from post-1980 Turkey. World Dev 31(8):1443–1458

Pamukçu T, Bertinelli L, Strobl E (2007) Technology spillovers due to foreign ownership and productivity of domestic firms: analyzing the evidence. Selected Papers from the 13th International Conference of ERF, Economic Research Forum, Egypt, pp. 187–230

Taymaz E, Ozçelik E (2004) Does innovativeness matter for competitiveness in developing countries? the case of turkish manufacturing industries. Res Policy 33:409–424

Taymaz E, Yilmaz K (2007) Productivity and trade orientation: turkish manufacturing industry before and after the customs union. J Int Trade Diplomacy 1:127–154

World Bank W (2006) Doing Business 2006. World Bank, Washington, DC

World Bank (2007) Turkey. Investment Climate Assessment. two volumes, World Bank, Washington, DC

Chapter 6
Economic Policies, Firms' Entry and Exit and Economic Performance: A Cross Country Analysis

Khalid Sekkat

6.1 Introduction

The change in the economic strategy, initiated in the mid-1980s and accelerated during the 1990s, of MENA countries aimed at putting their economies on a path of higher efficiency, and hence, fostering growth and development. The core of the new strategy was constituted around lowering trade barriers, privatizing public firms, and reforming the foreign-exchange market. Other reforms, such as the adoption of competition laws, aimed at improving the business climate were also on the agenda.

In the Region, four countries have especially sustained important efforts toward the implementation of the new strategy. These are Jordan, Morocco, Tunisia, and Turkey. The latter has even gone further under the framework of the Customs Union agreement signed with the European Union (EU), which came into effect in 1996. The agreement embraces a number of deep integration elements such as the harmonization of Turkey's competition policy legislation to that of the EU, the adoption of the Community's commercial policy toward third countries, and the adoption of the EU Acquis regarding the standardization of industrial products.

Recent analyzes of the impact of liberalization on efficiency in developing countries (LDCs) suggest that the major channel is natural selection among firms and reduction in X-inefficiency: less efficient firms are forced to downsize, improve efficiency, or exit, with more efficient firms expanding their market shares. For instance, Wacziarg and Wallack (2004) analyzed a set of 25 liberalization episodes in developing countries and found a very weak effect of liberalization on interindustry labor reallocation but a strong effect of intraindustry reallocation. Bernard and Jensen (1999) found that intraindustry reallocations to higher productivity exporters explain up to 20% of productivity growth in US

K. Sekkat (✉)
University of Brussels, Brussels, Belgium
e-mail: ksekkat@ulb.ac.be

K. Sekkat (ed.), *Market Dynamics and Productivity in Developing Countries: Economic Reforms in the Middle East and North Africa*, DOI 10.1007/978-1-4419-1037-0_6,

manufacturing. For developing countries, Aw et al. (2000) showed that exposure to trade forces the exit of the least efficient producers in Korea and Taiwan. Pavcnik (2002) finds that market share reallocations contributed significantly to productivity growth following trade liberalization in Chile.

Recent evidence for Jordan, Morocco, and Tunisia (Sekkat 2008) confirms that the 20 years of economic reforms in these countries have resulted in little inter-industry reallocation of activities. The manufacturing sector is still highly specialized in few "traditional" industries. More than 50% (less for Jordan) of the sector's value- added /employment depends on 3 industries the core of which includes textiles and wearing apparel, food products, and chemicals. However, these industries are, in general, inefficient and enjoying high market power suggesting that the process of entry and exit has not been in play in these countries. It is, therefore, important to examine whether this is true (i.e. economic liberalization has not improved productivity through the process of firms' entry and exit) and why.

The process of trade liberalization alone might not produce the expected gains if other reforms (e.g. product and labor market regulations) are not implemented. For instance, Revenga (1997) suggests that the small market responses found in developing countries may reflect restrictive labor market regulation. Harrison and Hanson (1999) argue that imperfect product markets may also be a relevant factor underlying the observed limited impacts of trade liberalization. Borjas and Ramey (1995) suggest that capital or financial market distortions or inefficiencies affect the ability of firms to expand or to enter. These variables may be more important than the labor market. Finally, studies of the determinants of investment (e.g. Wei 2000; Klapper et al. 2007) suggest that the institutional framework of a country could also have marked impacts on entry and exit.

This chapter provides a comparative analysis of the findings of 4 researches investigating the issue in Jordan, Morocco, Tunisia, and Turkey; i.e. Chap. 2–5. Given Turkey's higher progress in terms of economic reforms, its inclusion can serve also as a benchmark for comparison with the 3 other countries to shed useful lights on their potential weaknesses. The studies addressed the following specific questions:

- What are the intensity and determinants of firms' entry and exit in the 4 countries?
- What are the policy and institutional reforms that may have affected the process of entry and exit?
- What is the impact of firms' entry and exit on the manufacturing sector's productivity?
- Which policy recommendations follow from the answers to these questions?

The next section examines the extent of inter versus intra industry reallocation of activities in the 4 countries. Section 3 investigates the determinants of the process of firms' entry and exit. Section 4 assesses the effects of such a process on labor productivity. Section 5 summarizes the main findings and provides policy recommendations.

6.2 Inter- and IntraIndustry Reallocation

6.2.1 InterIndustry Reallocation

6.2.1.1 Aggregate Level Analysis

In the 4 countries, the importance of manufacturing Value Added (VA) in GDP is lower than in other developing countries and even lower than in other Middle Income countries, although the differences are less pronounced in the latter case.

In 2006, Turkey exhibits a markedly lower share of manufacturing in GDP than in the 3 other countries. While the shares remained relatively stable between 1995 and 2006 in Morocco, Tunisia, and Turkey, Jordan showed an important increase (from 12.32% to 18.19%). One reason behind this seems to be an increase is the establishment in Qualifying Industrial Zones (QIZs). These zones allow for the privileged access to the USA market and have resulted in the expansion of the exports of the garment and textile (Table 6.1).

One issue raised in the introduction is the fact that in Jordan, Morocco, and Tunisia the manufacturing sector is still highly specialized in few "traditional" industries despite 20 years of economic reforms. It is, therefore, interesting to see whether this is also a characteristic of the Turkish manufacturing sector, which seems to achieve better outcomes from liberalization (e.g. Taymaz and Yilmaz 2007; Pamukçu 2003). In order to do this, we should move to a more disaggregated level of the data and compute the Gini index of specialization of the manufacturing sector in each country. However, such move implies caution, because the industry classification in Turkey has changed since 2001.

Table 6.2 presents the Gini index and shows no clear contrast between Turkey and the other 3 countries. Morocco is more specialized than Turkey while Tunisia

Table 6.1 Share of manufactured value added in GDP (ISIC 311 to 390) (percentage)

Year	Jordan	Morocco	Tunisia	Turkey	Middle income	Developing countries
1995	12.32	18.14	18.50	13.60	18.60	19.45
2000	13.46	17.57	18.25	13.55	19.11	20.66
2006	18.19	17.10	17.17	13.94	19.19	22.24

Source: UNIDO, http://www.unido.org/index.php?id=4879

Table 6.2 Gini index of specialization in the manufacturing sector

	1995	2005
Jordan	0.48	0.56
Morocco	0.57	0.59
Tunisia	0.47	0.47
Turkey	0.49	0.48[a]

[a] = 2001

has a similar degree of specialization. However, with a same degree of specialization, there may be differences in performance because countries are not specialized in the same industries. We should, therefore, also examine the pattern of specialization at the industry level.

6.2.1.2 Industry Level Analysis

In order to overcome the problem posed by the change in industry classification in Turkey since 2001, we will proceed in 2 ways. First, we compare the structure of the manufacturing sector in Jordan, Morocco and Tunisia to that in Turkey in 1995. This allows assessing how far these countries were from the benchmark. Second, we analyze the evolution of the sector's structure between 1995 and 2005 in the 3 countries to identify possible "catch up" with the benchmark's specialization.

Table 6.3 presents countries specialization in comparison with Turkey in 1995. A positive figure means that the share of the industry in total manufacturing is higher in the country under consideration. The main differences between Turkey and the 3 other countries concern 9 industries out of 21. Jordan, Morocco, and

Table 6.3 Pattern of specialization: comparison with Turkey in 1995 (percentage points)

Industries	Jordan	Morocco	Tunisia
Food and beverages	2.44	8.00	1.65
Tobacco products	11.25	6.31	−2.32
Textiles	−9.95	−8.45	−2.86
Wearing apparel, except fur apparel	−3.13	4.48	14.40
Leather and footwear	0.44	0.78	4.60
Woods	0.15	0.78	5.67
Paper and paper products	−0.15	1.10	−1.47
Printing and publishing	1.51	0.85	:
Chemicals	2.43	0.13	−3.52
Rubber and plastic	−0.83	−1.14	−1.59
Non-metallic mineral products	8.83	3.01	1.44
Basic metals	−3.64	−4.92	−5.97
Structured metal products	1.47	0.57	0.53
Machinery	−4.86	−4.96	−6.26
Office and computing machinery	−0.04	−0.16	−0.95
Other electrical equipment	−1.59	0.65	:
Electronic equipment	−1.52	−2.57	:
Medical, optical, watches etc.	−0.28	−0.26	:
Vehicles and accessories	−4.76	−2.75	−3.79
Other transport equipment	−0.46	−0.62	:
Manufacturing n.e.c.	2.70	−0.85	0.46

Tunisia are much more specialized in non-metallic mineral products, food and beverages, tobacco (except Tunisia), and wearing apparel (except Jordan). Turkey is much more specialized in textiles, basic metals, machinery, and vehicles and accessories. It seems, therefore, that in 1995 Jordan, Morocco and Tunisia were mainly producing basic manufactured good while Turkey was producing more sophisticated goods (i.e. machinery and vehicle and accessories).

Table 6.4 sheds light on whether Jordan, Morocco, and Tunisia have succeeded in upgrading their manufacturing production toward more sophisticated goods over the period 1995-2005. A positive figure means that the share of the industry in total manufacturing has increased in the country under consideration. The results show that the changes are in general marginal. In all the countries, the most significant changes (more than 2% points) do not concern more than 4 industries over 21. If any upgrading should be mentioned, it concerns other electrical equipment in Jordan and office and computing machinery in Tunisia.

To sum up, it appears that the process of accelerated economic liberalization in Jordan, Morocco, and Tunisia has not resulted in any major change of the manufacturing sector specialization. This is in line with the recent literature that found that (e.g. Wacziarg and Wallack 2004) intraindustry reallocation seems to be more important than interindustry reallocation when discussing the effects of trade liberalization. We turn to this in the next section.

Table 6.4 Pattern of specialization: evolution between 1995 and 2005 (percentage points)

Industries	Jordan	Morocco	Tunisia
Food and beverages	−2.36	−2.19	−0.23
Tobacco products	−4.95	4.43	0.04
Textiles	−1.58	−1.31	−4.04
Wearing apparel, except fur apparel	7.48	−1.70	1.05
Leather and Footwear	−0.82	−0.11	1.07
Woods	−0.31	−0.36	0.05
Paper and paper products	−0.25	−1.32	−0.96
Printing and Publishing	0.00	0.01	:
Chemicals	0.60	2.17	−0.22
Rubber and Plastic	−0.42	−0.76	0.07
Non-metallic mineral products	−1.62	−0.44	0.31
Basic metals	3.13	0.80	−0.85
Structured metal products	0.10	−0.04	−0.69
Machinery	0.40	0.08	0.01
Office, computing machinery	0.00	0.02	3.20
Other electrical equipment	2.02	1.14	:
Electronic Equipment	−1.06	−0.06	:
Medical, Optical, Watches Etc.	0.43	0.06	:
Vehicles and Accessories	−0.33	−0.55	1.04
Other Transport equipment	0.21	−0.01	:
Manufacturing n.e.c.	−0.66	0.12	0.14

6.2.2 InterIndustry Reallocation

This section highlights the importance of intraindustry reallocations through the dynamics of firms' entry and exit. For a given year t, if a firm was present in t-1 but absent in t+1, it will be classified as an exitor. If a firm was absent in t-1 but present in t+1, it will be classified as an entrant. A firm that was absent in t-1 and t+1 (i.e. it is only present on t) is both entrant and an exitor. Finally, a firm that belongs to none of the three categories will be classified as a survivor. For comparability across sectors, we define entry and exit rates with respect to the current year's stock of establishments:

$$\text{Entry rate in } t = \frac{\text{Number of new firms in } t}{\text{Number of firms in } t\text{; including entrants but excluding exitors}}. \quad (6.1)$$

$$\text{Exit rate in } t = \frac{\text{Number of firms that exit in } t}{\text{Numbers of firms in } t\text{; including entrants but excluding existors}}. \quad (6.2)$$

6.2.2.1 Aggregate Level Analysis

Fig. 6.1 presents an index of "turbulence" in the manufacturing sector. The index is simply the arithmetic mean of entry and exit rates and highlights the intensity of market's dynamism. The index is much higher in Turkey than in the other countries. From 2000 on, it decreases or stabilizes in all countries. Splitting the index into its components, Fig. 6.2 shows that the entry rate is higher in Turkey until 1999 and

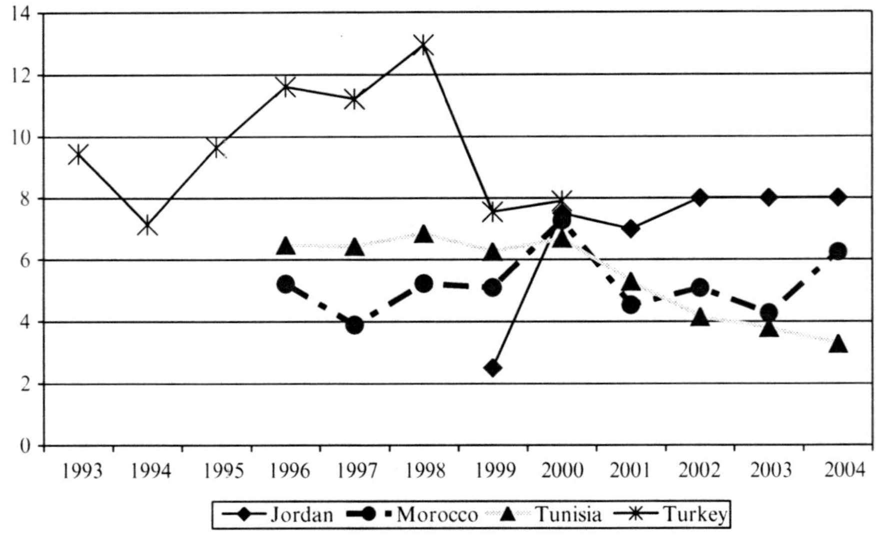

Fig. 6.1 Turbulence in the manufacturing sector

then fall under the Moroccan and the Tunisian. The entry rate in these two countries (especially in Tunisia) exhibits a decreasing trend from 2000 on. The exit rate (Fig. 6.3) gives a clearer contrast between the countries. It is the highest in Turkey and the lowest in Tunisia and remains stable around 10% and 3% respectively. The

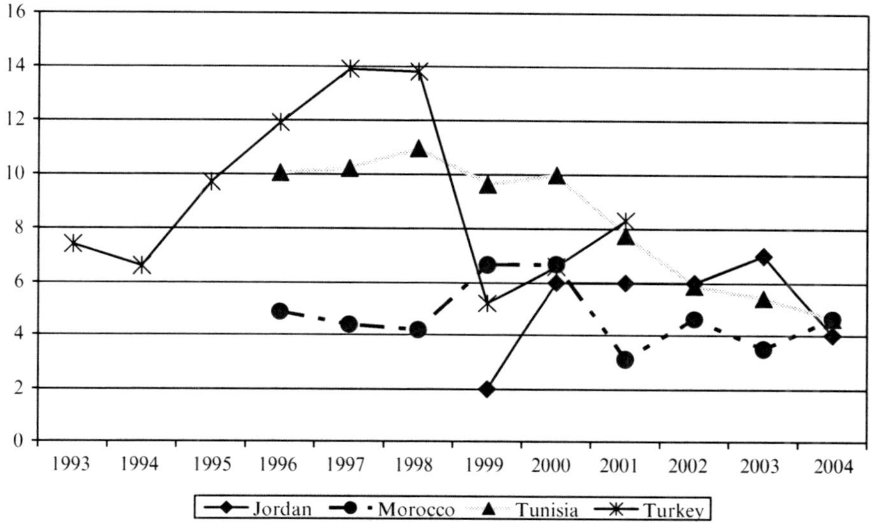

Fig. 6.2 Entry rates

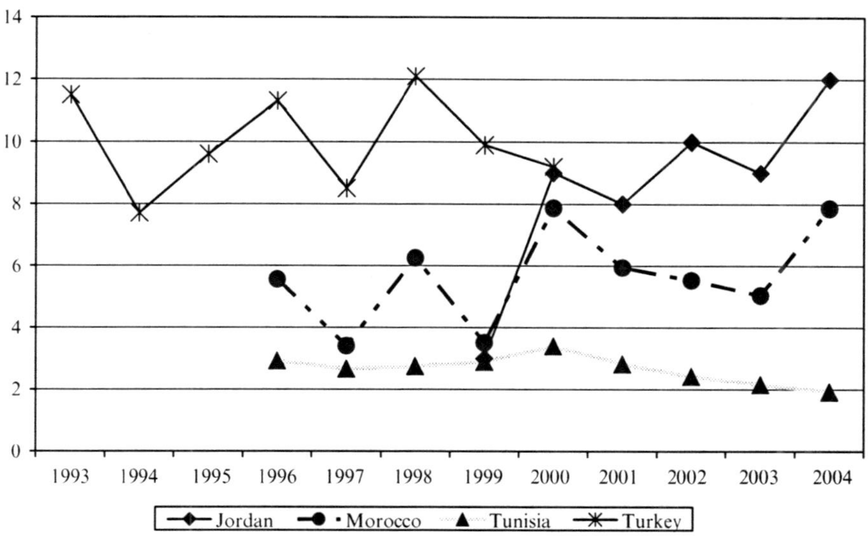

Fig. 6.3 Exit rates

exit rate in Jordan and Morocco has been steadily increasing since 2000 to be close to the Turkish by the end of the period.

In the 4 countries, the entry rate lies, on average over the period, between 4.73% (Morocco) and 9.27% (Turkey). This is comparable to the findings by Eslava et al. (2006) for Columbia (8%), but lower than in Brazil (13.86% following Campos and Iootty (2005)) and in Hungary and Poland (14.05% and 10.20% respectively following Klapper et al. (2007)). The exit rate in our sample lies between 2.66% (Tunisia) and 9.97% (Turkey), which is lower than in Columbia (11%) and (10%) Brazil.

Summing up, it appears that "turbulence" is the highest in the Turkish manufacturing sector, where it is comparable to other emerging economies. From 2000 on, turbulence has been the lowest in Tunisia. While in Turkey and Tunisia, the main driver of "turbulence" is the entry rate, in Jordan and Morocco, the main driver is the exit rate. Finally, entry and exit rates in Jordan, Morocco, and Tunisia are much lower than in other emerging economies.

6.2.2.2 Industry Level Analysis

The aggregate entry and exit rates hide sometimes considerable differences across industries. Table 6.5 presents industries with the highest and the lowest entry and exit rates over the period 1995–2005. In Jordan, the entry rate is the highest for the manufacture of rubber products (50%) and manufacture of wood and wood products (20%). It is below 5% for 20 industries out of 27. The exit rate is the highest for other manufacturing products (43%), manufacture of leather products (33%), and manufacture of wearing apparel (27%). It is below 5% for 13 industries out of 27. Two aspects are worth noting in Jordan. First, the highest entry and exit rates are due to industries, with very small number of firms. Second, except for these industries the distribution of entry and exit rates is almost flat.

Table 6.5 Industries with the highest and lowest entry and exit rates: 1995-2005 (rates in percentage)

	Entry	
	High	Low
Jordan	Rubber products (50%) Wood products (20%)	*8 industries exhibit 0%*
Morocco	Wearing apparel (7%)	Glass products (2%)
Tunisia	Textiles (26%).	Paper and printing (3%)
Turkey	Furniture (except metal) (17%)	Beverages (5.8%)
	Exit	
	High	Low
Jordan	Other manufacturing products (43%) Leather products (33%) Wearing apparel (27%).	*4 industries exhibit 0%*
Morocco	Wearing apparel (8%)	Non-ferrous metal (1%)
Tunisia	Textiles (5.39%)	Paper and printing (1%).
Turkey	Wearing apparel (15%)	Coke and refineries (4%)

In Morocco, entry rates lie between 1.89% in manufacture of glass products and 7.28% in manufacture of wearing apparel. Exit rates lie between 1.2% in nonferrous metal and 7.75% in manufacture of wearing apparel.

In Tunisia, the highest entry rate is comparable to the one found in Jordan and concerns textiles (25.98%). The lowest entry rate is 3.55% and concerns paper and cardboard industries and printing and related support activities. Note, however, that wood products and electric and electronic equipment exhibit high entry rates (around 10%). Exit rates are always lower than entry rates. They are also lower than in Morocco and Jordan. The maximum exit rate is found for textiles (5.39%) and the minimum for paper and cardboard industries and printing and related support activities (0.84%). These are the same industries than for entry.

In Turkey, there is a limited degree of variability of entry and exit rates across industries. Out of 28 industries, 27 have an entry rate higher than 5% (14 industries have a rate higher than 10%). Among the 27 industries, the maximum (17.7%) concerns manufacture of furniture (except metal) and the minimum (5.8%) concerns beverages. Exit rates lie between 4.5% (Coke and refineries) and 15.2% (manufacture of wearing apparel, except footwear).

It is worth noting that in the 4 countries entry and exit are mainly driven by small and medium sized firms. Moreover, textile-related products are those with high exit rates irrespective of the country. No specific pattern emerges for entry rates across the 4 countries. However, in Morocco and Tunisia, both the highest entry and the highest exit rates concern textile- related products. Such a high turbulence could be associated with the foreseen termination of the Multi Fibers Agreement in 2005.

6.2.2.3 Correlation Analysis

The analysis of the correlation between entry and exit rates, although a rough approach, allows shedding some light on two competing conjectures. If entry and exit rates at the industry level are mostly driven by industry specific demand shocks, then the correlation should be negative (Bartelsman et al. 2004). Alternatively, if entry and exit rates at the industry level are driven by a process of creative destruction (i.e. a supply side shock) within the industry, then the correlation of entry and exit rates should be positive

At the aggregate level, the average correlation between entry and exit is low in Morocco (around 20% in absolute terms) but with changing signs depending on the year. The average correlation is relatively high (around 50% in absolute term) in Jordan, Tunisia, and Turkey. It is, in general, positive in Tunisia and Turkey and negative in Jordan.

Table 6.6 summarizes the results at the industry level. The correlation is high and positive in the Jordanian food industry (81%), other manufacturing products (80%), and manufacture of wearing apparel (72%) and relatively low for the remaining industries. It is high and positive for the Moroccan transport equipment (65%), foods products (67%), other non-metallic mineral products (76%) and high and negative

Table 6.6 Correlation of entry and exit rates by industry: 1995–2005 (rates in percentage)

	Correlation	
	Significantly positive	Significantly negative
Jordan	Food (81%)Other manufactures (80%) Wearing apparel (72%)	
Morocco	Other non-metallic minerals (76%) Foods (67%) Transport equipment (65%) Other chemicals (54%) Rubber products (54%)	Wearing apparel (−65%) Pottery, China, etc. (−57%)
Tunisia	Fabricated metal (83%) Wearing (80%) Wood products (74%) Textiles (60%) Metallurgy (55%)	
Turkey	Non-ferrous metal (70%) Printing, and publishing (58%) Machinery electric (56%) Coke and refineries (55%)	

for wearing apparel (−65%). In Tunisia, it is high and positive for textile industries (60%), wood products (74%), clothing and lining industries (80%), and fabricated metal products (83%) and relatively low for the remaining industries. Finally, in Turkey, except for 4 industries out of 28, the correlation is relatively low.

At the industry level, there seems that no common pattern of correlation across countries exists. A negative correlation shows up only in Morocco. It concerns wearing apparel, one of the most important industries in the economy, which seems to be affected by a specific demand shock. In the other countries and for numerous Moroccan industries, the correlations are positive suggesting that the process of creative destruction (i.e. a supply side shock) is the main driver of entry and exit.

6.3 Determinants of Entry and Exit

The previous section shows that the intensity of firms' entry and exit in Turkey is comparable to other emerging economies having adopted trade liberalization. In Jordan, Morocco, and Tunisia, it is much lower. The fact that the process of trade liberalization in these countries has not induced a similar intensity of firms' entry and exit suggests that other factors might have slowed down such a process. To investigate this issue, this section summarizes the findings of national studies of the determinants of entry and exit.

The studies used a similar methodology (Sekkat 2007) where a series of firm, industry, and country specific factors determines the intensity of entry and exit. The econometric models for the entry and exit are respectively:

$$\begin{aligned}\text{Entry rate}_{i,t} &= \alpha_0 + \alpha_1 \times \text{average size of entrants}_{i,t} \\ &+ \alpha_2 \times \text{industry's characteristics}_{i,t} \\ &+ \alpha_3 \times \text{institutional environment}_{i,t} \\ &+ \alpha_4 \times \text{exit rate}_{i,t} + \mu_{i,t},\end{aligned} \tag{6.3}$$

$$\begin{aligned}\text{Exit rate}_{i,t} &= \beta_0 + \beta_1 \times \text{average size of exitors}_{i,t} + \beta_2 \times \text{average age of exitors}_{i,t} \\ &+ \beta_3 \times \text{industry's characteristics}_{i,t} + \beta_4 \times \text{institutional environment}_{i,t} \\ &+ \beta_5 \times \text{entry rate}_{i,t} + \upsilon_{i,t}.\end{aligned} \tag{6.4}$$

where i stands for industry, t stands for time, and entry rate is defined in Equation (6.1), exit rate is given by Equation (6.2).

Firm's characteristics include the average size of entrants and exitors in terms of employment or output and the average age of exitors.

Industry's characteristics include profit margin, concentration ratio, growth rate, average productivity, average wage rate, capital intensity, and openness to trade. Profit margin determines the attractiveness for new firms to enter into the industry but it could also be associated with imperfect competition. In the former case, the expected sign is positive, while in the latter the reverse is expected. The concentration is an indicator of the easiness to enter a market. It is easier to enter perfectly competitive industries in which many small firms produce standard products. Openness to trade captures the impact of foreign competition through imports and opportunities of business through exports. The growth rate of the industry is a proxy of its life cycle. New firms prefer to enter rapidly growing industries. The other variables aimed at capturing some "natural" barriers to entry. Capital intensity may discourage entry, because if the industry uses capital-intensive technology, the cost of the initial investment could be substantial. The average labor productivity reflects the dynamism of an industry. It can also be associated with investment. In the first case, it may encourage entry, while in the second case it could discourage entrants either because investment requirements are indivisible and massive or because of the risks of severe post entry competition. The average wage rate in an industry can be negatively correlated with the entry rate if it reflects the demand for industry-specific skills.

Regarding exit, the following signs are expected for the coefficients. Negative for profit margin (losses stimulate the decision to exit), capital intensity (sunk cots delay exit), growth rate (firms can survive in rapidly growing industries), and concentration ratio (high concentration reduces competition among firms).

Finally, since entry and exit rates tend to be correlated (Caves 1998), the exit rate is included in Equation (6.3) and the entry rate is included in Equation (6.4).

Country's variables include trade barriers, exchange rate, investment and labor market regulations as well as indicators of governance (e.g. political stability, corruption, democratic accountability, bureaucratic quality). Trade barriers protect from foreign competition: the expected coefficient for entry and for exit is negative. An increase in the exchange rate means an appreciation of the currency, which makes domestic firms less competitive. The expected sign is, therefore, negative for entry and positive for exit. The signs for regulations and governance depend on whether they are pro business or not.

Due to data availability, the exact definition of each explanatory variable varies from one country to another. However, the economic interpretation of the variable remains the same across countries (e.g. C4 versus Herfindhal for concentration). For this reason, the significance and sign of the coefficients can be compared across countries but not their levels. The estimation method is also the same across countries. Since the dependent variable cannot take values below zero (there is no negative entry or exit rate), econometric theory implies that OLS estimation gives biased results and one should use, instead, the Tobit method. The estimation was conducted using various combinations of the explanatory variables, of interactions terms, and of lags. To save on space, Tables 6.7 and 6.8 present only the results of the preferred regressions in each country.

The results for Jordan are counterintuitive both for entry and the exit equations. For instance, they show that entry decreases in expanding market and exit increases in expanding market, which is in contradiction with the earlier economic discussion. The reason for the counterintuitive results may be, as noticed, that the highest entry and exit rates are due to industries with very small number of firms and that the distribution of entry and exit rates is almost flat.

In Morocco, the only significant coefficient (apart from lagged entry) is the one of the Real Effective Exchange Rate (REER). Entry is affected significantly and negatively by the REER. As an increase in the REER means an appreciation of the dirham (i.e. a loss of competitiveness of Moroccan firms with respect to foreigners both on the domestic and on international markets), new firms do not enter. The coefficient of the lagged entry rate is positive and significant. This implies that if entry is feasible into a given market (less barrier to entry or expanding demand), there will be more and more entry.

Characteristic of entrants plays a role in explaining the entry rate in Tunisia. Entry is higher is those industries where entrants need to be big. *Industry's characteristic* pertaining to profit has a negative and significant coefficient. This is compatible with the interpretation of this variable as an indicator of imperfect competition which deters entry. In the same vein, concentration and capital intensity discourage entry. High productivity fosters it.

In Turkey, the coefficient of concentration is negative and significant implying that the entry rate is lower in more concentrated industries. The coefficient of industry growth is positive and significant, confirming the positive influence of greater business opportunities and possibly of the industry life cycle on entry. Coefficient estimates of the average wage level are significant and negative. Import duties exert a negative and significant effect on the entry rate. This could be interpreted as entry into sectors where firms are sheltered from foreign competition is more difficult than in less protected sectors. Hence, tariff reductions that took place in the Turkish economy sine the early nineties must have eased entry of firms in the

Table 6.7 Estimations results: Determinants of the entry rate

	Jordan	Morocco	Tunisia	Turkey
Firm's characteristics				
Average size of entrants	0.00		0.02	
	2.14		**3.21**	
Industry's characteristics				
Profit margin	0.00		−0.10	−0.01
	1.83		**−3.43**	**−0.05**
Concentration ratio	−0.01	−0.11	−0.26	−0.13
	−3.14	**−0.62**	**−2.61**	**−2.61**
Growth rate	−0.01	−0.04	0.04	0.08
	−1.99	**−0.08**	**1.27**	**5.94**
Average productivity	0.00		3.09	0.00
	2.64		**1.96**	**0.27**
Wage rate	−0.00			−0.02
	−4.21			**−1.91**
Capital intensity	−0.00	−0.08	−0.03	0.00
	−2.91	**−0.77**	**−1.93**	**0.77**
Imports from developed countries				−0.01
				−1.21
Imports from less developed countries				0.01
				3.69
Exports to developed countries			0.01	−0.00
			2.07	**−1.01**
Exports to less developed countries				0.02
				3.60
Institutional environment				
Tariffs	−0.05	0.17		−0.06
	−1.50	**0.93**		**−2.19**
Real effective exchange rate		−0.16		
		−2.78		
Exit Rate	0.04		0.69	0.20
	1.67		**3.40**	**5.99**
Lagged entry rate		0.44		0.09
		3.10		**2.46**
Period	2000–2004	2001–2004	1998–2003	1992–2001

manufacturing sector. The direction of foreign trade apparently plays an important role in the entry process. Growth rates of imports of goods originating from developed countries and exports toward these countries have no significant effects but the same variables when focused on developing countries have positive and significant coefficients. It seems that trade with developing countries facilitates the creation of new (small) firms because of the fact that local entrepreneurs

Table 6.8 Estimations results: determinants of the exit rate

	Jordan	Morocco	Tunisia	Turkey
Firm's characteristics				
Average size of exitors	–0.00		0.00	
	–3.17		**0.20**	
Average age of exitors	–0.00			
	–0.66			
Industry's characteristics				
Profit margin	–0.00		0.01	0.01
	–1.89		**0.63**	**0.08**
Concentration ratio	0.05	–0.41		–0.13
	–1.46	**–3.49**		**–2.61**
Growth rate	0.13	–1.10	–0.01	0.01
	2.73	**–3.28**	**–2.16**	**0.45**
Average productivity	00.0		0.20	0.04
	–0.60		**0.69**	**1.86**
Wage rate	–0.03			–0.08
	–2.28			**–4.31**
Capital intensity	–0.00	–0.03	–5.38	0.00
	–1.20	**–0.46**	**–2.46**	**0.12**
Imports from developed countries				–0.01
				–0.92
Imports from less developed countries				–0.01
				–1.98
Exports to developed countries			–0.00	–0.01
			–0.23	**–1.34**
Exports to less developed countries				0.01
				0.78
Institutional environment				
Tariffs	0.54	–0.15		–0.08
	10.96	**–1.32**		**–1.78**
Real effective exchange rate		–0.03		
		–0.82		
Entry Rate	–0.35		0.10	0.04
	–0.74		**3.71**	**0.83**
Lagged exit rate		–0.04		–0.15
		–0.31		**–2.29**
Period	2000–2004	2001–2004	1998–2004	1992–2001

believe that the business prospects are better in sectors in which developing countries tend to specialize.

The other institutional environment variables collected in each country (e.g. investment regulations, labor regulations and other trade and non-trade barriers) do not exhibit significant coefficients. The reason is that these variables do not vary enough across time and industries (i.e. have a low variance) and hence the estimates of their impact cannot be precise enough.

In Morocco, demand plays an important role in the process of firms' exit. The corresponding coefficient is negative and significant. When demand is increasing, firms stay in the market. Concentration, reflecting the intensity of competition, has a significant and negative coefficient. Firms operating in poorly competitive environment are more likely to survive than those in highly competitive environment. In Tunisia, both industry's growth and capital intensity have the expected negative sign. Exit is lower in growing industries and when capital intensity (i.e. sunk costs) is high. In Turkey, the level of concentration has a negative and statistically significant coefficient. Labor productivity has a positive and significant coefficient. If we see (as for entry) productivity as an indicator of industrys' dynamism, this means that the exit rate is higher in dynamic industries. Wage rate, trade protection, and imports from LDCs have negative and significant coefficients. The exit rate is lower in more protected markets but also in industries competing with LDCs. Although surprising at first sight, the latter result is coherent with the findings for entry rate. Like for entry rate and for the same reason, the coefficients of the other institutional variables are nonsignificant in the 4 countries.

To summarize, the findings that are consistent across the 4 countries are that entry is higher in those industries offering some opportunities, either sales or productivity improvement. These are in general characteristics of new and growing industries. Entry is discouraged by natural (capital intensity and wage level) and strategic barriers (concentration of incumbents). Exit is lower when demand is growing, there are high sunk costs, and competition either foreign or domestic is limited. Once the control for the other determinants is done, entry rates are, in general, positively related to exit rates, lending support to the hypothesis of creative destruction in the countries.

6.4 Entry, Exit, and Productivity

The main interest in the process of entry and exit concerns its impact on productivity (Wacziarg and Wallack 2004). This section investigates the impact of the process of entry and exit on labor productivity in the countries under consideration. If the process is found to be conductive to higher productivity, the fact that its intensity is low in these countries means a loss of opportunities to improve economic performance.

There are two commonly used methods to assess the impact of the process of entry and exit on productivity. The accounting method decomposes labor productivity into the contribution of "internal restructuring" (i.e. productivity growth within the surviving establishments, or the "within" effect), changes in the market shares of the survivors (i.e. productivity grows further if the shares of higher productivity establishments increase, or the "between" effect), and contribution of entry and exit. The other method is econometric and is motivated by the fact that the accounting one may not measure precisely the impact of entry and exit on productivity growth of survivors. Practically, it consists in a regression of the change in output of survivors on the change in their inputs and on the state of present competition and entry and exit rates.

The results of the accounting method are in Table 6.9. Due to data problems, the method could not be applied to Tunisia. Moreover, in all the countries, the between effect was almost zero. So the column survivors concern mainly the within effect. In Jordan, clearly the incumbent plants are on average more productive than entrants and exitors. New entrants play a minor role in enhancing productivity. In contrast, in Morocco and Turkey, improvement in productivity is mainly driven by entrants. The contribution of survivors is positive but much lower than entrants. In the 3 countries, exitors have contributed negatively to productivity growth over the period. Hence, exit seems to clean industries from their less productive plants. Entry allows replacing these plants by more productive one. The results at the industry level are in general in accordance with Table 6.9.

Table 6.10 presents the results of the econometric method. It concerns the impact of entry and exit on the productivity of survivors. Hence, if the coefficients of entry and exit rate are significant, this means that these variables have an additional effect on aggregate performance through their impact of the productivity of survivors. If the coefficients are not significant, this means that the whole impact of entry and exit is captured in Table 6.9. The typical regression is:

$$\begin{aligned}\Delta \log\left(Y_{it}\right) = \eta_0 + \eta_1 \times \text{firm's characteristics} \\ + \eta_2 \times \text{industry's characteristics} \\ + \eta_3 \text{institutional environment} \\ + \eta_4 \times \text{impact of entry and exit} + + \xi_{it}.\end{aligned} \quad (6.5)$$

where $\Delta\log(Y_{it})$ is the change in output of survivor i at time t, firms' characteristics concern the change in its inputs, industrys' characteristics include the state of present competition and openness and the institutional environment covers various policy variables.

Like in Section 6.3, the exact definition of each explanatory variable varies across countries (due to data availability), but its economic interpretation remains the same. The estimation method is also the same: the GMM estimation method, which takes account of simultaneity. To save on space, Table 6.10 presents only the results of the preferred regressions in each country.

Here again and may be for the same reason as before, the results for Jordan are counterintuitive. In Morocco, investment has a positive and significant coefficient.

Table 6.9 Contributions to productivity growth

	Entrants	Exitors	Survivors	Total
Jordan	0.15	-9.70	109.56	100
Morocco	120.18	-51.76	31.58	100
Turkey	111.59	-84.63	73.04	100

The coefficients of the concentration ratio is significant and negative implying that less competitive industries are also less productive. Finally, net entry exerts a positive and significant impact on productivity. In Tunisia, the output growth rate is highly dependent on labor and capital. There is no significant relationship between firm entry and exit (actual or lagged) and output growth of survivors. In Turkey, labor and capital have positive and significant coefficients. The coefficient associated with the degree of concentration is negative but not significant. Variables measuring the extent of foreign competition (i.e. growth rate of imports from developed and from developing countries) both exert a positive and significant effect on survivors' productivity growth. In contrast, the exit rate variable has a coefficient that is negative and significant.

Table 6.10 Estimations results: determinants of productivity

	Jordan	Morocco	Tunisia	Turkey
Firm's characteristics				
Change in capital	0.48	0.01	0.28	0.09
	2.67	**1.71**	**2.60**	**18.25**
Change in employment	1.18	−0.16	0.93	0.54
	2.39	**−1.05**	**5.40**	**38.71**
Industry's characteristics				
Concentration	0.24	−0.03		−0.01
	5.35	**−1.97**		**−0.14**
Imports from developed countries				0.05
				4.12
Imports from less developed countries				0.01
				2.68
Exports to developed countries				−0.01
				−1.56
Exports to less developed countries				−0.01
				−0.54
Institutional environment				
Tariffs	0.14			−0.04
	3.71			**−0.80**
Impact of entry and exit				
Entry rate	−0.12		−1.22	−0.12
	−1.96		**−1.62**	**−1.42**
Lagged entry rate			0.75	−0.06
			0.95	**−1.08**
Exit rate	0.00		2.39	−0.26
	−0.08		**1.15**	**−3.20**
Lagged exit rate			2.20	0.00
			1.11	**−0.02**
Net entry		0.56		
		1.66		
Period	2000–2004	2001–2004	1998–2004	1992–2001

To conclude, it seems that across the 4 countries, there is a weak support to the hypothesis that entry and exit have an effect on survivors' productivity. In contrast, the latter depends heavily on factors of production availability, especially capital and on actual competition. Both the factors of production availability and actual competition (either foreign or domestic) improve survivors' productivity.

6.5 Conclusion and Policy Recommendations

The starting point of the analysis is the confrontation of two results in the literature concerning the impact of trade liberalization on firms' efficiency. On the one hand, evidence shows that, after more than 20 years of liberalization, the main manufacturing industries in which Jordan, Morocco, and Tunisia are specialized suffer high degree of inefficiency. On the other hand, the recent literature suggests that the major channel by which liberalization affects firms' efficiency is natural selection in the same industry: less efficient firms restructure or exit, while more efficient ones enter or expand in the market. The question is, therefore, whether or not the process of entry and exit has played a similar role in these countries and why. Given Turkey's similarity (e.g. level of development, same region, comparable culture, adoption of liberalization) and difference (i.e. better economic performance) with the 3 other countries, it is used as a benchmark for comparison.

The analysis showed that over recent years, the process of entry and exit has, indeed, contributed to improving industries' productivity in Jordan, Morocco, and Turkey. This improvement took place through exit of the less productive firms (Jordan), entry of more productive firms, or both (Morocco and Turkey). The effect on industries' productivity operates through entry and exit in their own and not through their impact on the productivity of survivors. Exit seems to clean industries from their less productive plants, while entry allows replacing these plants by more productive ones. Productivity is also driven by other factors such as factors of production availability (especially capital) and actual competition.

Although the process of entry and exit has improved productivity in a similar way in the countries of interest as in other emerging economies, the question remains about the relative persistence of inefficiency in the corresponding manufacturing sector. The response might be found in the intensity of the process.

Comparison of the intensity of entry and exit across the 4 countries and with other emerging economies (both at the sector and at the industries level) shows that the intensity is the highest in the Turkish manufacturing sector, where it is comparable to other emerging economies. From 2000 on, intensity has been the lowest in Tunisia. In Jordan, Morocco, and Tunisia, entry and exit rates are much lower than in other emerging economies. Hence, it seems that while the process has played a similar role as in other emerging economies, its limited impact on industries' productivity is due to its weak intensity. It is, therefore, important to study the determinants of entry and exit in the 4 countries.

Regressions of the intensity of entry and exit rates on a series of firm, industry, and country specific characteristics show that entry is higher in those industries offering some opportunities (sales or productivity improvement) and lower in industries with high natural (capital intensity and wage level) and strategic barriers (concentration of incumbents). Exit is lower when demand is growing, there are high sunk costs, and competition either foreign or domestic is limited.

These results are in accordance with the literature (see the introduction) and suggest a number of policy recommendations. First, intense competition either foreign or domestic seems to affect productivity directly and indirectly through higher entry and exit rates. Hence, enforcement of competition policy seems to be a good instrument for improving productivity. The 4 countries have adopted a competition policy. However, its enforcement varies greatly across countries: Tunisia and Turkey went significantly further in this respect than Jordan and Morocco. The latter should urgently improve their record in term of enforcement of competition policy. Moreover, higher openness to trade seems also in order especially in Jordan, Morocco, and Tunisia. The 3 countries are member of the WTO and have, in particular, signed a free trade agreement (FTA) with the EU. Jordan and Morocco also have a FTA with the USA. Morocco and Tunisia have a FTA with Turkey. It seems, however, that their FTA induces faster dismantling of barriers to trade than their participation to the WTO. Their continuous and firm commitments to such agreements could, therefore, have a very beneficial impact on productivity. Second, better access to factors of production also appears to affect productivity directly and indirectly through higher entry and exit rates. This is especially true for capital. The cost of using capital encompasses a number of components such as getting credit, protecting investors, paying taxes, enforcing contracts. Comparisons with around 170 countries show that in 2005 (see Appendix B), Turkey performs fairly well in this respect, Jordan has an "average record" but Morocco and Tunisia exhibit in general disappointing records. The latter have, however, recently implemented a number of reforms to address the problem of access to capital. Third, industries offering demand opportunities witness higher entry but lower exit rates. Since the positive effect of entrants on productivity improvement is found to be much higher than the negative effect of potential exitors, the net effect is expected to be positive. Abstracting from internal demand, which is a macroeconomic issue, it seems that productivity improvement can also be achieved through more export orientation of the economy. Interestingly, comparison with major exporters from Asia (Korea and Japan) shows that although the obstacles to exporting are higher in the 4 countries (see Appendix B), the differences are not dramatic. The problem may come from the export strategies, which seem less active in terms of promotion, advertising, lobbying, etc.

6.6 Notes

1. A theoretical foundation of such a process is provided by Melitz (2003) who showed how changes in the relative performance of firms as a response to foreign competition occur
2. Presents the structure of the manufacturing sector in the 4 countries
3. Coke and refineries, manufacture of machinery electric, printing, and publishing and non-ferrous metal

6.7 Appendix A: Structure of the manufacturing sector in the 4 countries

Industries	Jordan		Morocco		Tunisia		Turkey	
	1995	2005	1995	2005	1995	2005	1995	2001
Food and beverages	17.50	15.13	22.18	19.99	16.70	16.47	15.06	14.18
Tobacco products	14.32	9.36	13.40	17.82	0.74	0.79	3.07	7.09
Textiles	3.08	1.50	5.52	4.21	10.16	6.13	13.02	13.97
Wearing except fur	2.65	10.13	11.20	9.50	20.18	21.23	5.78	6.72
Leather and footwear	1.17	0.34	1.39	1.28	5.32	6.39	0.72	0.61
Woods	0.95	0.64	1.41	1.05	6.48	6.53	0.81	0.63
Paper and paper products	3.08	2.82	2.98	1.66	3.54 [a]	2.58 [a]	3.23	1.88
Printing and publishing	3.29	3.29	1.37	1.38	:	:	1.78	0.52
Chemicals	15.91	16.50	12.61	14.78	9.96	9.74	13.48	12.48
Rubber and plastic	3.50	3.08	2.76	2.00	2.73	2.80	4.32	3.90
Non-metallic mineral products	16.76	15.13	10.27	9.83	9.36	9.67	7.92	7.27
Basic metals	4.14	7.27	2.22	3.01	1.81	0.96	7.78	7.14
Structured metal products	4.77	4.87	3.87	3.83	3.83	3.14	3.30	3.30
Machinery	1.91	2.31	0.85	0.93	0.51	0.52	6.77	5.80
Office and computing machinery	0.00	0.00	0.02	0.04	4.61 [b]	7.81 [b]	0.04	0.18
Other electrical equipment	1.06	3.08	3.26	4.40	:	:	2.65	2.61
Electronic equipment	1.06	0.00	1.07	1.01	:	:	2.58	3.63
Medical, optical, watches etc.	0.00	0.43	0.12	0.18	:	:	0.28	0.38
Vehicles and accessories	1.27	0.94	2.03	1.49	2.70 [c]	3.75 [c]	6.04	4.79
Other transport equipment	0.00	0.21	0.36	0.35	:	:	0.46	0.98
Manufacturing n.e.c.	3.61	2.95	1.11	1.23	1.37	1.50	0.91	1.95

a = Paper and paper products + Printing and Publishing

b = Office and computing machinery + Other electrical equipment + Electronic Equipment + Medical, Optical, Watches Etc.

c = Vehicles and Accessories + Other Transport equipment

6.8 Appendix B: World Bank's indicators of the cost of doing business

See Tables 6.11–6.13

Table 6.11 Ranking of countries in 2005

	Jordan	Morocco	Tunisia	Turkey
Ease of doing business	73	117	77	84
Starting a business	127	63	52	47
Dealing with licenses	68	130	113	145
Employing workers	30	158	93	148
Registering property	110	53	69	48
Getting credit	76	143	96	59
Protecting investors	114	114	151	58
Paying taxes	16	125	138	61
Trading across borders	85	70	36	69
Enforcing contracts	72	126	38	69
Closing a business	79	58	30	137

Table 6.12 Change of ranks 2005–2006

	Jordan	Morocco	Tunisia	Turkey
Ease of doing business	5	−2	3	7
Starting a business	6	−16	7	6
Dealing with licenses	2	3	−3	3
Employing workers	0	−2	−1	−2
Registering property	0	−8	2	6
Getting credit	7	0	5	6
Protecting investors	4	4	0	2
Paying taxes	2	3	1	4
Trading across borders	−7	7	3	10
Enforcing contracts	3	1	2	1
Closing a business	5	3	−1	1

Table 6.13 Trading across borders 2006

Country	Jordan	Morocco	Tunisia	Turkey	Korea	Japan
Requirement to export						
Number of documents	7	6	5	8	5	4
Number of days	28	18	18	20	12	10
Cost (US$ per container)	720	700	770	513	780	989
Requirement to import						
Number of documents	12	11	7	13	8	5
Number of days	28	30	29	25	12	11
Cost (US$ per container)	955	1,500	600	735	1,040	1,047

References

Aw BY, Chung D, Roberts M (2000) Productivity and turnover in the export market: micro-level evidence from the republic of Korea and Taiwan (China). World Bank Econ Rev 14:65–90

Bartelsman E, Haltiwanger J, Scarpetta S (2004) "Microeconomic evidence of creative destruction in industrial and developing countries". Tinbergen Institute Discussion Paper (TI 2004-114/3)

Bernard A, Jensen J (1999) "Exporting and productivity". NBER Working Paper No. 7135, National Bureau of Economic Research, Cambridge, Mass

Borjas GJ, Ramey VA (1995) Foreign competition, market power, and wage inequality. Q J Econ 110:1075–1110

Campos NF, Iootty M (2005) "Firm entry and exit in Brazil: cross-sectoral evidence from manufacturing industry." In the Proceedings of the 33th Brazilian Economics Meeting

Caves RE (1998) Industrial organization and new findings on the turnover and mobility of firms. J Econ Lit 36(8):1947–1982

Eslava M, Halti wanger J, Kugler A, Kigler M (2006) "Plant Turnover and Structural Reforms in Colombia". IMF Staff Papers, Vol. 53, Special Issue

Harrison A, Hanson G (1999) Who gains from trade reform? Some remaining puzzles. J Dev Econ 59:125–154

Klapper L, Laeven L, Rajan R (2007) Entry regulation as a barrier to entrepreneurship. J Financ Econ 82:591–629

Melitz M (2003) The impact of trade on intra-industry reallocations and aggregate industry productivity. Econometrica 71:1696–1725

Pamukçu T (2003) Trade liberalization and innovation decisions of firms: Lessons from post-1980 Turkey. World Dev 31(8):1443–1458

Pavcnik N (2002) Trade liberalization, exit and productivity improvements: Evidence from Chilean plants. Rev Econ Stud 69(1):245–276

Revenga A (1997) Employment and wage effects of trade liberalization: the case of Mexican manufacturing. J Labor Econ 15(3):S20–S43 Part 2

Sekkat Kh (ed) (2008) Competition and efficiency in the Arab World. Palgrave Macmillan

Taymaz EA, Yilmaz K (2007) Productivity and trade orientation: turkish manufacturing industry before and after the customs union. J Int Trade Diplomacy 1:127–154

Wacziarg R, Wallack JS (2004) Trade liberalization and intersectoral labor movements. J Int Econ 64:411–39

Wei S-J (2000) "How taxing is corruption on international investors?". Rev Econ Stat 82(1):1–11

Index

Breinigsville, PA USA
23 December 2009

229339BV00005BD/2/P

9 781441 910363